The Slave Trader

Bryan Blundell (1674–1756). (*Courtesy of the Liverpool Blue Coat Foundation*)

The Slave Trader

The Story of Bryan Blundell, Master Mariner, Philanthropist and Slave Trader

Ben Shaw

PEN & SWORD
HISTORY

First published in Great Britain in 2026 by
Pen & Sword History
An imprint of Pen & Sword Books Limited
Yorkshire – Philadelphia

ISBN 978 1 03613 803 5

A CIP catalogue record for this book is available from the British Library.

Typeset by Mac Style
Printed in the UK by CPI Group (UK) Ltd, Croydon, CR0 4YY.

MIX
Paper | Supporting responsible forestry
FSC www.fsc.org FSC® C013604

The Publisher's authorised representative in the EU for product safety is Authorised Rep Compliance Ltd., Ground Floor, 71 Lower Baggot Street, Dublin D02 P593, Ireland.
www.arccompliance.com

For a complete list of Pen & Sword titles please contact:

PEN & SWORD BOOKS LIMITED
47 Church Street, Barnsley, South Yorkshire, S70 2AS, England
E-mail: enquiries@pen-and-sword.co.uk
Website: www.pen-and-sword.co.uk
or
PEN AND SWORD BOOKS
1950 Lawrence Road, Havertown, PA 19083, USA
E-mail: uspen-and-sword@casematepublishers.com
Website: www.penandswordbooks.com

For Sam and Lucy,
May you always learn from the past,
have courage in the present, and hope for the future.

Contents

Acknowledgments

This book stands on the shoulders of many others. While I have spent countless hours tracing sources and piecing together records, it is the work of historians, archivists, and researchers that has made this story possible.

First and foremost, I owe an immeasurable debt to the late Harry Hignett, the distinguished maritime historian, author and long-serving Vice-President of the Liverpool Maritime Society. His meticulous transcription of Bryan Blundell's journal and accounts laid the very foundation on which this book has been built. Without his patient labour, it could not have been written. All quotes from Bryan Blundell's journal are taken from Hignett's transcription, held at the Liverpool Record Office. Where dates are unambiguous in the text, they have not been separately referenced.

My sincere appreciation also goes to Bryan Biggs, Director of Cultural Legacies at the Bluecoat Arts Centre, and to Dr Paul Wainwright of the Liverpool Blue Coat School, both of whom read this work in draft and offered thoughtful feedback, sharpening its accuracy and deepening its insight. Their own publications on the history of the Blue Coat School and Bryan Blundell have also been invaluable and are duly cited throughout. I also wish to thank the Liverpool Blue Coat Foundation for kindly granting permission to reproduce a number of images in this book.

I am also grateful to the Historic Society of Lancashire and Cheshire and the Liverpool Maritime Society, whose preservation efforts and archival collections have been hugely helpful.

In shaping this book, I have used every tool available to me, including emerging AI technologies, which assisted with structure, research synthesis, and refinement, though the interpretation, voice, and responsibility remain entirely my own.

To the many scholars whose published work has guided, challenged, and inspired me, I extend my sincere thanks; their dedication to the historical record underpins these pages.

Finally, I owe my warmest gratitude to those closest to me for their patience, support, and thoughtful questions throughout. I also wish to thank family and friends who read early drafts and offered encouragement and suggestions along the way; their fresh eyes and honest reactions helped shape the book more than they know.

Author's Note

Bryan Blundell began his life at sea as a cabin boy and rose steadily, first to master mariner, then to merchant, philanthropist, and twice Mayor of Liverpool. But he made much of his fortune through the Atlantic trade, beginning with goods like sugar and tobacco, and later through direct investment in the trafficking of enslaved people.

This book seeks to reconstruct that life, not simply as a chronology of events, but as a work of narrative historical non-fiction, drawing together the surviving evidence to explore both the man and the world that shaped him.

In instances where the records are incomplete, I have consulted contemporary accounts, sermons, and various historical sources to reconstruct what Bryan Blundell may have seen, heard, and felt. These reconstructions are grounded in the practices of the time but are not intended as literal transcripts of events. For readability, I have written in the past tense, without repeatedly signalling with "would have" or "likely," though those cautions remain implicit.

In places, I have drawn upon a 1711 sermon by Reverend Christopher Bassnett, who knew Bryan Blundell personally and dedicated the sermon to him and his crew (Appendix A).[1]

Each chapter opens with a short passage from the sermon, offering a glimpse into the moral and spiritual language of the time. Where the historical record falls silent, I have also drawn on his vivid imagery to help imagine what those lost moments might have felt like. Whether Bassnett's own words was inspired by Blundell's own accounts we cannot know; but his words help convey the atmosphere and emotion of a world now out of reach.

Some sections, such as the Prologue and Chapter 21, move more fully into reconstruction, using contemporary sources to imagine scenes not recorded directly but which allow Blundell's story to be told as a continuous narrative.

To support readers unfamiliar with maritime language, I have included a glossary of terms in Appendix B, together with a diagram of a Royal Navy ship-of-the-line, see Figure 4. While I have explained terms in the text wherever possible, these references are intended to aid orientation without breaking the flow of the story. Six family trees are provided in Appendix C to help identify individuals mentioned and clarify their relationships.

The result is not a novel, nor a bare chronology, but an attempt to tell Bryan Blundell's story as fully and faithfully as the evidence allows: not just what happened, but how it happened, and why.

Note on Currency:

Throughout the book I refer to sums of money as they appear in Bryan Blundell's journal and other contemporary records.

These are given in pounds (£), shillings (s), pence (d), and occasionally farthings (¼d), the pre-decimal currency used in Britain before 1971. There were 20 shillings in a pound, and 12 pence in a shilling, meaning 1 pound equalled 240 pence (d).

To give a sense of scale: in the late seventeenth century, an ordinary sailor might earn £12–£18 a year, while a naval captain on a smaller vessel could earn £80–£120. A modest gentleman might live on £40–£60, while a successful merchant's fortune could range from several hundred to several thousand pounds. A townhouse in a port town might cost £100–£300, while a labourer's cottage might be valued at £10–£30.

Exact sums varied widely depending on region, occupation, and time, but these ranges offer a general sense of the monetary scale in Bryan Blundell's world.[2]

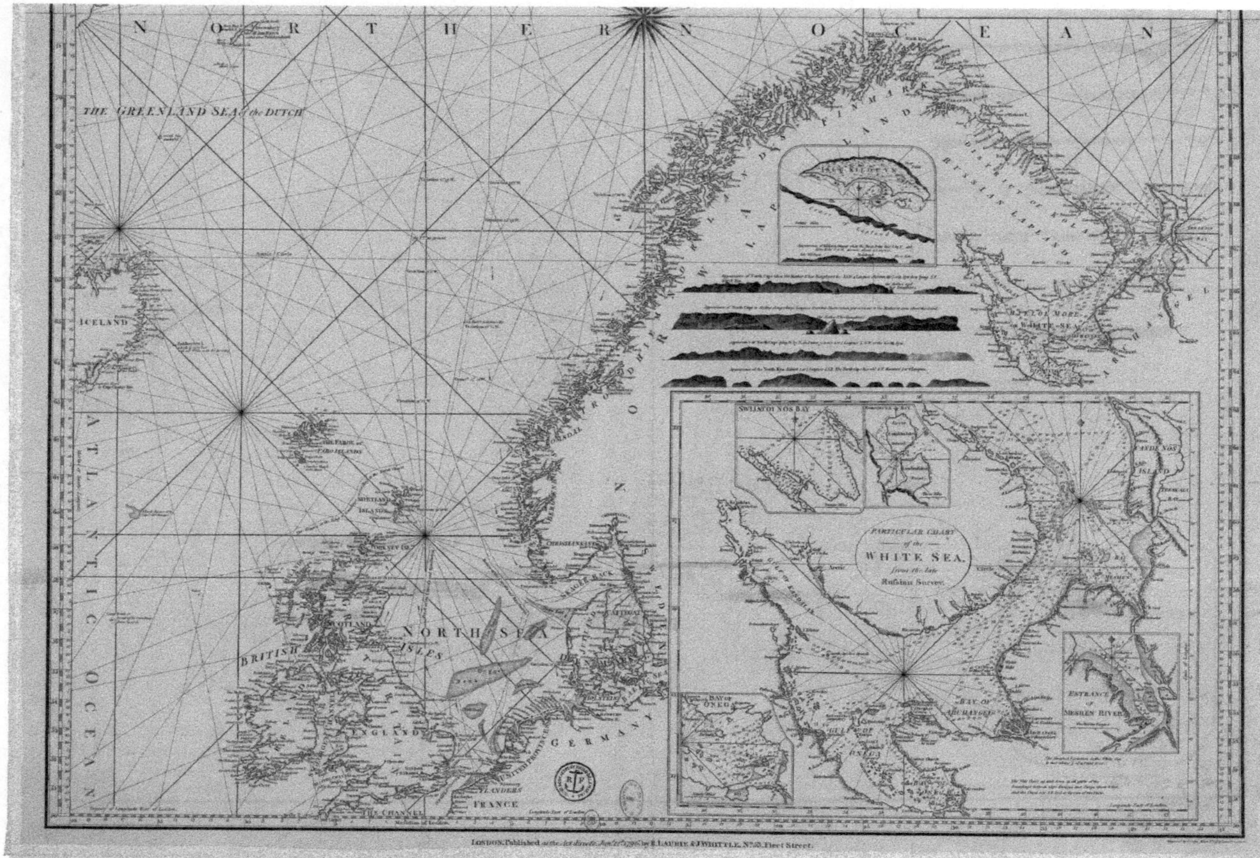

Map 1. R. Laurie and J. Whittle. *A New Chart for the Whale Fishery and the Archangel-Traders…* London, 1796. (*Bibliothèque nationale de France, Département Cartes et plans, GE SH 18 PF 2 DIV 1 P 19/1. Public domain*)

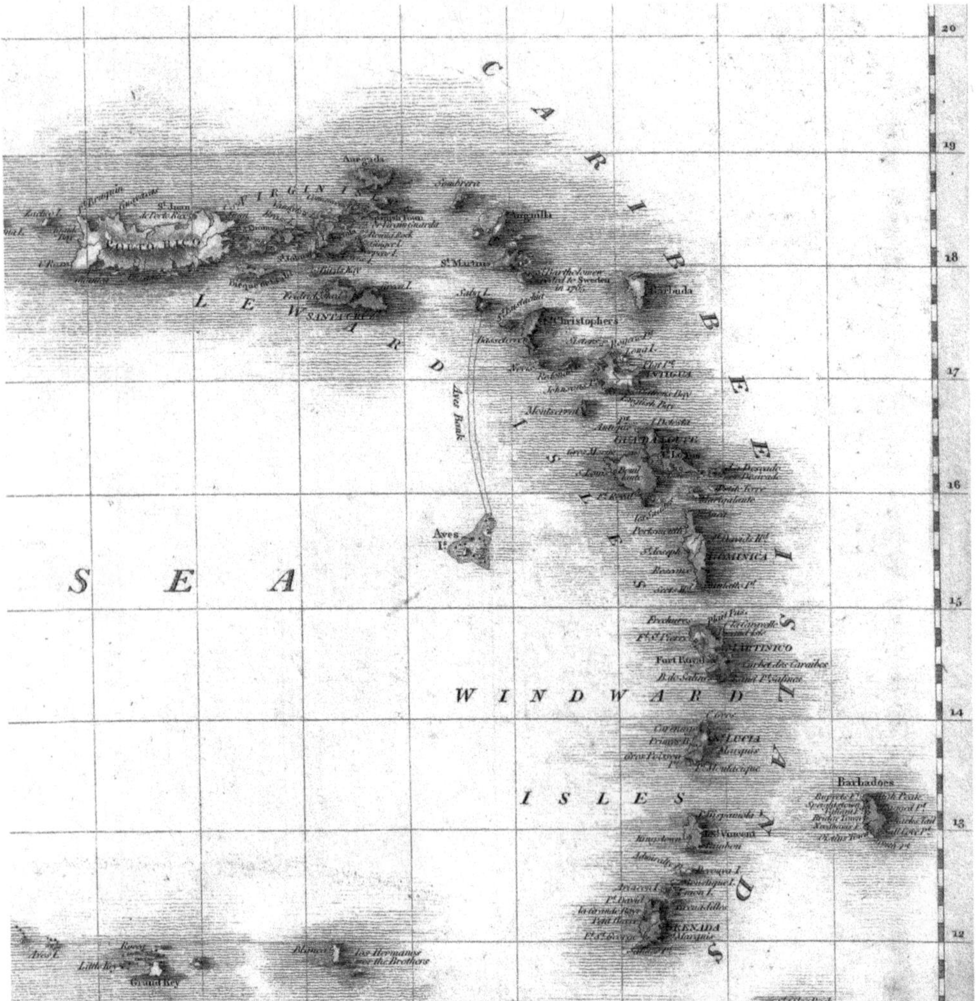

Map 2. John Pinkerton. *West Indies.* Philadelphia: Thomas Dobson, 1818. Engraved map drawn by L. Herbert and engraved by Samuel Neele. From *A Modern Atlas, From the Latest and Best Authorities.* (*Public domain*)

Map 3. Map of Barbados, 1657, from Richard Ligon's *A True and Exact History of the Island of Barbados*. The map marks St Michael's Towne (later known as Bridgetown) and Spickes Towne 12 miles to the north. The latter is now Speightstown, and may correspond to the "Spickles" mentioned in Bryan Blundell's diary as the port from which he first departed for home. Maycock's Bay is shown to the northwest of the island. (*Public domain*)

Map 4. *Virginia und Maryland*, hand-coloured engraved map, c. 1737. Engraved by Johann Baptist Homann; based on original cartography by Herman Moll. Published by Homann Erben. (*Digital image courtesy of the Maryland Center for History and Culture, Resource ID 3996. Public domain*)

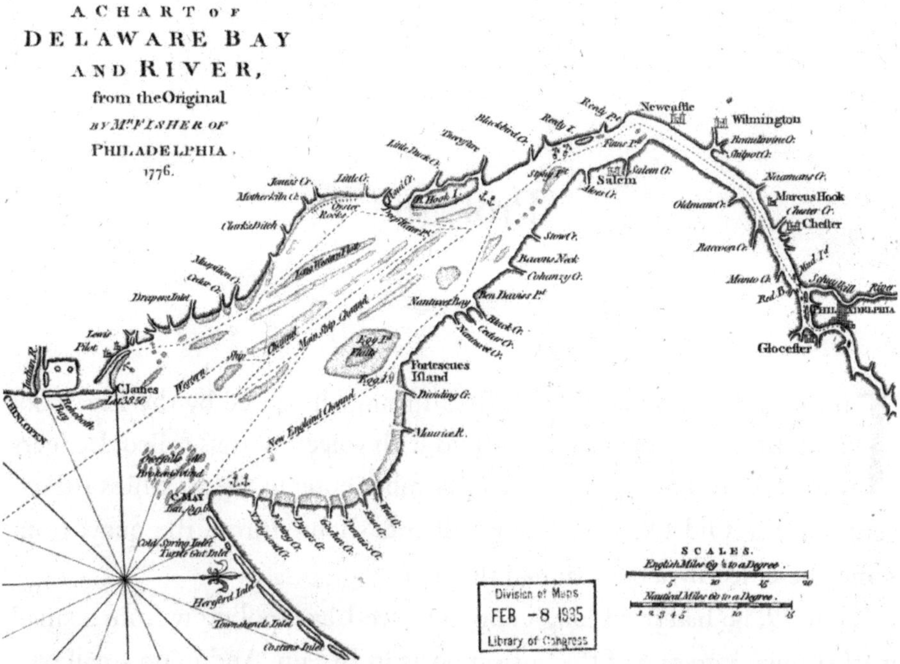

Map 5. *A Chart of Delaware Bay and River*, 1776, by Joshua Fisher. (*Library of Congress, Geography and Map Division. Public domain*)

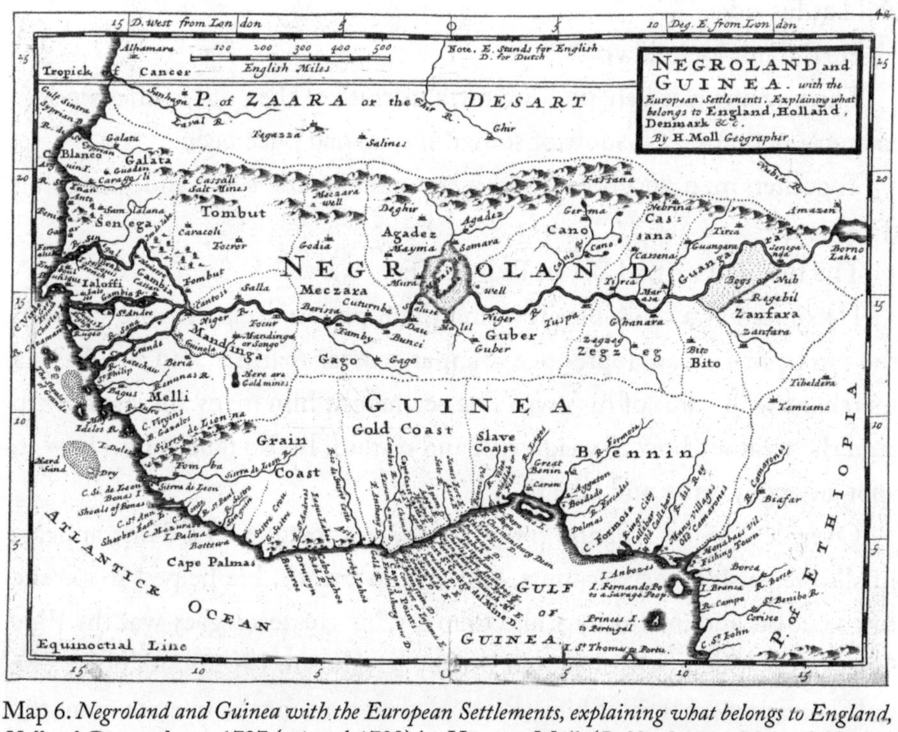

Map 6. *Negroland and Guinea with the European Settlements, explaining what belongs to England, Holland, Denmark, etc.*, 1727 (printed 1729) by Herman Moll. (*Public domain: Maps of Africa to 1900, Map Library, University of Illinois at Urbana-Champaign Library*)

Prologue

In the early summer of 1754, Bryan Blundell paused by the Liverpool waterfront. The dockside was loud with voices. Barrels rolled. Ledgers were tallied. The scent of salt and timber hung in the air. Ships rocked gently in the Old Dock. A few merchants shouted from the quay; from somewhere nearby, a bell chimed the hour.

Now 79, he had lived long enough to see Liverpool grow from a small market town into one of the busiest ports in Britain. And in no small way, he had helped shape it.

He watched for a while – then felt, distantly, the presence of a small child at his side.

He did not look down. Not yet.

The boy was just a shape, a sound, a warmth at the edge of the wind. A memory, perhaps. A shadow of something he had once been.

Together, man and boy, stood a moment in the salt wind, watching the ships.

The tide had carried Bryan Blundell far.

He started as a cabin boy, learning the ropes on deck. He rose through the ranks, first as an apprentice, then as master mariner, and finally as a merchant with ships of his own. The sea taught him many things: how to read the weather, how to weigh risk and reward. It also taught him how to spot an opportunity and take it.

Over decades of Atlantic trade, he made a fortune. His name appears in ship registries, port accounts, and civic petitions. He helped shape the town's docks and institutions, and to many, his greatest legacy was the Blue Coat School, built with his own money to educate Liverpool's poor. The only surviving portrait of him (Plate 1) shows a sober, deliberate man: the image of the prosperous merchant he had finally become.

But it wasn't all success. He buried three wives. Lost ships and men to storms and war. Lived long enough to outlast many of his friends. And now, in his old age, he watched his children and grandchildren step into his shoes, securing their own fortunes as merchants. The town and places he helped transform would endure long after he was gone.

For generations, Bryan Blundell was remembered as one of Liverpool's builders and benefactors: a man of industry and faith, of discipline and generosity.

But the past, like the sea, holds more than what is seen on the surface.

More than 250 years after his death, Blundell's life is being looked at afresh. And a more difficult picture is coming into view.

The fortune he built, and the town he helped shape, were tied to a trade that brought immense human suffering. His early wealth came from goods like sugar and tobacco, grown by enslaved people. Later, he invested directly in the slave trade. Ships he owned, cargoes he financed, partners he trusted all played their part in Liverpool's growing involvement in slavery. His descendants would continue in the trade for decades to come.

Even in his own time, there were voices that questioned the trade. One came from Christopher Bassnett, a nonconformist preacher whose chapel stood near the waterfront. He knew Blundell personally and would later become related to him by marriage. A man of sharp intellect and spiritual conviction, Bassnett believed the sea was as much a test of conscience as of skill. Excerpts from one of his sermons, delivered directly to Blundell and his crew in 1711, appear throughout this book.

To understand Bryan Blundell is to understand eighteenth-century Liverpool, a place of energy, ambition, and contradiction. His life reflects not just his choices, but the values of the world around him.

His journal is one of the richest surviving sources for Liverpool's early maritime history. Yet like many documents of its kind, it is far from complete. His early entries are concise and businesslike: focused on dates, sea conditions, profits, delays, and losses. Only in later years, especially in his writings about the Blue Coat School, does he offer deeper insight into his values and reasoning.

The chapters that follow draw not only on Blundell's own records, but on the wider evidence of his time: shipping manifests, port books, sermons, and civic archives. Where his journal falls silent, other voices help fill the gaps.

Through the pages of his journals and ledgers, we trace Bryan Blundell's journey, from humble cabin boy to master mariner, from prosperous merchant to slave trader, and eventually twice mayor of his town. His own words offer rare glimpses into his ambitions, his choices, and his silences.

But this is not just his story. It is the story of Liverpool, a place growing fast and looking outward. A place where faith and profit sat side by side, and charity flourished, but not for all.

It is a story of people; named and unnamed. Of fortunes made, and the human cost behind them.

A story not only of Liverpool's past, but of the values it honoured, the truths it buried, and the legacy it left behind.

Part I

Apprentice of the Sea

Chapter 1

Where the Tides Turned

"Shipping is a great and noble invention. It is the strength and bulwark, the riches and ornament of a nation – especially such a one as ours, encompassed by the sea and surrounded by the vast deep."

Christopher Bassnett, 1711

The Pool, Liverpool | 1648

The tide had slipped out fast that morning, leaving the merchant crew of the *Friendship* riding at anchor off the mouth of the Pool. With no dock in sight, they ferried their cargo ashore in lighters, small flatbottomed boats used to navigate the shallows. The men then picked their way along rough wooden planks laid across the exposed mud, hauling barrels of tobacco from the New World to the waiting carts.[1]

Thirty tons of Virginia tobacco were landed, "a fairly good consignment in those days," as one later historian noted.[2]

Hard labour for the crew; quiet triumph for the town's elders, who no doubt looked on with satisfaction. It was the first recorded cargo to cross the Atlantic and land on Liverpool's shore. It would not be the last.

Among those watching, perhaps, stood a young merchant named William Blundell,[3] just 20 years old. He may have realised what others already had: that the scene before him was not just a challenge to overcome, but a future taking shape.

Back then, Liverpool had no dock, no grand civic buildings. But it had ambition. And it had the tide.

Mud and Money

Chartered by King John in 1207, Liverpool had for centuries remained a backwater: a small, windswept borough on England's north-west coast, huddled beside a tidal creek.

By the mid-seventeenth century, Liverpool remained unremarkable, better known for ferry crossings than for long-distance trade. A cluster of narrow streets twisted toward the shore, their surfaces churned by livestock and rain. Timber-framed houses leaned unevenly over open drains.[4]

Swine were a common sight, often unringed, without the nose-rings used to stop them rooting through earth and refuse, which made them especially destructive. In 1648, the town appointed swineherds to keep the animals in check.[5]

On market day the streets grew even more chaotic: carts jammed the narrow-crooked lanes, voices rose over the clatter of hooves, and farmers from the outlying villages came to barter eggs, cloth, and gossip. Shoemakers

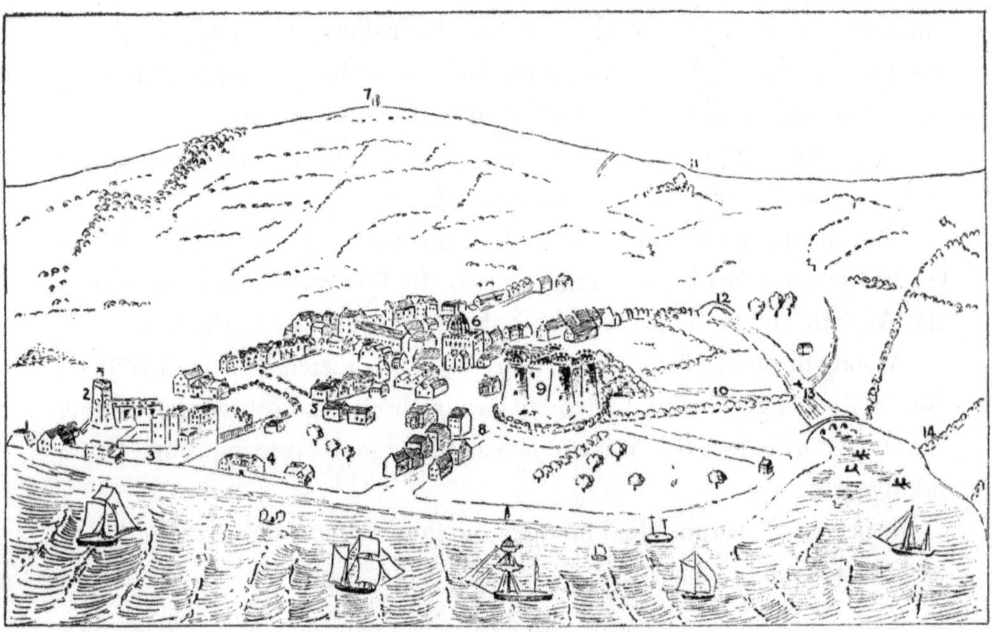

Fig. 27—Liverpool from the River in 1650.

1—The Battery
2—Old Church
3—The Tower
4—Custom House
5—Water Street
6—Town Hall
7—Everton Beacon
8—James Street
9—Old Castle
10—Pool Lane
11—Low Hill
12—Towsend Bridge
13—The Pool
14—Road to Park

Figure 1. William Ashton. *The Evolution of a Coast-Line*, 1920. *Liverpool From the River in 1650.* (*Public domain*)

and salt merchants hawked their goods from crowded stalls. Herrings, caught off the Irish Sea, were sold cheaply by the barrel. The air carried the familiar mix of smoke, saltwater, fish, and dung. It was a scent as much a part of town life as the tide itself.[6]

The town's common hall, near the market cross, was little more than a timbered structure with a leaking roof. It also served as the community's small warehouse, and in 1653 the council ordered that it be "lathed and tiered over with lime and hair, and made handsome above, at the town's expense".[7]

That same year, the town made its first attempt at street lighting: two lanterns with candles were set out nightly at the High Cross and White Cross during the dark of the moon, burning until past 8 pm. Their faint glow offered little illumination, but it was a start.[8]

The stone walls of Liverpool Castle loomed over the ferry crossing and market below. For centuries, the fortress had been held by the Molyneux family, hereditary constables appointed by the Crown, whose influence touched nearly every aspect of town affairs.[9]

Nearby stood the Chapel of Our Lady and St Nicholas Church; its tower was long a landmark for mariners and townsfolk alike. Dedicated to the patron saint of sailors and commonly known as St Nicholas Church, it had served Liverpool since at least the fourteenth century, its spire guiding vessels home across the water.[10] Its bells tolled the rhythms of the waterfront, marking time, warning of storm, and calling the town to prayer.

Just beyond its churchyard stretched the River Mersey, broad, tidal, and mercurial. Along its edge ran a narrow, muddy inlet. This unassuming feature, once used to beach small fishing boats and shelter river barges, gave Liverpool its name: Liuerpul, the "pool with muddy water". Crude but functional, the Pool offered just enough shelter to serve as a working harbour.

The great ports of Bristol and London dwarfed Liverpool in scale, wealth, and reputation. In the mid-1600s, its population stood at barely 2,000.[11]

And yet, even in this period of obscurity, the tides of transformation were rising.

In 1648, the *Friendship* anchored in the Mersey, the very consignment that had first turned heads among the town's elders.[12] It was the first recorded shipment of tobacco into Liverpool, arriving more than half a century after Sir Walter Raleigh first introduced the leaf to England. The consignment also stands as the earliest known transatlantic cargo from the New World to reach the town's shore.[13]

Three years later, Parliament passed the Navigation Acts (1651), a set of mercantile laws designed to cut out Dutch intermediaries and secure English control over seaborne trade. Only English ships, or those from a cargo's country of origin, could now trade with English ports.[14]

For Liverpool's merchants, it was an open door.

Then came the crises: disasters that, paradoxically, created opportunity. In 1665, the Great Plague devastated London; the following year, the Great Fire gutted its commercial heart. Amid the chaos, Liverpool's traders began to seize new routes, markets, and prospects.

That same year, the *Antelope*[15] returned from Barbados with a cargo of sugar, rum, and molasses: a dark, treacly by-product of sugar boiling, most profitably distilled into rum. The sugar imported would have been largely muscovado, the coarse, semi-refined product that dominated West Indian exports at the time.[16]

Twelve months later, the Dutch launched a daring raid on the Medway, crippling England's fleet and sending shockwaves through the southern ports. With London and the Thames exposed, merchants began to look northward for safer harbours and fresh opportunity. Among them was Liverpool: a port that had, until then, lingered on the periphery of national trade, but was uniquely poised to exploit the new maritime order taking shape.[17]

Capital followed. Southern merchants brought with them investment, contacts, and commercial experience. At the same time, the East India Company's monopoly on routes to Asia left independent traders few options but to look west, and to the sugar islands of the West Indies and to Britain's emerging colonies in America.[18]

In 1668, Liverpool's first sugar refinery was established by a London merchant, who leased the land from Sir Edward Moore. Moore described the plans for this ambitious project in Dale Street: a grand stone house four storeys high, with a passage leading through to "a house for boiling and drying sugar, otherwise called a sugar baker's house."[19]

Behind the elegant façade, shipments of muscovado sugar were boiled, refined, and dried into white sugar for the English market. Any residue or molasses extracted during refining was often sold to local distillers for rum production.

"If this be once done," Moore predicted, "it will bring a trade of at least £40,000 a year from the Barbadoes, which formerly this town never knew."[20]

He was not wrong. Within a few years, the town had become one of the principal centres for processing sugar in England, supplied from Barbados and other West Indian islands.

By the early 1670s, Liverpool's waterfront thrummed with activity. Ships bound for the New World departed loaded with metalware, textiles, and finished goods; those returning brought cotton, sugar, and tobacco.

The town's rise did not go unnoticed. In 1673, the traveller and cartographer Richard Blome noted that Liverpool contained "divers eminent merchants, whose trade and traffick, especially with the West Indies, make it famous."[21]

The prosperity was marked in stone the following year, when a new Town Hall was raised at the High Cross. Built on pillars and arches of hewn stone, with rooms above and an open arcade beneath, it served as a Customs House, prison, and meeting place. Merchants gathered under its arches to strike bargains, swap shipping intelligence, and arrange ventures, making it the centre of civic as well as commercial life.

Figure 2. The Old Exchange and Town Hall, 1754, as pictured in James Touzeau's *The Rise and Progress of Liverpool from 1551 to 1835*. (*Liverpool: J. Irvine, 1910, p.259. Public domain*)

Between 1669 and 1686, customs revenue jumped from £1,875 to £14,850, a near eightfold increase in less than two decades.[22] But as trade increased, the town's makeshift harbour could barely cope. Without a proper dock, larger vessels were anchored mid-river, their cargoes ferried ashore in smaller boats. The process was slow, labour-intensive, and increasingly out of step with Liverpool's growing ambitions.

The Family Ledger Begins

In this climate of rising fortunes, William Blundell established himself among the town's most capable traders.[23] He also seemed to understand the value of alliance. In 1661, he married Mary Preeson,[24] daughter of the prominent merchant Alderman Thomas Preeson, one of the wealthiest men in Liverpool.[25]

Together, William and Mary raised at least six children.

On Sunday, 30 December 1674, their son Bryan was born, named in honour of his grandfather.[26]

In his later years, William Blundell held civic standing, serving as Town Clerk of Wigan, and contributed visibly to the public life of Liverpool. In 1687, a year before his death, he funded the construction of a gallery in St Nicholas Church, securing a permanent seat for his family.[27]

Such gestures were common among wealthy merchants: a public blend of piety and prestige, designed to anchor their legacy not only in profit, but in the institutions of the town.

However, it was Bryan, his surviving son, who would soon carry the family name into Liverpool's emerging fortunes. In time, the Blundell's influence would grow alongside the town itself, shaping its civic, commercial, and philanthropic life in ways that would echo for generations.

Liverpool's small size made it nimble; its merchant class made it bold.

It was a town built for trade. Adaptive, opportunistic, and eager to profit from whatever tides came in.

Chapter 2

A Childhood Shaped by the Sea

"The Seaman's Calling: They that go down to the Sea in Ships, that do Business in great Waters — these see the Works of the Lord, and his Wonders in the Deep."
Christopher Bassnett, 1711

St Nicholas Church, Liverpool | Saturday, 9 January 1675

That day, in the nave of St Nicholas Church, Bryan Blundell was baptised.

On the Sundays that followed, young Bryan would have walked there with his mother and father, as the bellringers called the town to prayer, their chimes carrying across the rooftops and out over the river, slowly dissolving into the morning air.[1]

Figure 3. *The Tower and Old St Nicholas's from Mann Island, after Richard Wright* (oil painting, c. 1735–1765), reproduced in Gregson's *Portfolio of Fragments*. (*Public domain*)

Within its stone walls, he would have sat quietly, listening to the prayers offered for those bound for "the great waters,"[2] and for the souls who would never return.

Liverpool by now was still modest in size: a few thousand inhabitants, a few narrow streets, and a harbour little more than a muddy inlet (Figure 3). It was a town where faith and trade moved together.

Its waterfront was Bryan's classroom, and the merchants who lined its bustling quays were his tutors in trade. In the language of the time, he was being "bred to the sea",[3] raised in a world where trade across the oceans was understood not merely as commerce, but as a divine calling.

From a young age, Bryan would have watched in awe as ships arrived, sails weathered, hulls packed with cargo. The men who came ashore would have moved with the weary rhythm of lives shaped by sea and weather.

Their clothes bore the same marks: patched, salt-stained, and streaked with tar. Beneath the grime lay the familiar dress of the sea: a rough seaman's coat thrown over a shirt of coarse linen, while wide, baggy breeches fell in many folds below the knee. On their heads sat Monmouth caps, stout knitted hats favoured by sailors, or else broad-brimmed felt hats tugged low against the wind. The tar that blackened their cuffs and seams was more than filth: it was a seaman's armour, smeared into canvas and cloth to harden it against rain and spray.[4]

No sooner had their ships moored than the town stirred into life. Bryan would have watched as barrels were unloaded, merchants haggled over their latest ventures, and shipwrights toiled over repairs.

As evening approached, the town's taverns came alive, warm with lamplight and loud with drink. Ale sloshed in mugs, brandy was poured freely, and boots scraped against sawdust-covered floors.[5] The air was thick with the sweet, heavy smoke of Virginian tobacco.

Then came the stories of masts split by lightning and ships that vanished without a trace. Of men lost overboard, and fires at sea that turned night to terror. There were whispers of pirates too, swift and merciless.

Bryan would no doubt have heard them all, some echoing from open tavern doors, others told by his father, retold and half-whispered at the fireside.

By now, Liverpool was changing. Ships still came from Ireland and Europe, but more and more arrived from the American colonies and the

West Indies, brimming with barrels of molasses, sugar, and bales of tobacco. Bryan could hear it, see it and smell it too, as the cargo rumbled along the cobblestone streets.

At age 10, Bryan's path seemed assured: he inherited a house from his grandfather, Alderman Thomas Preeson.[6] But in a town on the rise, inheritance alone was never enough. Success demanded sharp judgment, resilience, and the courage to seize opportunity.

Before long, Bryan was preparing to set sail, leaving behind his parents and the narrow streets he had always known. The world that awaited was vast, uncertain, and unforgiving, but it was the world in which fortunes were made.

In His Own Hand

While historical records and family connections offer glimpses of Bryan's rise, it is his own words that provide the most vivid account of his journey.[7] He recorded them in a large, leather-bound volume measuring 15 by 10 inches, parchment-like pages purchased, as he later noted, for 5 shillings. It was both a working journal and a personal ledger, and over time, it became the written spine of his career.

It offers a rare window into his progression from cabin boy to master mariner. More than a ledger of ports and cargoes, it captures the evolving mind of a young man carving a place for himself in Liverpool's expanding maritime world.

Bryan's ascent epitomises the archetype of the shipmaster-merchant in the late seventeenth and early eighteenth centuries, driven, resilient, and shrewd. Even his handwriting tells the story. Early entries show a "youthful, deliberate round hand";[8] over time, the script grows vigorous and fluid, the language of a businessman, confident and in command.

After each voyage, he recorded what seemingly mattered most with practical care, his wages, his share of the profits, and the steady growth of his stock.

Today, his diary stands as a rare and valuable insight into the financial strategies of a rising Liverpool merchant.

The Boy Who Sailed

Bryan's maritime journey began at the age of 12, when he embarked on his first transatlantic voyage aboard the *Reserve* of Liverpool, under the command of Captain Christopher Moore. As a cabin boy, he held the lowest rank aboard, a servant to the ship, unpaid and expected to perform the most menial tasks while gradually learning the ways of the sea.

On Sunday, 30 November 1687, the *Reserve* weighed anchor, departing for Barbados with a small crew of eight hardened sailors and apprentices.

For a boy from Liverpool, the departure of a fleet would have been a spectacle unlike any other. The quayside teemed with life, merchants shouting orders, labourers loading final barrels, apprentices lashing down sails with raw fingers. And then, as one, all eyes turned to the sky, waiting for the breeze.

As one observer later recalled: "The wind ruled supreme, without a rival. When, after a long stretch of contrary winds, a change took place and a favourable breeze set in, a whole fleet of ships would at once be hauled out of dock and start upon their several voyages. It was a glorious spectacle."[9]

Bryan would have gripped the ship's rail, his pulse quickening as he took in the organised chaos. The language of sail filled the air, ropes tightening, canvas unfurling, as Liverpool's merchant fleet slipped their moorings and leaned into the morning wind. Though he would cross these waters many times in his life, that first departure must have felt momentous.

To merchants, sailing in convoy was both a necessity and a test of allegiance. The dangers were real enough. The seas in the late seventeenth century teemed with predators, privateers prowled the Channel, the Atlantic, and the Caribbean. These privately owned vessels were authorised by governments through letters of marque to attack enemy shipping during wartime. They were legal in theory, but often indistinguishable from piracy in practice. Many used deception as part of their trade: flying false colours to approach unsuspecting targets, only hoisting their true flag at the last moment. For merchant crews, a single silhouette on the horizon could spell disaster.[10]

A naval convoy offered protection against such threats, but it also demanded patience. Usually guarded by one or more Royal Navy men-of-war, large, heavily armed warships crewed by professional sailors and built

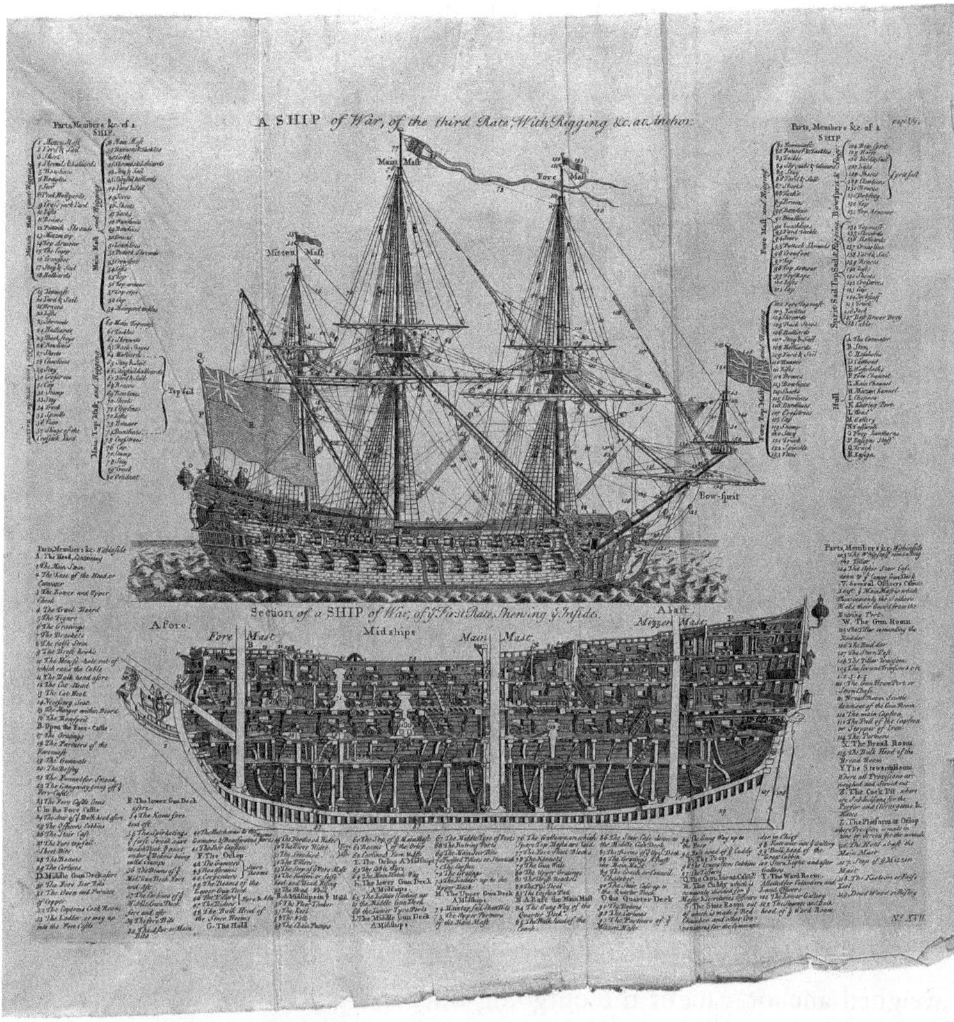

Figure 4. Diagram of a Royal Navy ship-of-the-line, late seventeenth century. Such vessels often escorted merchant convoys, their presence a deterrent to privateers. "A Ship of War, of the third Rate" and "Section of a Ship of War, of the first Rate" (1728). (*Public domain*)

for battle rather than trade, each vessel was bound to the pace of the slowest. (Figure 4). Their course was dictated not just by wind and tide, but by the need to stay together.

For a restless young apprentice, the slow, methodical pace of travel was an education. He would learn the rhythms of maritime life, how to anticipate shifting weather, navigate treacherous waters, and endure the long, monotonous stretches between ports.

As their sails caught the wind and the tide pulled them out to sea, young Bryan would have watched the skyline of Liverpool slowly fade from view. And as the tower of St Nicholas Church vanished into the haze, so too did the boy's old life.

The Edge of Routine

His first stop was Dublin, an important port for transatlantic voyages. There, they would have restocked the hold with essential supplies: barrels of salted beef and pork, ship's biscuit, dried peas, oatmeal, and fresh water carefully stored in wooden casks. Markets also provided butter, cheese, and smoked fish, goods that could endure weeks at sea. Casks of ale were also likely stowed, not as a luxury but a necessity, safer than water on longer voyages.

But these provisions were not only for the crew. Many were also intended for sale or exchange in Barbados, where Irish produce, especially salted beef, pork and butter, was in steady demand. Alongside supplies, the ship may have loaded Irish linens, wool, and tallow candles, cheap, sturdy, and made from animal fat. They were the staple lighting aboard most merchant vessels.

Provisioning was as much physical labour as it was planning. Bryan would have hauled casks and fetched orders barked from the galley or quarterdeck. The stink of dried meat, the scrape of rope, and the clang of iron on deck filled the air. He might have paused now and then, to take it all in. But mostly, he worked, eager to prove himself, and to earn his place among the crew.

Once the hold was full and the final inspections completed, the *Reserve* weighed anchor, caught the outgoing tide, and braced for the vast and unpredictable Atlantic.

Whatever anticipation Bryan may have felt as the ship cleared Dublin Bay, it would soon be replaced by something else. For the seasoned crew, this was routine: the discomforts, the danger, the discipline. But for someone so young, it was something else entirely: his first step inside that floating "wooden world,"[11] part prison, part kingdom, a realm unto itself.

Baptism by Salt

The voyage from Dublin to Barbados usually took six to eight weeks, depending on wind conditions and currents. A well-rigged merchant vessel of the time could average 4 to 5 knots, roughly 100 to 120 nautical miles per day, but storms, calms, or unfavourable winds could slow progress considerably.[12]

The *Reserve* would have made her way south along the western coasts of France and Spain, catching the prevailing westerlies. If conditions were favourable, they might have stopped briefly in the Azores or Madeira to take on fresh water before turning westward across the Atlantic.[13]

The small crew would have worked to a strict watch system, dividing the day into rotating shifts to keep the ship manned, the sails trimmed, and the course steady. Each man had his station and routine, from pumping seawater and scrubbing decks to hauling lines and standing lookout. It was relentless, repetitive work.

As a young apprentice, Bryan would have been expected to assist wherever needed, learning the ropes in the most literal and lethal sense. Each knot, line, and sail had to be mastered on the fly, often in storm conditions, and always under pressure. One misstep, and a man could vanish overboard without a sound. And often it wasn't a man at all, but someone barely in his teens.

Bryan would have been sent aloft in rough weather, climbing the ratlines, rope ladders strung between shrouds, his fingers stiff with cold, his body swaying high above the deck. His task: to reef the sails, wrestling canvas against the wind, braced against every lurch. Perched high on the yardarm, he would have leaned out over open sea, the topmast yawing beneath him, spray lashing his face as he wrapped the sail with numbed fingers.

Below deck, he might be tasked with crawling into the bilge, the lowest, foulest part of the ship, where stagnant "bilge water" pooled with every leak and spill. Here he would clear blockages or hammer in fresh caulking wedged between timbers, lantern flickering in the dark, the air thick with brine, rot, and tar. The stench was infamous. Men of the seventeenth and eighteenth centuries sometimes collapsed or even died from the foul vapours rising there.[14] These were the duties given to boys: the nimble, the expendable.

On such a voyage, seasickness was almost inevitable, especially for those on their first crossing. The rolling Atlantic swells, coupled with the stink of bilge water and tar, could reduce even the strongest to weakness.

Hugh Crow, another Liverpool apprentice, later recalled of his first passage that they "experienced stormy weather and contrary winds, and I for one was very sea-sick the greater part of the time."[15]

The ordeal didn't end there.

"The ship being leaky I was kept almost constantly at the pumps, and my sensations, both of mind and body, were extremely mortifying; for my illness excited only the derision of the older sailors, who, in those days, treated the young with great harshness and severity."[16]

For Bryan, too, seasickness would have been no protection: work continued regardless, and weakness was met not with sympathy but with scorn.

Hardtack and Hardship

After long hours of hot, exhausting work, staying hydrated was as essential as it was difficult. Water stored in wooden casks quickly turned stagnant and foul, often leaving sailors to rely on beer or watered-down spirits instead.

When thirst became overwhelming, they resorted to desperate measures. Some strained rainwater through scraps of cloth, catching what they could before it ran off the deck. Others even licked dew from railings or rigging, anything that might yield a few drops to soothe cracked lips and swollen tongues.[17]

Meals offered little relief. Shipboard fare was endured, not savoured. For the old hands, this was routine. For a boy, it was initiation. Yet, for someone unused to hunger or hardship, even coarse rations held a kind of comfort. He would soon learn what could be stomached and what had to be chewed through. Ship's biscuit, hardtack, was a staple of sea life: little more than flour, salt, and water, baked until rock-hard and left to dry. It lasted for months, even years, and was rarely eaten without soaking, softening, or swearing.[18]

By the second or third week at sea, rations often began to deteriorate. Meat grew rank, biscuits crumbled with black-headed weevils, and barrels of peas turned sour in the heat. Maggots were common. Rats gnawed through sacks and scuttled overhead in the dark. The rare appearance of fresh food, an onion, a turnip, or a hen's egg, was cause for celebration, and quickly gone. Hunger flattened expectations. Sailors ate what they could, when they could, and learned not to look too closely.[19]

Given such conditions, it is hardly surprising that disease followed. The threat loomed over every voyage, not just scurvy, caused by vitamin deficiency, but a host of illnesses bred in the ship's damp, airless quarters.

Fevers, dysentery, and infections spread quickly among exhausted men, and with no real medical care, even minor ailments could turn deadly.[20]

Worst of all was "ship fever", a broad term sailors used for typhus or typhoid, spread by lice, stagnant water, and poor sanitation. Symptoms included high fever, chills, severe headaches, and a mottled rash that often spread across the chest and back. With no effective treatment, the disease could be as deadly as it was swift. In severe outbreaks, mortality rates reached up to 40 per cent, decimating a ship's company before it ever reached port.[21]

And layered over all of it was a constant, gnawing dread. Life at sea on a seventeenth-century merchant vessel was not merely hard, it was hierarchical, punishing, and often cruel. Aboard ship, the captain's word was law, and discipline was dealt in lashes.

A later associate of Bryan's, William Hutchinson,[22] recalled a tyrannical Jamaican trader who drank and gambled with his officers, "abused and ill-used" his crew, and ordered men aloft in storms simply for punishment.[23] Others spoke of masters who lashed cruelly for the smallest offences, their authority unchecked, their tempers sharpened by hunger, weather, and fear of mutiny.[24]

Not every voyage was governed with the same severity. Conditions on naval warships, with their crowded crews and stricter discipline, could be especially harsh; on later slave ships, the brutality reached another order entirely.[25]

Even so, a young boy like Bryan would have learned quickly that silence, obedience, and speed might spare a man's back, though not always. There were no courts on the ocean, no appeal, no redress. The price of a mistake could be a blow, a lost ration, or days chained in the dark.[26]

It would have been a harsh and formative initiation: every groan of the hull, every flap of the sails, every shouted order from the captain.

Wonders in the Deep[27]

Not all of it was hardship. There must have been moments, amid the hunger and the fear, when the Atlantic offered something else entirely.

Between the fury of storms and the hush of calm, Bryan would have stood at the deck's edge and taken in a view few on land could ever know.

Sometimes the sea was bright, smooth, and clear. The water shimmered with life, shoals darting below, flying fish lifting from the waves, and dolphins cresting in the ship's wake.

What could be more beautiful than a calm evening, when the sun set in splendour upon the waters? Or on a clear night, when the moon rode high, the stars shone, and the ocean turned glassy beneath the light, its surface broken only by the occasional gust or distant gull.

Storms were terrible, yes, but the aftermath brought its own strange stillness. Rainbows arched over retreating clouds, and the water, newly churned, glittered in their colours.

To the boy aboard the *Reserve*, these moments must have seemed miraculous, etched into memory with the quiet weight of wonder.

His body ached, his hands were raw, and yet his eyes remained wide.

Chapter 3

The Sound of the Drums

"Though 'tis a trade that the laws of our country allow us to follow, yet it carries considerable difficulties along with it, to which it is not easy to return clear and satisfactory answers."

Christopher Bassnett, 1711

Barbados | January, 1688[1]

Now, as Bryan and the crew of the *Reserve* neared Barbados, the easternmost of the Caribbean islands, the deep Atlantic blue lightened to the bright, glassy-green shallows. Coral beds glinted just below the surface, and lush, green islands rose on the horizon.

As the coastline of Barbados came into view, Bryan would have glimpsed the high, lofty trees of the island's interior, their branches flourishing in the tropical light, the whole island seeming to offer itself in beauty and bounty.[2]

By the time they entered Carlisle Bay off Bridgetown (see Map 3), he would have seen how fields and sugar plantations climbed one above another, each open to the sea breeze and looking out across the water.[3]

In the bay, dozens of ships lay at anchor, while small boats plied to and fro under sail and oar, carrying goods and passengers and moving with the bustle of a busy port.[4]

As Bryan and the exhausted crew stepped ashore, they would have found the quays alive with noise and motion. The local yards, warehouses and market stalls teemed with planters and factors (local agents who bought and sold goods on commission) bargaining hard. Their reputations for quarrelsome dealings and heavy drinking were already well known. One early observer dismissed them as "such great drunkards that they will find the money to buy their drink all though they goe naked."[5]

There was no time to linger. Bryan set to work, helping to unload textiles, tools, and goods for planters. In return came barrels of raw sugar, dark thick molasses, and casks of rum, bound for eager buyers in England. He might also have carefully stowed smaller crates of cotton, and ginger, their strong aroma mingling with the ever-present tang of salt and tar.[6]

The process of loading was back-breaking work, requiring balance and precision as the crew carefully manoeuvred heavy barrels and crates into the ship's hold, ensuring the weight was evenly distributed to maintain stability at sea.[7] Though still an apprentice, Bryan would have already begun to understand the value of accuracy, of records kept, deals struck, and cargo tallied.

But beneath all of this, something darker hung in the air.

The island was a paradox: immense wealth built on unimaginable suffering. Its plantations fuelled fortunes, while enslaved men and women laboured under the sun. By the late 1680s, the imbalance was stark: more than 46,000 enslaved Africans lived on Barbados, outnumbering the white population by more than 2 to 1.[8]

In Plain Sight

Bryan did not need to look far to see the system that underpinned the island's wealth. The arrival of a slave ship often announced itself on the wind, thick with waste, sickness, and human despair. The stench, they said, could carry for miles.

Once in port, some captives were sold directly from the deck, their buyers climbing aboard before the ship had even finished unloading. Others were kept aboard for inspection before being sent to market.[9]

Many were sold at the waterfront or in nearby yards and houses, where buyers gathered to examine and bid. Bryan could not have missed the rows of naked men, women, and children standing barefoot and silent, their skin sometimes oiled to suggest health and to mask the exhaustion of the voyage, a cosmetic deceit meant to make them more saleable.[10]

Here he would have seen human beings bought and sold, their fates determined by the highest bidder. Traders poked arms, pulled mouths open to check teeth, and prodded abdomens and thighs with the practiced

Figure 5. Julien-Léopold Boilly. *The Slave Trade in Martinique*, c. 1826. Illustration from Alcide Dessalines d'Orbigny, *A Picturesque Journey Through the Two Americas* (1836). (*Public domain*)

detachment of livestock buyers.[11] Among those on display were children younger than himself, small boys and girls with wide eyes, all torn from their homes across the ocean and brought here to be sold. There was no privacy.

The scrutiny was public, and merciless.

Amid these scenes, he likely witnessed one of the most brutal forms of sale: a violent spectacle known as the "scramble." The enslaved were herded into a yard, arranged like merchandise beneath the Caribbean sun.[12]

Then came the signal: the beating of a drum.[13]

At once, buyers surged forward in a frenzy, rushing "with the ferocity of brutes," clawing to claim the strongest before anyone else could.[14]

Olaudah Equiano, who experienced such scenes firsthand, described how the "noise and clamour"[15] overwhelmed the captives, who believed the buyers meant to kill them, not claim them. Husbands were torn from wives, children from their mothers. The chaos was not incidental, it was orchestrated. A performance of power. A tool of disorientation and control.

And after the frenzy, the machinery resumed.

Slavery in Barbados was not hidden behind plantation walls. It was part of the street scene, visible in the cart drivers, the labourers on the wharves, and the enslaved attendants carrying baskets or watching silently as their masters and mistresses haggled for goods.

Freshly landed Africans, their speech still unfamiliar, stood apart from those who had already been "seasoned" on the island, those who had survived the brutal transition into plantation life.[16] This period often lasted from one to five years and involved relentless labour, language suppression, and harsh discipline. Many did not survive it. Disease, malnutrition, and mistreatment claimed countless lives before the process was complete. Bryan would have seen these people too, marching past the quay in chains, hauling loads, or unloading barrels, their movements watched closely by armed overseers.[17]

Back on the plantations, the Great Houses perched like citadels on high ground, overlooking the slave quarters below. Most enslaved people lived in crude wooden huts clustered around a central yard. Planters called it the "Negro yard." These dwellings, made from wattle and daub or rough timber, had thatched roofs and earthen floors. They were overcrowded, poorly ventilated, and offered little protection from tropical rains, sweltering heat, or the sting of mosquitoes and sandflies. The estate layout was no accident: the slave quarters were always deliberately placed by the planters, close enough to watch, far enough away to avoid the stench.[18]

In the fields, Bryan would have witnessed the enslaved labouring from dawn to dusk under the lash. He would have seen how the gangs cut sugarcane under a remorseless sun, with only two brief breaks for food. Men, women, and children alike were expected to work. Beyond the fields, others were set to endless tasks: felling wood, heaving supplies, or attending the "ingenio." The complex of mill, boiling house, still house, and curing house where cane was crushed, boiled, distilled, and packed into raw sugar. The boiling houses were the worst of all, stifling with heat and steam, and dangerously unforgiving.[19]

To the planters, this cruelty was not excessive, it was efficient. Across the Caribbean, they applied ruthless arithmetic to human life.

One slaver recalled a debate about their treatment. Should the "appoint them [the enslaved] moderate work... and such treatment, as might enable them to protract their lives," or "rigorously drain their strength...before they became useless, and then to buy new ones to fill up their places"? The latter, he was told, was the cheaper option.[20]

It was a cold calculation, made "with all possible exactness". On some estates, it was rare for an enslaved person to live more than nine years.[21]

The brutality Bryan witnessed was not random; it was protected and perpetuated by law. The Barbados Slave Codes of 1661[22] had already cemented a grim legal foundation: enslaved people were treated not as humans, but as property. Stripped of all rights, they were subjected to their owners' total control, including punishments without legal restraint. Children born to enslaved mothers inherited their status, ensuring the system reproduced itself across generations. These codes would serve as a template across the Caribbean and the Americas, making slavery not just permitted, but permanent, a legal institution woven into every facet of colonial life.

Bryan, by now just 13, may not have grasped the full scope of what he was witnessing, but he would have seen it, heard it and smelt it. The cries from the pens, the lash of the whip, the blank stares of the unsold: slavery revealed itself not in rumour, but in noise and motion, in routines of cruelty performed in plain sight. It was physical, immediate, and unrelenting.

And though his thoughts went unrecorded, the memory of this place – the blistering heat, the sugar, the salt, and the sound of the drums – would surely have travelled home with him.

The Wake Behind Him

On Friday, 22 June 1688, with the ship fully loaded and the final dealings concluded, Bryan would have taken a final glance at the busy waterfront before the *Reserve* prepared to depart. As the anchor was raised and the convoy drifted from the coast, he could at last begin to dream of the Mersey wind and familiar shores.

In one of his first entries in his journal, Bryan carefully recorded their departure: "at 3 of the clock in the afternoon we set sail from the town of Spickles," a small settlement west of Bridgetown. Catching the steady trade winds, the *Reserve* turned northward, beginning the long and uncertain voyage back to England.

Just five weeks later, they had drawn close enough to the English coast to begin taking soundings, measuring the depth of the water with a weighted line to ensure safe passage as they neared land. These depth checks usually took place near the continental shelf, where the ocean floor rose sharply to around 200 metres.[23] On Friday, 30 July, Bryan noted carefully in his journal: "This day at 6 in the afternoon we sounded and took ground at 60 fathoms" (approximately 360 feet).

Two days later, they rounded the Isles of Scilly off Cornwall and, then finally, on Saturday, 14 August, after nearly two months at sea, Bryan Blundell and the crew of the *Reserve* reached their destination, making their way upriver past dockyards and wharves, into the teeming heart of London.

As they approached the city, the Pool of London unfolded before them, a bustling stretch of the Thames between London Bridge and Limehouse, a riverfront district dense with timber yards, ropemakers, and seafarers' inns. From the deck of the *Reserve*, Bryan would have taken it all in: a skyline splintered with masts, ships moored side by side, their hulls creaking as they jostled for space along the crowded quays.[24]

On the north bank, the imposing Custom House stood guardian over the legal quays where cargoes were offloaded, weighed, and taxed.[25] Nearby, Billingsgate Market rang with a cacophony of barking traders and the cries of gulls overhead. Brine and coal smoke clung to the air, laced with the scent of foreign goods newly arrived.

To Bryan, it must have seemed overwhelming: a city where commerce flowed on a scale Liverpool could scarcely have imagined.

The crew remained there for ten weeks, tending to business, repairs, and cargo. By December, they had returned to Liverpool, Bryan no longer a sailor in name alone, but in experience hard-won.

When the Wind Changed

The end of 1688 brought both personal tragedy and national upheaval, events that would shape not only Bryan's future but also the fortunes of Liverpool and the wider British kingdom.

He returned from his first voyage to find that his father, William Blundell, had passed away. At 13, Bryan had spent months at sea, growing used to danger and routine. But nothing could have prepared him for this loss. The boy who had sailed away was not the boy who came back. His childhood, such as it was, ended that day.

Now under the care of his mother, Mary, Bryan returned briefly to family life, surrounded by his three surviving siblings: Elizabeth, Dorothy, and William.[26] Yet Liverpool itself was teeming with father figures of a different kind. The town's merchants, rough-handed and self-made, were shaping a new order. Their influence surrounded him: in the timber yards and ropewalks near the Mersey, in the shipyards ringing with the sound of hammer, and in the counting houses where fortunes rose and fell.

That same year, a new figure stepped into Liverpool's spiritual life: the Reverend Robert Styth.[27]

He was appointed Rector of St Nicholas Church, and it is possible he was among those who officiated at William Blundell's burial, a moment of quiet formality that may have marked the beginning of a lasting association between young Bryan and the reverend.

While Bryan was setting his course at sea, Styth was beginning a ministry that would one day be woven tightly with the Blundell name, and with the founding of one of Liverpool's most enduring institutions.

Yet even as Bryan laid his father to rest on Monday, 6 December, events were unfolding far beyond Liverpool's streets that would change the course of his life.

At the Edge of History

Just three weeks later, on Thursday, 23 December, King James II abandoned the throne and sought exile in France. In his place, the Dutch prince William of Orange and his wife, Mary, assumed power, ushering in what would come to be known as the Glorious Revolution (Figure 6).[28]

James had been a king at odds with his own people. A Catholic ruler in a predominantly Protestant kingdom, his attempts to reassert royal authority had sparked deep unease.

When his wife gave birth to a son earlier that year, a Catholic heir, Protestant nobles feared a dynasty. They invited William of Orange, the husband of James's Protestant daughter Mary, to intervene.

That December, William landed in England with a powerful fleet, said to be nearly three times the size of the Spanish Armada of 1588 (Figure 7). James fled.

Figure 6. *William III.* (*Wellcome Collection, public domain*)

Parliament declared the throne vacant, and in February 1689, William and Mary were jointly crowned as monarchs.

The following month, James landed in Ireland. Backed by French arms and Irish support, he rallied his Jacobite[29] forces, determined to reclaim the crown.

William responded swiftly, unleashing a campaign to crush the Jacobite cause. He oversaw preparations at Hoyle Lake, a sheltered anchorage off the Wirral coast, now known as Hoylake, which became the mustering point. Soldiers and supplies poured in.

Figure 7. *Formation of the Fleet with Which William III Sailed to England*, 11 November 1688. Etching by Adriaan Schoonebeek, Amsterdam. (*Public domain*)

The first major test came in 1689 at Derry, referred to by most English contemporaries as Londonderry. The Siege of Derry began on Thursday, 18 April 1689, when James, leading a predominantly Catholic force, laid siege to the fiercely Protestant stronghold (Figure 8). The city's inhabitants, nearly 30,000 in number, endured unimaginable hardship, suffering from starvation and disease over the course of 105 desperate days.[30]

As the siege dragged on, a relief effort was launched by sea.

Among the fleet of merchant vessels sent to aid the besieged city was the *Reserve* of Liverpool, with young Bryan among its crew.

His journal records that they carried soldiers to Londonderry and "had them aboard for two months whilst lying at anchor off the town."

The mission was fraught with risk. The warship *Dartmouth* attempted to force a path through the River Foyle but was repelled by a formidable boom of timber and chain laid across the water by Jacobite forces.[31]

The turning point came on Sunday, 28 July, when the merchant ship *Mountjoy*, commanded by Captain Michael Browning, rammed the barrier, splintering it apart. Though Browning was killed in the attempt, the breach allowed much-needed provisions to reach the starving defenders.

Figure 8. *The Siege of Derry. From British Battles on Land and Sea*, Vol. 1 (1873). (*Public domain. Image credit: British Library, digitised 201*)

Morale inside the city surged. Outside, Jacobite forces, already stretched and demoralised after months of failed assaults, were unable to mount a renewed attack.

The Jacobite troops began to fall back. Four days later, they withdrew entirely, marking the end of the siege and securing Londonderry for William's cause.[32]

A Tide Unleashed

The campaigns of 1689 to 1691 broke Jacobite resistance in Ireland. The war's turning tide not only cemented William and Mary's rule over the Three Kingdoms; it altered the balance of power across the British Isles.

It was in the aftermath of these hard-won victories that Liverpool erupted in celebration. For many English towns, the changing fortunes of war brought relief. But in Liverpool, barely 100 miles across the Irish sea, it felt personal.

As troops returned from Ireland, the town erupted. Barrels of turf and coal were rolled into the street and set ablaze, their thick smoke rising through the narrow lanes around the Exchange. Soldiers were welcomed with ale, and townsmen gathered with mugs of punch, laughing and shouting as firelight danced across the brickwork. The festivities were raucous, a jubilant embrace of victory and the new Protestant order.[33]

"Men laugh and riot till the feast is o'er. Then comes the reckoning, and they laugh no more."[34]

For Protestant townsmen and mariners like Bryan Blundell, it was a moment of triumph, a new king, a new future, and the loosening of old constraints.

But not everyone was rejoicing. In the shadow of the old castle, Caryll Molyneux, the 3rd Viscount Molyneux, remained a staunch Catholic and loyalist to the deposed King James II. In the wake of the revolution, Parliament outlawed him for his Jacobite sympathies.[35] Though Liverpool Castle itself was already crumbling into obsolescence, Molyneux's decline marked a deeper shift, as power passed quietly from aristocratic hands into the grasp of a rising merchant elite.[36]

The town had aligned itself firmly with the new political and religious order. The Whig party, champions of constitutional monarchy, commerce, and Protestant succession, gained control of Liverpool's Corporation. In a region largely loyal to the old Catholic and Tory elite, Liverpool became a Protestant stronghold, backing the new dynasty with fervour. It reaped the rewards of this allegiance: political favour, legal protection, and a rising commercial profile.[37]

It was a striking symbol of a broader English transformation. Freed from feudal constraints, traders reshaped towns to serve their ambitions, expanding trade routes, investing in ships, founding banks, and laying the foundations of empire.[38]

These changes were not confined to politics. The Glorious Revolution also redefined the relationship between church and state. In 1689, Parliament passed the Toleration Act, granting freedom of worship to Protestant dissenters, nonconformists who worshipped outside the Church of England, for the first time. Though it excluded Catholics and still demanded allegiance to the established church, it marked a quiet revolution in religious life.[39]

The revolution also redrew the economic map.

It broke monopolies such as the Royal African Company, opening the way for private merchants to stake their claim in the transatlantic slave trade. It was this shift that would soon bind Liverpool's fortunes to the brutal logic of the triangular trade.

At the same time, it triggered the Nine Years' War[40] (1688–1697), drawing England into continental conflict. For Liverpool, the war brought peril but also opportunity. French privateers prowled the seas, making southern routes treacherous. Ports like Liverpool, far from the Channel and closer to Ireland, found themselves in sudden demand.

For Liverpool's merchants, the overthrow of James II was more than a political shift; it marked the dawn of a new economic order.

The town's transformation had begun, and its merchants were at the helm.

Chapter 4

The Far Shore

"For if the ship springs but a leak, or if but a plank chance to fly, down you go — whence you shall not return..."

Christopher Bassnett, 1711

The Town of Liverpool | Monday, 6 November 1690

Finally, the wind turned.

At 10 am the *Reserve* slipped from her moorings and eased down the River Mersey, sails drawing full in a brave southeast gale, her bow cutting through the cold, slate-grey water under a clear sky.

Bryan, now 15, stood aboard. He was no longer a boy, but a seaman earning his keep. "I was cabin boy but I had 20 shillings per month, for I knew my labour very well, and to my strength could do as well as any."

The voyage had been long in coming.

For more than a year, wars had held the ship in port. England was locked in a wider conflict with France, part of the Nine Years' War, a global struggle that stretched from Flanders to the Caribbean. The Atlantic had become even more dangerous without escort. Trade routes were disrupted by naval blockades, privateers, and the constant threat of enemy capture. Merchant vessels now waited weeks for safe passage.

Despite the risks, Bryan's next journey would carry him further than ever before – to the American colonies, to the plantations of Virginia, and to the world of tobacco.

Learning the Hard Way

The *Reserve* sailed in company with two other ships, the *Merica* and the *Unicorn*, their sails bright against the November sky.

However, those first days at sea were a test of endurance.

By morning, their ship had made its way south and was now off the coast of Wales near Holyhead. That night, they battled hard westerly winds. The sea was unforgiving, forcing the crew to reef the sails, partially lowering and fastening them to reduce their area, as the gales intensified. It was the only way to prevent the canvas from tearing and the masts from giving way.

The following morning, St David's Head loomed into view, but the wind, shifting southwesterly, pressed them dangerously close to shore. Bryan and the men worked tirelessly, hauling ropes, adjusting sail, fighting back to keep the ship steady.

The storm roared around them. The wind howled. The waves frothed white against the hull, and the *Reserve* groaned under the weight of it all.

Eventually, the gusts grew so intense that the mainsheets and the main tack, the lines anchoring and shaping the mainsail, couldn't withstand the pressure and gave way. In the chaos, the foresheet blocks split, and the clew-garnets snapped. The crew scrambled across the deck, struggling to regain control. For a time, it seemed they might be driven ashore.[1]

For days, the *Reserve* wrestled with the sea, tacking northward and southward, battered by a relentless barrage of wind and spray. Again and again, they sighted the Isle of Man and Holyhead, trapped in a battle between wind and tide.

They soon sought refuge at Hoylake on the Wirral, anchoring within the protective rocks. Despite all they had endured, they had barely made it more than a few miles from Liverpool. For nearly a month they remained marooned there – weather-beaten, watchful, but determined – until Thursday, 4 December, when they tried again.

But the weather turned against them once more. Their next stop was near Piel Castle,[2] a fourteenth-century fortress perched on a tidal island near Barrow-in-Furness, where they were forced to stay until late December.

For Bryan and the crew of the *Reserve*, the New World still seemed an impossible dream. Six weeks after leaving Liverpool, they found themselves still stranded in Britain. But with every passing day, Bryan was learning more than just navigation; he was learning how to endure, how to adapt, and what it truly meant to be a sailor.

Four days before Christmas, they finally set sail again. By nightfall, a fresh easterly wind picked up, pushing the ship southwest. Over the next few days, they made their way down the east coast of Ireland, passing Greenore Point and then finally Cape Clear, Ireland's southernmost inhabited island. They left Irish waters behind at last, on Christmas Day 1690.

Not long after, the crew discovered that a musket had been hung too close to the ship's binnacle, the wooden housing for the ship's compass. The iron in the musket had disturbed the compass needle, throwing their course off and sending them further south than intended.

New Year's Day brought heavy gales forcing them to reef the topsails. Over the next few days, they battled shifting winds, rough seas, and frequent rain. Positions recorded on 4 and 5 January placed them well into the Atlantic.

The coming weeks brought little relief, only more squalls and strong gales. One day, they encountered two ships, one a Plymouth flyboat, a fast, shallow-drafted vessel, originally Dutch in design and prized for its speed and agility. A brief exchange followed, but worsening weather soon forced them apart. It was the only contact they would have for weeks, each vessel carried onward into the deepening Atlantic swell.

The journey neared its next phase on Thursday, 5 February. Soundings at 22 fathoms, then 14, signalled approaching land, but poor visibility kept the coast hidden. Still, the crew held their course, their destination drawing closer.

Landfall and Ledger: First Steps in the New World

For more than two months, the *Reserve* had battled both the Irish Sea and the Atlantic – gales, calms, driving rain, and biting cold. The crew had reefed and loosed the sails more times than they could count, their hands left raw by salt and rope.

At sea, time lost all meaning. Days blurred into each other; weeks could pass beneath the same grey canopy. The ocean became their world – vast, indifferent, capable of delivering fortune or ruin.

Deep down, fear must have lingered among the crew: fear of storms, sickness, and the ever-present dread that they might never sight land again. Such feelings could not be shared aloud. Doubt had to be buried deep, silence was survival, and uncertainty a risk no one could afford.[3]

They followed their course, checked the compass, read the stars, and trusted the wind to shift in their favour.

They waited. And hoped.

Then, at 7 am on Friday, 6 February 1691, a smudge appeared on the horizon. The crew gathered, willing it to be real. At last, certainty – a low, dark line where sea met sky. Cape Henry, Virginia (see Map 4).[4]

A wave of relief must have surged through Bryan and the crew. The journey had been long and punishing, but here was proof they had made it.

As they drew nearer, the outline sharpened. Behind the cape rose the thick forests of the Chesapeake – vast, unbroken, and still. Pines, oaks, and hickories crowded the shoreline, their winter-bare limbs dark against the pale morning sky.[5]

Soon they were navigating cautiously up the eastern side of the Chesapeake Bay, feeling their way through shifting depths. Snow and rain swept the deck, the wind forcing them to anchor. The weary men took down the yards and topmasts, the upper sections of the mast that carried additional sails higher into the wind, waiting for the weather to break.

When it did, the *Reserve* pressed onward, sailing past the mouth of the York River until they reached Watt's Island, safe waters at last. Once known as St Gabriel's Island, it had been renamed in 1670 after a local landowner, John Watts,[6] and now served as a familiar landmark for ships progressing up Chesapeake Bay (see Map 5).[7]

The following week, they slowly navigated into Chesconessex Creek, a quiet inlet on Virginia's Eastern Shore.[8] Here, along the banks, the signs of settlement were plain. Fields of tobacco stubble[9] stood beside raw-hewn cabins, smoke drifting from brick chimneys where settlers dried maize and salted pork. Canoes slipped across the shallows, while hogs rooted on the shore and cattle grazed at the edge of new clearings.[10]

When Bryan finally stepped ashore, his legs, shaped by months at sea, must have faltered on the solid earth. But one thing was certain, he was far from the boy who had first left Liverpool. He had been hardened by the fury of the Atlantic and the trials of the voyage. The world before him now was vast, uncertain, full of both opportunity and danger.

Creeks and Backwaters

Once safely on land, the crew swiftly turned to business, unloading English goods: textiles, tools, and other manufactured wares, ready to trade with Virginia's planters. They often set up makeshift stores or hired space in existing warehouses to facilitate these exchanges.[11]

Yet the colony did not revolve around towns. Its life was stretched along the waterways, where plantations of 400, even 1,000 acres, reached down to the riverbanks. From these wharves and creeks, planters rowed or sailed their own craft – small pinnaces, shallops, and canoes – to carry tobacco out to the anchored ships and bring back the goods that sustained their households. The same vessels also tied the colony together, ferrying families to church, neighbours across the water, and fishermen to the oyster beds.[12]

Here boats were not luxuries, but lifelines, as necessary as the land itself. Whether rowed by the planter, an indentured servant, or an enslaved African, they stitched together the fabric of daily life in the Chesapeake.

Foremost among them were shallops – open, versatile boats, rigged with oars and sometimes one or two masts. They slipped into narrow creeks, hauling corn and ferrying 4-foot-high hogsheads of tobacco, vast wooden barrels, to the waiting ships. Their handiness made them indispensable, the everyday workhorses of the rivers.

By the early eighteenth century, larger Virginia-built sloops began to dominate the longer runs. Sharp-lined and swift, they carried tobacco south to the West Indies, where ship and cargo were often sold together. Speed was their safeguard: quick enough to outpace pirates, shallow enough to dodge Spanish patrols, they were the traders' best defence as well as their livelihood.[13]

Figure 9. A colonial shallop, as illustrated in Willis J. Abbot, *American Merchant Ships and Sailors.* (*New York: Dodd, Mead & Company, 1902; Project Gutenberg eBook #15648*)

Figure 10. Sloops on the York River between Yorktown and Gloucester Point, after an original 1755 drawing. From Cerinda W. Evans, *Some Notes on Shipbuilding and Shipping in Colonial Virginia* (*Jamestown 350th Anniversary Historical Booklet*, No. 22, Williamsburg, 1957). (*Reproduced via Project Gutenberg eBook #15648*)

All of it, however, turned on the crop that filled the boats and fixed the colony's place in the Atlantic world.

A World Built on Tobacco

On this first voyage, Bryan soon discovered how tobacco ruled everything;ordering the lives of merchants and sailors alike, setting the rhythm of their years and the length of their voyages. It dictated the weight of every cask thudding across a deck, and even served as currency in which debts, wages, and fines were paid.

The land itself seemed shaped for tobacco. A sandy loam stretched mile upon mile, easy to clear and quick to yield. Even with crude methods, two crops could be drawn from the same ground in a year.[14]

At the landings Bryan saw the results of those harvests. He now watched as hogsheads were prised open, the leaf inside telling its own story.

Two varieties dominated: Orinoco and sweet-scented. Orinoco, coarse and pungent, thrived in the lowland soils of the Eastern Shore where Bryan first came ashore. Packed loose and sold cheaper, it was favoured on the continent. Sweet-scented, finer and more aromatic, clung to upland plots and commanded higher prices in London.[15]

For now, Bryan leaned close, learning as every merchant must to tell them apart by scent and texture: Orinoco's sharp bite rising when a hogshead was opened, sweet-scented softer, more delicate.[16]

Only after the inspections and bargaining were done did the heavy work begin. With smaller growers the leaf came loose, and the men had to pack the hogsheads themselves – layer upon layer, pressed tight with iron screws until the staves bulged against their hoops.[17]

Once sealed, the casks began their journey from the fields to the water's edge, hauled sometimes for miles across rough tracks. In winter when the ground was frozen hard, the great barrels lurched forward step by step.

At the riverside Bryan helped wrestle them onto canoes and shallow-draft sloops one by one. Each weighed 400 to 800 pounds, so heavy it took two men straining together to shift one.[18] From there they were taken to the waiting ships in deeper water. Ropes were looped and tightened around each cask, the pulleys groaning under the weight. And slowly, they began to rise. As the hatches opened, the thick reek of tobacco rose into the air, before each barrel was swung over and slowly lowered into the dark, airless hold.

The merchant's schedule was fixed with the seasons. Ships sailed from England in late autumn, reached the Chesapeake by January, and aimed to sail home by May. This allowed them to purchase and load tobacco that had been harvested, cured, and packed into hogsheads during the

Figure 11. *Rucker's Tobacco Boat*, 1771. From Percy's Piedmont Apocalypse. (Reproduced in Willis J. Abbot, *American Merchant Ships and Sailors* (*New York: Dodd, Mead & Company, 1902*; *Project Gutenberg eBook #15648*)

autumn months. It also avoided the peak months of July and August, when shipworms – teredo navalis, a type of marine mollusc resembling a reddish worm – posed the greatest threat.[19]

These creatures, often several inches long, bored into the wooden hulls of ships, riddling the planks with tunnels and honeycombing the timber until it could crumble without warning. Some vessels were lost before the damage was even detected. The risk was greatest in the warm, saline waters of the Caribbean and Chesapeake Bay. Until copper sheathing became widespread in the late eighteenth century, captains would, if delayed, move their ships into upstream freshwater rivers to wait out the danger until September.[20]

Fire and Water

After three months in Virginia, the crew of the *Reserve* finally prepared to make the long voyage home. On Wednesday, 20 May 1691, they left their anchorage and headed toward the James River to join their convoy.

When it came to convoys, the Virginia tobacco fleet stood in a league of its own. No other colonial trade demanded such elaborate protection. The sheer size of the crop, and the revenue it yielded, made the Chesapeake convoys the largest and most closely watched in the English Atlantic. War, piracy, and privateering made the Atlantic crossing perilous, and the government was determined to protect the £200,000 in customs revenue that each year's cargoes brought to the Exchequer. That year, for example, nearly half of England's permitted merchant tonnage was assigned to the Virginia fleet, 125 out of 300 ships.[21]

But convoy protection came at a cost. Ships might lie at anchor for weeks, their holds idle, as masters and merchants fumed at the delay. Wages drained away, expenses mounted, and in the warm waters of the Chesapeake shipworms gnawed through planking while sailors waited at the river mouths for the navy's signal.[22]

At last, on Saturday, 20 June, Bryan and his crewmates were permitted to set sail from Cape Henry, Virginia. They were part of a massive convoy of 130 merchant ships. Their escorts for the perilous Atlantic crossing were two formidable Royal Navy men-of-war: *Experiment Galley* and *Woolf*.

Even so, power at sea did not always mean safety. The crossing proved anything but smooth. Three days in, dark clouds swallowed the horizon, and a fresh gale tore through the convoy.

Bryan and the crew scrambled to hand the topsails as the wind took them aback. By 2 pm the storm struck with full force, bringing a downpour so heavy it blurred the line between sea and sky.

Thunder cracked overhead, deafening above the howling wind.

Amid the chaos, a small pink, a narrow-sterned vessel, built for coastal manoeuvrability, "lost her main-mast to [a] thunderbolt", the splintered wood vanishing into the waves.[23]

By morning, the worst had passed, but the sea was eerily still. Bryan watched uneasily as the ship drifted without wind or steerage, their sails slack. The stillness was as dangerous as the storm: vessels were at the mercy of currents alone. Nearby ships floated closer, threatening to collide.

The crew grew tense, fearful they might "come foul of one another, for we had no command of the ship, but the sea hove her not without it."

Then, three days later, horror unfolded before their eyes.

At 1 pm a flyboat carrying 1,000 hogsheads of cargo caught fire. The flames began aft, creeping through the ship's quarters as smoke billowed into the sky. The crew of the *Reserve* could do nothing but watch as it "smouldered and smoked" through the afternoon, a slow, merciless destruction. By early evening, "the fire flared up and continued all night".[24]

Fire was the unspoken terror of every sailor. A single spark – a dropped pipe, a galley fire left smouldering, or a candle burning after its owner had fallen asleep – could turn a ship into an inferno. In a world of tarred ropes, oak timbers, and loose powder, the smallest carelessness might mean sudden ruin.[25]

Fire at sea left little chance of rescue. To bring another vessel too close risked sparks or falling timbers setting her alight as well. The flyboat's blaze had begun "aft," likely in the crew's quarters. With few sailors able to swim,[26] and no one willing or able to risk rescue, escape was all but impossible. All Bryan and the *Reserve* could do was stand off and watch.

By sunrise, the vessel had either vanished from view or sunk beneath the waves. There was no trace of wreckage, no sign of survivors. Bryan stared out over the empty water, shaken. He wished he would "never see the like again".

The Measure of Success

After seven weeks at sea, the convoy finally neared home waters.

On Thursday, 6 August 1691, the *Reserve* parted ways with the London fleet, sailing northward toward St George's Channel alongside thirty other vessels. By dawn, the Irish coast emerged through the mist. Bryan noted the sighting in his journal – Mizen Head lay east-northeast, about 8 leagues away, while the jagged Bull, Cow, and Calf Rocks[27] rose to the north-northeast.

With the winds now in their favour, they pressed on toward home.

At last, on Sunday, 30 August 1691, after more than two months at sea, the *Reserve* reached Lancaster and Liverpool. By then, Bryan had crossed the Atlantic four times, braving fierce storms, shipwrecks, and the endless uncertainty of the open ocean.

The journey had tested him, but it had also paid off.

This was his first voyage earning both wages and a share in the cargo, and the outcome pleased him. He had cleared £18, "which I thought a brave business," and with the £40 from his last journey, his total stock now stood at "£120 or better."

It was a modest return, earned through skill, resolve, and no small measure of luck.

Chapter 5

Forged by the Sea: The Making of a Master Mariner

"It seems to require a great deal of skill and good conduct, to be clear masters of it — to be able to carry a ship to any part of the world, and to any port in it, that a man has a mind to. This looks like no ordinary talent."

Christopher Bassnett, 1711

Rathlin Islands | Sunday, 16 October 1692

The wind struck without warning.

As the *Reserve* approached the northern coast of Ireland, a sudden gale tore across Rathlin Sound,[1] snapping the mainsail and leaving the ship to limp forward under reduced canvas. At midnight the wind shifted again, forcing yet another change in direction. The work was relentless; the sea gave no quarter.

Their course had taken them past the Calf of Man, a small islet just south of the Isle of Man, and then north between Ireland and Scotland, but now the narrow channel became a trap of shifting winds and heaving seas.

At 17, Bryan Blundell stood on deck, exhausted and soaked to the bone, second mate now, with real responsibilities and no room for fear. He and the crew fought through the night, their destination, Montserrat in the West Indies, still an ocean away.

The storm would come. But first came the waiting.

Twelve months earlier, war had kept Bryan's captain, Christopher Moore, ashore. Apart from a brief voyage to Dublin, the *Reserve* remained moored in Liverpool through the winter of 1691.

It was not until March the following year that a new master, William Webster, took command. Under his leadership, they set sail for Bergen,

Norway. The voyage proved a short interlude. The real opportunity, and the greater risk, lay ahead: a voyage back to the sugar islands of the West Indies.

As second mate, Bryan now earned 35 shillings a month. It was a defining promotion for a teenager, and one that set him firmly on the path to command. It was also a role of real consequence, demanding far more than muscle or obedience. He was now responsible for navigation, the upkeep of charts and instruments, and the supervision of the crew's daily routines.

But to chart a safe course across vast and often treacherous waters, knowledge alone was not enough. In an age before modern instruments, survival depended on a mariner's ability to read the stars, the sea, and the shifting winds.

Sailing by the Stars

His journal suggests a solid education in astro-navigation, the practice of using celestial bodies to determine a ship's position. Using mathematical calculations, charts, and instruments such as the cross-staff and backstaff, sailors like Bryan were able to estimate their position and navigate across vast stretches of ocean.[2]

Every ship Bryan sailed carried a magnetic compass, housed in the binnacle beside the helm. It was the mariner's most trusted guide, allowing him to steer with remarkable accuracy: within 2.8°, an impressive feat for the time.[3] The compass needle, drawn by a magnetised mineral known as lodestone, pointed north with an uncanny consistency that had guided sailors for centuries.

But to many of his generation, the compass was both tool and enigma. As the Liverpool minister Christopher Bassnett later observed, "The lodestone carries such a mystery in it that naturalists can't give a just and clear account of it – it remains mysterious and hidden."[4]

Bryan soon learnt its quirks well, taking care to keep iron objects away from the binnacle to preserve the needle's accuracy – in the open sea, even a slight deviation could mean the difference between safe harbour and disaster. A compass off by a few degrees might seem nothing at first, but over time, it carried you far from where you were meant to go.

To estimate his ship's speed and distance, Bryan relied on the seaman's old standby, the log and line. The method involved casting a weighted wooden log astern, attached to a rope knotted at regular intervals. Each length of line measured roughly 50 feet to a knot, and a small sandglass, calibrated to about 28 seconds, was turned as the log drifted out behind. The number of knots that slipped through the sailor's hands before the last grain of sand fell gave the ship's speed in nautical miles per hour: hence the word "knots". Even a slight stretching of the wet rope could throw a reckoning off, so the line was checked often for accuracy.[5]

By this simple ritual of line and glass, Blundell and his crew could gauge their progress across the Atlantic. One knot equalled roughly one nautical mile an hour, about one and one-seventh of an English mile, and a steady passage under sail might average 4 to 6 knots.[6]

The sandglasses, sometimes called hourglasses, were essential tools for sailors to measure time at sea. While some were calibrated for short spans like the log-and-line, others tracked longer periods and were turned routinely to regulate watches, daily tasks, and pumping schedules.

To determine latitude, the ship's position north or south of the equator, Bryan relied on instruments such as the cross-staff and quadrant, gauging the angle of the midday sun above the horizon. By consulting navigational tables listing the sun's declination for each day of the year, he could calculate his position with reasonable accuracy. It was a delicate process, dependent on clear skies, accurate tables, and a steady hand.[7]

For earlier sailors, though, theory met reality in squinting eyes and blistered hands. A cross-staff forced the observer to look directly into the sun, often leaving him half-blinded (Figure 12). By Bryan's time, the Davis quadrant had softened the task. Sliding a vane along its arc, the sailor aligned shadow with horizon, fixing the sun's altitude without staring into the glare. Even so, it was awkward in a heaving sea: one foot braced, one hand gripping the instrument, the other scratching down the angle before it slipped away.[8]

Longitude, however, posed a far greater challenge. The precise measurement of east-west position remained one of the great unsolved problems of the age. It was a gap in knowledge that could, and often did, prove costly.

Instead, sailors relied on a method known as dead reckoning, estimating position based on speed, direction, and elapsed time – always vulnerable to

SEVENTEENTH CENTURY MARINER USING A CROSS-STAFF
From Seller's "Practical Navigation," London, 1676.

SEVENTEENTH CENTURY MARINER USING DAVIS' QUADRANT
From Seller's "Practical Navigation," London, 1676.

Figure 12. Seventeenth-century mariners using a cross-staff (left) and Davis quadrant (right). From John Robinson and George Francis Dow, *The Sailing Ships of New England, 1607–1907*. (Salem: Marine Research Society, 1922. After John Seller, Practical Navigation, London, 1676).

current, wind, and cumulative error. "By guess and by God," as they wryly called it, dead reckoning was more faith than precision, especially on long Atlantic crossings.[9]

The towering volcanic peak of Pico in the Azores served as a critical waypoint for transatlantic crossings, and Bryan meticulously recorded longitude estimates between London, The Lizard, Cape Clear, and Pico.[10]

But ultimately, even the most careful calculation could not replace a mariner's senses. Land was often felt before it was seen: the cry of seabirds, the change in wave pattern, the shift in water colour or temperature. Mariners confirmed their instincts with the lead line, casting for soundings to gauge depth, essential when threading into the English Channel or unfamiliar rivers.[11]

Just as crucial was the ability to read the weather, an art passed down through generations. Long before barometers or forecasts, sailors watched the sky's colour, the drift of clouds, and the roll of the swell.[12]

The techniques Bryan mastered were not merely tools of trade, but instruments of survival. It was said that this system of navigation depended on three Ls, Lead, Latitude, and Look-out, a triad capturing the science and skill of seventeenth-century seamanship.[13] What seems rudimentary today was, for him, the height of maritime expertise: a discipline rooted in mathematics, tempered by instinct, and paid for in lives when it failed.

Trial by Water

On Friday, 14 October 1692, under Webster's command, the *Reserve* finally departed Liverpool, bound once again for Montserrat. Bryan's route took them north around Ireland before turning west into the Atlantic.

Two days after leaving the crew passed the Calf of Man, and that afternoon faced the storm that would tear their mainsail and test their seamanship to its limits. They adjusted course as the winds shifted, struggled on under damaged canvas, and fought to hold position through a long, harrowing night.

The Atlantic offered no reprieve, just two months of open sea. At last, on Thursday, 15 December, they sighted land: the island of Désirade, a narrow strip off Guadeloupe's eastern coast.[14]

The next morning, they turned westward and by 9 am, Bryan noted Montserrat on the horizon, bearing west by south. It was, he wrote, "a very high island and makes with 4 or 5 hills upon it." The hills Bryan counted were, in fact, the island's volcanic spine – peaks that had shaped its valleys and soils for centuries. From those rich soils came the sugar that bound Montserrat to the Atlantic economy.

As they drew nearer, he would have seen steep ravines cutting through its lush slopes. Plantations dotted the hillsides, hemmed in by cane and jungle. A few stone buildings lined the harbour, half-swallowed by green. Closer still, he might have caught the smell of woodsmoke drifting in the tropical air.[15]

The *Reserve* was soon safely at anchor, the crew weary but unharmed. In Montserrat's bustling markets, goods sold for fine prices: barrels of beef at £3, soap and candles fetching up to 12 pence per pound. There was money to be made, and Bryan wasted no time turning a profit from his own venture.[16]

But trade did not always run smoothly. When they arrived, sugar was scarce: "we being early in the year, there was not much made so that we were forced to stay long for it."[17]

In the end, Bryan and the *Reserve* lay trapped on Montserrat for six long months, waiting to fill her hold.

When loading finally began in June, fresh trouble struck.

The *Reserve* "would break out in leaks," her timbers straining under the weight. Again and again the crew patched her, but the water kept coming. Some began to fear she was no longer seaworthy, that she might never leave the island at all.

Still, they pressed on.

They eventually set sail on Sunday, 18 June, but were forced to pump the bilge twice every half-hour, turning their sandglass each time to keep the rhythm.

By Tuesday, the leaks had worsened. The crew worked without pause. The ocean offered no reprieve, only resistance. It would be a long, hard passage home.

Despite the hardships, the voyage, with Bryan now serving as second mate, proved a success. They kept the pumps going throughout, suffering no further damage. "Blessed be the Lord," Bryan later wrote, "all things well with us."

Bryan finally returned to Liverpool in August 1693 with £50 in wages and profits, an impressive sum for a young sailor.[18]

But the voyage had earned him more than money. It had brought him the respect of his captain and crew. Captain Webster, recognising his skill and dedication, offered him the position of first mate once the *Reserve* was repaired and sheathed, a process of covering her hull with protective material, such as tar or planking, to guard against shipworms and rot. It was a prestigious step, second in command, a role that carried real authority and responsibility.

Yet Bryan was restless. Waiting in port while repairs dragged must have felt intolerable. Another captain, Lewis Jenkins, preparing his ship for departure, persuaded him to sign on as second mate on the *Amety*, with pay of 35 shillings a month, along with 18 shillings for portage, an allowance for carrying personal cargo to sell abroad.[19]

It was a decision that would shape his future. The West Indies had been a land of fortune but also of risk. In his diary he notes that Montserrat was often ravaged by sickness, and "a man, after 6 or 7 months being sick, he was put ashore with his goods and so left there."[20]

This fate was not uncommon. Sailors who fell ill were often left behind, deemed too great a burden to carry home, their names quietly struck from the muster roll and their stories lost to the sea.

Profit and the Press

His new ship, the *Amety*, set sail from Liverpool in early December 1693, bound once more for Virginia and the American colonies.[21]

Weeks into the voyage, the risks of life at sea made themselves known. On the night of 28 January 1694, under a moonless sky, a sharp cry rang out. John Robinson had slipped from the main topsail yard, a horizontal spar high on the mainmast, and plummeted to the deck.

In his journal, Bryan acknowledged their good fortune: "wherein God's great mercy was that he was not killed or drowned." It was a stark reminder of the ever-present dangers aboard a merchant vessel; one loose line, one mistimed step, and a man's soul could be lost to the sea forever.

Within three weeks they reached Cape Henry. From here the *Amety* steered inland, threading her way along the western shore of Chesapeake Bay. Their destination was Hobb's Hole some 70 miles up the Rappahannock River.[22] Established in the 1680s as a small river port, it took its name from the deep anchorage in midstream. Here Bryan could safely anchor in the "hole," sheltered from the river's shifting currents, while he spent three weeks ashore storing and arranging cargo.[23] Tobacco sold at "8s 4d per hogshead", and within two months the *Amety* was fully laden and ready to join the James River fleet for the journey home.

They departed Cape Henry in the second week of May[24] "in company of 24 sail," and under the protection of two letters-of-marque from London, each armed with twenty guns.

For three days they sailed together, but then the weather turned. "We had very thick rain and wind," Bryan wrote, "and in the morning we had lost the fleet except 4 ships that had made the same sail that we did."[25]

On the page it reads like accident. Yet there are hints of calculation. The *Amety* was a quick vessel, and its captain and crew knew the value of being first home. For the master, pressing ahead of the fleet meant securing the best prices before Liverpool's market was flooded with Virginian goods. For the crew, it meant something just as valuable – avoiding the press, the Royal Navy's gangs who prowled the ports to seize sailors by force and drag them into service.

Whether by chance or intent, the separation changed everything. From that point, they steered their own course across the Atlantic, no longer shielded by the guns of the fleet but no longer bound to its delays.

They arrived safely back in Liverpool at the end of June.[26] Only days later Bryan learnt that the rest of their fleet had been ambushed off the Irish coast by two powerful privateers, one armed with fifty-six guns, the other with thirty. Outgunned and outmatched, six of the finest ships in the convoy were seized, while the others scattered in desperate flight.

If the decision to split from the convoy was strategic, then the captain could not have had a better man in charge of navigation. Bryan's ability to handle a ship with exceptional speed and efficiency was fast earning him a reputation. Among his contemporaries, he would go on to be regarded as the "finest shallop racer from the Mersey to the West Indies."[27]

Captain William Hutchinson, a fellow mariner, later recalled an episode that captured Bryan's mastery of a vessel. The two were assigned to survey neighbouring ports, commanding one of two pilot sloops. Theirs was widely regarded as the worst in the fleet, slow and sluggish.[28]

But Bryan, undeterred, ordered the heaviest materials moved amidships. The result was immediate: the vessel, once outpaced by its rival, now cut cleanly through the water. "Without so much as adjusting the mast, sails, or rigging," Hutchinson recalled, "he made her sail better than the other."[29]

Through Wind and Current

Bryan's next voyage aboard the *Amety* departed from Liverpool on Thursday, 22 November, bound for Virginia under the command of Captain Lewis Jenkins.

His journal, precise and restrained, records "thick dirty weather" in early January, with violent gusts from the southwest and frequent thunderstorms. The crew tracked compass variation, logged sightings of distant ships, and fought through days of strong easterly currents. "Here is a great rippling and overfalls," he wrote near the Virginia Capes, "which betokens a great current…"[30]

After more than eleven weeks at sea, they finally sighted land.[31] As the Virginia capes rose ahead, Bryan took his bearings – first with the quadrant, then with the cross-staff. His quadrant fixed Cape Henry at 37° 10′ N, his cross-staff at 37° 05′ N. The near agreement must have been reassuring.

The following day they reached the mouth of the Potomac River; and three days later, they entered the Wicomico, a smaller river winding through the plantations of Maryland's Eastern Shore. There, Bryan helped load tobacco and acted as assistant to the supercargo, the officer responsible for managing the cargo and overseeing trade on behalf of the ship's owners.

After four months in Virginia, the *Amety* sailed home in mid-June[32] as part of a convoy of 120 vessels under the protection of the Royal Navy's *Norwich*.

The homeward leg brought its own hazards.

At 10 am one morning, four weeks after departing Virginia, they sighted sixteen French "bankers", fishing vessels armed for privateering, standing to the westward.[33] The French squadron fell in with the English convoy. One of their ships, the same that carried the French squadron's light, drifted dangerously close to the commodore's stern lantern, the beacon the English convoy used to steer by at night. Letting an enemy light mix with your own was risky: in the dark, ships might follow the wrong master, plunging the convoy into chaos and leaving stragglers exposed.

As the day drew on, the commodore ordered his ship to bout, and the *Amety*, with the rest of the fleet, followed. A brief stand-off ensued. Then, as the British line pulled away, the French ship fired a parting broadside at the commodore before slipping into thick weather.

By the end of July, the *Amety* had parted company with much of the fleet and was running up the Channel in heavy weather.[34] Off the north coast of Cornwall they picked up soundings and sighted land, judging it to be Padstow before passing Hartland Point.[35] Not long after, Grassholm rose into view, a small, uninhabited rocky island off Pembrokeshire, a marker of home waters. A few days later they cleared into Liverpool, completing the round trip in just over seven months.[36]

In his final line, Bryan wrote simply: "All things well with us. Blessed be the Lord, for he is who kept us out the hands of our enemies. I cleared this voyage £60."

Not a Cable's Length

That December, Bryan embarked on his third and final journey aboard the *Amety*. At just 21, he was earning £3 per month and was responsible for 4,000 lbs of portage.

By then, he was well-acquainted with the perils of the Atlantic, yet nothing could have fully prepared him for the dangers that lay ahead.

On Thursday, 5 December, Bryan and his company – Jonathan Livesly,[37] John Nomas, Coulthbert Sharples, Henry Brown, and Randell Galaway – departed from Liverpool, bound for Virginia.

A fresh east-northeast wind carried them down the Formby Channel, a narrow, shifting channel off the Lancashire coast just north of Liverpool. But as night fell, the wind shifted north-northeast and strengthened. Unable to make headway to the north and wary of privateers patrolling the southern waters, they were forced to take refuge in Beaumaris just three days later, where they remained trapped by fierce winter winds for eight frustrating weeks.

At last, in early February, the weather shifted. After a brief stop in Belfast for provisions, the *Amety* set sail again, making careful progress through narrow channels with the wind at their backs.[38] By 6 am the following morning, they were near the Scottish shore, ahead of the other vessels in the convoy. The wind, now northeast by north, made sailing difficult, but with the first of the ebb tide, the outgoing current, in their favour, they attempted to pass through the North Channel, between Ireland and Scotland.

Then disaster struck.

By mid-morning, the wind intensified, and without warning, the foretopsail yard snapped. Struggling to control the damaged rigging, Bryan and his crew fought to keep the ship from drifting. They narrowly cleared the treacherous Maiden Islands, two small islets surrounded by skerries, sharp, submerged reefs off County Antrim that had wrecked many a ship.

But the wind shifted again, forcing them away from the channel. They were now headed straight toward the jagged coastline of Lough Larne, a narrow inlet on the Antrim coast notorious for its reefs and shifting tides.

As they bore away for the harbour, a thick snowstorm descended, completely obscuring the shore. With no visibility, they sailed blind, relying only on instinct and experience. By noon, convinced they were dangerously close to land but unable to see any sign of the harbour, Bryan ordered the ship to "heave to", bringing her nearly to a standstill, riding out the storm as best they could.

Then, in what he would later call "a very great mercy," the snow lifted just enough to reveal their position: the *Amety* was "not a cable's length from the rocks eastward of the mouth of the harbour."

The ship's master, desperate to avoid wrecking on Magee Island,[39] ordered the crew to loosen the main topsail, hoping to force her out of danger. But the sea was running too high; the manoeuvre failed.

At that moment Bryan glimpsed the narrow entrance to Larne Harbour. Acting instantly, he let fly the mainsheet and threw the helm hard to windward, "putting it aweather."

The *Amety* answered at once, pivoting away from the rocks. Two crashing waves propelled her forward, and before the crew could even lower sail, they had shot safely into the harbour.

Later, Bryan recalled "had we stood two minutes longer, we could not have worn clear of the rocks, but must have lost the ship, if not our lives." He called it "the most imminent danger that ever I was in before, and I hope I never shall be again."

In words shaped by awe as much as faith, he recorded his gratitude for "the Lord's great mercy in giving us light, not only to see our danger, but also the way to escape."

It was a narrow deliverance, but there was no time to dwell. The Atlantic still lay ahead.

Once clear of Larne, the *Amety* continued her course toward Virginia. The voyage was fraught with strong westerly gales and rough seas, but after nearly two months, the ship finally entered the Potomac River in early April.[40]

At Nanjemoy, a small settlement on the north bank of the river, he divided his cargo with Mr John Hopkins, who took charge of selling half.

Meanwhile, Bryan pushed 20 miles further inland to negotiate on his own account. There he secured 150 hogsheads of tobacco. Though late in the season, he and his crew managed to fill the ship's hold through purchases and freighted cargo, ensuring a full load for the return journey.

In early July the *Amety* set sail from Virginia as part of a convoy of seventy ships. The journey home proved just as challenging as the outbound voyage, with persistent westerly winds and turbulent seas forcing the fleet to separate. By 18 August land was sighted off the Irish coast, and they reached Kinsale the next day.

They remained in Irish waters for several weeks, delayed by weather, repairs, or trade, before finally making for home.

Bryan arrived safely back in Liverpool on Friday, 13 November. The ship was fully loaded, and tobacco fetched a high price, making the voyage a financial success. He cleared £130 in wages and venture profits.

The *Amety* had carried Bryan through three testing voyages. But this would be his last aboard her.

The Master Mariner

By the end of 1696, Bryan Blundell had become more than a sailor, he was a seaman of rare skill and discipline. He had crossed the Atlantic multiple times, learned to read the stars with precision, to chart courses that balanced risk and return, and to manoeuvre with a strategist's instinct.

But mastery at sea was only part of the equation. To succeed in Liverpool's rising merchant class, one also had to navigate the waters of land-based power – alliances sealed by trade, partnership, and often by marriage.

That same year, he took another decisive step: taking Samuela Williamson,[41] daughter of one of Liverpool's leading merchant families, as his wife. Her grandfather, Edward Williamson, a draper and former mayor, had issued trade tokens during the Commonwealth, each stamped with the emblem of the Worshipful Company of Drapers: three radiating clouds crowned in gold.[42] Such tokens were common during the mid-seventeenth century, when political upheaval and the collapse of royal authority led to an acute shortage of small denomination coinage. Merchants, unable to rely on consistent national minting, issued their own local currency to maintain trade – coins that served as instruments of both value and trust.

Bryan's own connections were no less formidable. His uncle, William Preeson, was now serving as Mayor[43] of Liverpool and he also owned the *Mulberry*. It was the vessel that would soon grant Bryan his first command.[44]

In the seventeenth century, marriage was rarely just a private affair. It was a transaction, a consolidation of power. With Samuela, Bryan joined bloodlines with one of the town's commercial dynasties.

He was no longer just a mariner. He was becoming a man of the town.

Part II

The Pursuit of Fortune

Chapter 6

Master of Ship, Apprentice of Fortune

"The Business of Authority and Command:
The ship's crew is the master's household — they are his sea-family…'Tis a great thing to have so weighty a concern reposed in one — it requires great care and attention, vigour and presence of mind, and an extraordinary conduct to discharge it aright."

Christopher Bassnett, 1711

Off the Isle of Arran, Scotland | Tuesday, 26 January 1697

A cold wind swept across the deck of the *Mulberry*.

Bryan Blundell stood at the helm for the first time, 22 years old, master of a vessel bound for Virginia. His ship carried a crew of thirty-four, every one of them now under his command.[1] Around him the men trimmed sail and held their course, every order now his to give.

It was a defining step. A ship was a world unto itself, and its captain required not only skill in navigation but the steadiness to govern men, keep order, and enforce discipline at sea. For Bryan, this was the moment he had worked towards for years: the moment he became master of all that moved beneath the sails.

With responsibility came reward: £5 a month in wages, and 6,000 pounds of portage for his own venture. It also brought space of his own. At the stern lay the "great cabin," the captain's quarters: a partitioned space enclosed by bulkheads, furnished with a table for charts, a sea chest for accounts, and a cot, a light framed or canvas bed for sleep.[2] It was no admiral's suite, but it marked a distinction. Here Bryan would dine with his officers, receive merchants, and weigh decisions that might shape a voyage's fortune.

The *Mulberry*,[3] entrusted to Bryan by his uncle William Preeson, was more than an opportunity, it was a statement. Preeson was signalling to

Liverpool's merchant elite that his nephew was a man to watch, a rising force in the world of transatlantic trade. Alongside Bryan sailed Thomas Preeson, the shipowner's son and Bryan's cousin.[4]

However, whilst Bryan possessed a rare understanding of seamanship, mastery of the ocean was now only half the battle.

As captain, a successful voyage did not end when the anchor was dropped in port; true success lay in what came next, the art of commerce. Here the greatest dangers were not always found in storms or treacherous shoals, but in the unpredictability of business. A missed opportunity or a misjudged venture could cost a captain just as dearly as a shipwreck.

By the mid-1690s, the Virginian tobacco trade was thriving, but prices fluctuated wildly depending on supply, weather conditions, and demand in Europe.[5] Successful merchants needed to be shrewd negotiators, adaptable risk-takers, and, above all, relentless opportunists.

The Merchant of Virginia

As Bryan Blundell took command, his crew knew that every order, and every outcome, now rested on his judgement.

After leaving Liverpool, they cleared the Isle of Arran on Tuesday, 26 January 1697. February brought uncertain weather and fierce gales, with two of the ship's main shrouds, thick ropes that braced the mast from side to side, giving way. Without them, the entire rig was at risk.

Progress slowed, as strong easterly currents and shifting winds forced constant course corrections to maintain westward momentum.

Eight weeks later, as they neared the American coast, the ship encountered a Plymouth brigantine, a small two-masted trading vessel, also bound for the Chesapeake.

Their final approach, however, was far from easy. Foul weather battered the ship, bringing gusting winds, squalls of hail, and sharp cold spells, delaying their entry into port.

When they arrived,[6] Bryan found a convoy already preparing for the return journey. "We got into Virginia," he wrote, "and find that here is a fleet near ready to sail home." He added: "They think to sail in 10 days' time, but as we have always known fleets to be long in getting ready, so we have some hope of getting ready to sail with them."

He was right; those extra days gave him and his crew the chance they needed to complete their trading.

Yet commerce in Virginia was rarely straightforward. A poor harvest had led to a tobacco shortage, driving prices to unprecedented highs and much of the local stock had already been sold. Captains unwilling to pay inflated rates faced returning home with near-empty holds.

Wasting no time, Bryan and his cousin split their cargo and established trading posts in Pungoteague and Nassawadox,[7] determined to secure what tobacco remained. It was a calculated risk; if prices in England fell before their return, the entire voyage could end in ruin.

But Bryan understood the rhythms of the trade: speed was everything. Not just to avoid storms or outrun pirates, but to beat the convoy home and reach Liverpool before prices dropped, before the port overflowed with barrels and bales.

Despite the shortage, within three weeks he managed to purchase 150 hogsheads of tobacco at 9 shillings and 6 pence per hundredweight, a steep price, but one he was willing to pay.

Then, determined to move quickly, he hired extra hands and small sloops to ferry the massive tobacco hogsheads from inland creeks to his ship, eventually securing 250 hogsheads and another 50 on freight at £11 per ton.

On Friday, 7 May, with loading finally complete, their vessel was due to join a fleet of 140 ships, sailing under convoy protection.

But by the time they were ready, the fleet was already gone. The convoy had slipped away early, departing at 7 am that morning and leaving Bryan and his crew behind.

Determined to catch up, Bryan and the *Mulberry* cleared the coast at 4 pm and sailed hard E by S through the night. The wind held, and they pressed on, covering 50 miles in little more than a day, scanning the horizon for the faintest glimpse of canvas.

Later the following day, they sighted movement: "we saw three or four of the sternmost ships."

And at last, at 2 am on Sunday, 9 May, they had rejoined the fleet, "without the least knowledge of the Commodore."

They hailed a nearby vessel: "So spake with our William Chauntrell for to copy his sailing orders, which we did." Such orders were essential, laying out the course, signals, and rules for keeping formation. Without them, a ship risked confusion, isolation, or even being taken for an enemy.

Though the *Mulberry* had made up the distance with surprising speed, it may not have been down to sailing skill alone. Within days Bryan was complaining of "some foul ships" in the convoy, vessels so slow or illkept that they made the fleet "very tedious."

The Atlantic soon presented other challenges. Strong westerly winds and sporadic storms forced the fleet to scatter, straining navigation and leaving each vessel to fend for itself.

Then, one day, sails appeared on the horizon. Twenty-eight ships, their intentions unclear.

Bryan, no doubt, squinted through his spyglass, scanning the waterline for colours, for rigging, for any sign of friend or foe. He watched and waited.

As the distance closed, tension gave way to relief, they were merchant vessels arriving from Barbados. But the encounter was a stark reminder of how vulnerable they remained on the open ocean.

After a long and arduous passage, Bryan sighted the Irish coast in mid-June, identifying Cape Clear and the Old Head of Kinsale in the distance. A few days later he navigated past Lundy Island,[8] approaching the Bristol Channel. However, strong tides forced him to adjust course, and rather than sailing directly for Liverpool, the ship first docked in Dublin Bay, where they remained until Thursday, 1 July.

After six months and eight days, the *Mulberry* arrived back in Liverpool on Saturday, 3 July, two days after leaving Dublin.

The timing was perfect, the tobacco shortage had driven prices up across the supply chain, and demand in England remained strong. The ship's cargo fetched a high price, sold "at the mast" in a dockside auction, for between 3½ and 3¾ pence per pound. Buyers gathered as soon as the hatches were opened, allowing merchants to inspect and bid on the goods fresh from the hold, often before unloading had finished.

For the captain, selling at the mast offered speed, visibility, and sometimes a share of the profits; but just as importantly, it helped avoid spoilage and ensured the cargo fetched its best price.

It was exactly the outcome Bryan had hoped for. Six months at sea had earned him £184; several times a common sailor's annual wage, and a clear sign he was rising fast.

That Saturday was a day of both triumph and quiet joy for Bryan. He arrived home from another successful voyage just as his daughter, Hannah, was born.[9]

In a world where so few children lived beyond infancy, Hannah's survival would make her all the more precious. Of his four children with Samuela, only Hannah would survive to adulthood. Her siblings, William, John, and Mary, were among the many lost to the harsh realities of early modern England, where high child mortality was a tragic norm. In this period, nearly one in three children died before the age of 5, their lives cut short by disease, poor sanitation, and the limits of early medicine. Wealth offered no guarantee.[10]

Even as Bryan braved the perils of the open sea, he carried with him the weight of these private sorrows. Perhaps it was this stark contrast, the hard-won victories at sea and the profound losses at home, that fuelled his relentless drive to seize every opportunity Liverpool's expanding trade had to offer.

Bound to the Crop

Bryan's first command taught him that markets were volatile, shaped by weather, war, and demand beyond the reach of any single planter or port.

He learnt that the most successful traders were those who could secure supply swiftly and position themselves ahead of the market. Bryan quickly began honing his skills as a negotiator, seeking out reliable planters, guaranteeing quantity and quality, offering favourable terms, and building relationships that could outlast a single voyage.

Just as vital was his grasp of credit. Most transactions were not settled in hard currency, but in promises. Promissory notes, future cargoes, and deferred payments created a web of obligations stretching across oceans. Wealthy merchants advanced funds or goods in exchange for crops not yet harvested. In effect, they became bankers, using credit to secure first access and drive out competition.[11]

Liverpool's merchants excelled at this system. Their willingness to trade on credit, more so than their counterparts in Bristol or London, would become a defining feature of the town's commercial character.[12]

As Bryan's grasp of trade deepened, so did his understanding that the true wealth of empire lay not only in cargoes – tobacco, sugar, and timber – but in the labour that produced them.

Throughout the seventeenth century, the plantations of the Chesapeake had relied on indentured servants: men and women from Britain and Ireland who agreed to years of labour in exchange for passage across the Atlantic. For some, it offered hope of a better future. A debtor in Liverpool, a widow in Bristol; each might sign away years of freedom to escape hardship at home.

Liverpool played a role in this transatlantic migration. Between 1697 and 1707, more than 1,400 indentured servants passed through its waterfront on the way to the Americas or the West Indies.[13] Some came by choice. Others were children bound by parishes, sent out by local authorities to reduce the burden of poor relief, or petty criminals seeking to avoid harsher punishment. Shipowners, captains, and merchants all stood to profit.

The journey was prohibitively expensive. Most could not afford their own passage, so merchants paid the fare in exchange for control of their labour. Upon arrival, contracts were sold to plantation owners, treated not as promises, but as property. These agreements could be extended through punishment or loophole, their holders bought, bartered, and resold.

Bryan recognised the opportunity early. At first, he simply transported servants as part of mixed cargo. But over time, he began to record their sale directly. On his 1697 voyage, he noted the sale of two servants in Virginia for £44.[14]

In subsequent voyages to Barbados and Montserrat, he repeated the practice. Though the numbers remained modest, one or two individuals per voyage, it marked a quiet but deliberate engagement in the economics of labour.

However, as Bryan established himself in the trade, the labour system that had supported the tobacco economy for decades was beginning to unravel.

Indentured servitude, once the backbone of Virginian and Maryland plantations, was in decline. Britain's improving economy meant fewer men and women were desperate enough to risk years of hardship abroad. Tales of abuse, deception, and exploitation had spread, discouraging all but the most desperate.[15]

At the same time, planters were growing impatient with a workforce that was temporary, mobile, and increasingly demanding. Contracts ended; and with them came expectations of land, wages, and opportunity that many landowners were unwilling to meet.[16]

In response, colonial elites turned increasingly to a more permanent, and profitable, solution: enslaved Africans. The shift had begun earlier, but by the 1690s it was gaining speed. Laws inspired by the Barbados Slave Codes formalised lifetime servitude, binding not only the enslaved but their descendants.

The future of the plantation economy was being written in racial terms, backed by statute and violence. The very tobacco Bryan purchased and transported was now more likely than ever to have been cultivated by enslaved hands. The shift would have been hard to miss. Each voyage would have brought more signs: the auctions, the tightening laws, the changing tone among planters.

Between Wars and Winds

That autumn, the Nine Years' War finally came to an end. For nearly a decade, conflict with France had made transatlantic voyages perilous; privateers prowled major routes, and insurance costs soared. The Treaty of Ryswick, signed in September 1697 between France and the Grand Alliance,[17] which included England, brought a fragile but welcome peace.[18]

For Liverpool's merchants, peace proved a double-edged sword. It ushered in safer seas, fewer naval threats, and less disruption to shipping. Freed from the constraints of war, traders like Bryan could now plan their voyages with greater confidence and capitalise on the stability of a rebounding Atlantic economy. But peace also reopened southern routes, reviving competition from London, Bristol, and other long-established ports.

Just weeks after the Treaty of Ryswick was signed and ratified, and as peace took hold on the Atlantic, Bryan departed Liverpool on his second voyage as master of the *Mulberry*.

He set sail on Tuesday, 9 November 1697, bound for Pungoteague in Virginia. The journey was rough from the outset; gales off the Welsh coast forced the ship back to Hoylake. Just over eight weeks later, the *Mulberry* finally reached the Capes of Virginia.[19]

Though they arrived safely, bitter weather soon set in. "That night came on freshly bad weather, with snow," Bryan wrote, "and continued a whole month, so that we could do little but get our firewood." It was not until the first day of March that they began loading tobacco.

The homeward passage in May was no easier. Off the Banks of Newfoundland they caught cod in icy seas. Then the mist thinned just enough to show what lay around them.

"We came past several great islands of ice," Bryan noted, "very near them... it cleared up a little and we counted 20 islands all round us, very dangerous things they are, and especially in thick weather as it here commonly is."[20]

For days they threaded cautiously through fog and floes, half-seeing, half-guessing their way clear.

He safely returned to Liverpool in mid-June, having cleared £340 in venture and wages.[21]

Despite the easing of naval threats following the war, transatlantic voyages remained fraught with peril. Violent storms, navigational errors, illness, and the sheer unpredictability of the open sea continued to test even the most experienced captains. Bryan, despite his growing reputation as a master mariner, was not immune to the sea's trials.

Dead Reckoning – Latitude Without Longitude

Bryan's 1698 voyage to Virginia began in mid-October,[22] when the *Mulberry* left Liverpool with the wind at north and the tide at a quarter ebb. The venture was a joint one, the cargo shared between Bryan and two of his cousins, his previous travelling companion Thomas Preeson, and Walter Brice.[23]

On board were nearly seventy passengers, along with a load of coal and provisions bound for Dublin. Bryan is also recorded as having three indentured servants aboard for this voyage. By the following day, they had reached Dublin, where the cargo was discharged and new provisions taken on in preparation for the Atlantic crossing to Virginia. They finally sailed from Dublin in early November.[24]

Then, a week before Christmas, disaster struck.[25]

In the rough waters of the mid-Atlantic, Bryan recorded the harrowing moment in his journal: "We lost our cook's boy overboard in the latitude of 31° 18' N." There was no time for rescue, no hope of retrieval. Only the grim reality of a life claimed by the deep.

Death at sea was often swift and silent.

No grave. No last words. Just a name in a logbook, and a ship that sailed on.

Following tradition, the boy's few belongings would have been auctioned off on deck. The proceeds, often raised generously by shipmates, were, where possible, sent to his family.

In the weeks that followed, the winds held steady from the northwest. Without any reliable way to fix their position, they were left to rely, as always, on judgement, instinct, and dead reckoning.

But unbeknownst to Bryan, the wind had been slowly pushing him further off course than he realised.

Then one clear January night, under a bright moon, Bryan peered over the ship's side and noticed something unsettling, the colour of the water had changed.[26]

"We thought the water looked very white, and, looking upon the lee bow, saw land, which startled us, not thinking but we had been a good way to the westward of Bermudas."

Panic gripped the crew. They had not expected to be anywhere near land. Bryan feared the worst.

In the confusion, a cry came from the rigging; someone had spotted breakers ahead. He wasted no time.

"I was afraid that we had got within some leagues of rocks."

He called all hands to turn the ship, shaking out the reefs from the sails and setting the topsails as quickly as possible. A lead line was cast into the water, 12 fathoms.

They were perilously close to disaster.

"But blessed be the Lord we was upon the clear side of thc Island, that's the East side of it."

Had they approached from any other direction, they might have struck the reefs before ever seeing land. The east side had spared them; not through skill or foresight, but through luck, providence, or both.

After their good fortune, they cautiously made their way back towards Bermuda two days later, hoping to enter a safe harbour. As they neared the eastern shore, they raised their ensign in a signal for assistance, and soon a boat approached offering to guide them in.

But Bryan hesitated. He had learned from experience that in poor visibility, shifting winds, and uncharted waters, it was often safer to remain at sea.

When the wind rose once again, he made his decision. "It came to blow and away we were forced to run N by E away 3 or 4 leagues about a long shoaled white water point with foul rocks to the northwestward."

Finally, after eleven weeks at sea the *Mulberry* reached the capes of Virginia. The long voyage had cost them dearly – rations were depleted, men were weak, and the tobacco they had hoped to trade was far more expensive than expected.[27]

The homeward passage in April was far kinder, though not without incident. The crew endured one violent gale, forcing them to sail under a reefed foresail.

Then, suddenly, a massive wave struck the stern, "and a sea came and stowed in all our cabin windows and spoiled most of our beer."

Of all the hardships they had faced, this was surely the most unforgivable.

Despite the trials of the journey, Bryan turned a modest profit. Yet misfortune followed him even on land.

"I cleared about £100 but left it in Ireland by selling some tobacco to some men that broke [i.e. went bankrupt], so that I made but a sorry year's work."

Still, he pressed on, each voyage teaching him something new about risk, return, and the hidden patterns of profit.

For now, peace held across the Atlantic. But it was a fragile calm.

Tensions with France simmered beneath the surface, and a new conflict, one that would reshape Europe's imperial fortunes, was already drawing near.

Interlude

On the Edge of a Century, 1700

By the turn of the eighteenth century, Liverpool was no longer a minor port clinging to the edge of Lancashire.

Tobacco and sugar poured in. The population had more than doubled in a generation, and customs revenue had increased eightfold.[1]

But the town's growth had outpaced its foundations.

Drainage was poor, roads churned to sludge in winter, and waste piled in alleys and yards.

The single chapel could no longer contain its congregation. In 1699, the Corporation petitioned Parliament to establish Liverpool as its own parish.[2] They won.

A new church, St Peter's, was planned, and a two-rector system was agreed. For the first time, Liverpool would manage its own spiritual and civic affairs, separate from Walton and its Catholic patron.[3]

At the dawn of the new century, more than 100 registered vessels jostled for space along the waterfront, their masts rising like a forest against a darkening sky.[4]

The town of Liverpool was growing – steadily, and with purpose.

Chapter 7

The Fevered Tide

"It is indeed exceeding wonderful to be preserved in the midst of such amazing dangers — when the winds blow, when the floods beat, when the billows rage and roar."

Christopher Bassnett, 1711

Blundell's Great Cabin, Off Nevis | Friday, 19 December 1701

In the dim light of the captain's cabin, a bowl was laid upon the table. A blade was produced. A vein opened. And dark blood trickled out, watched in uneasy silence by the crew.[1]

Bryan Blundell was sick. With no real remedy at hand, he resorted to one of the age's most trusted treatments: bloodletting, followed by forced sweating. Heavy blankets were piled high. The galley fire was stoked until the cabin thickened with heat. The air grew stifling.

The disease had moved fast. One man had already been buried. Another two were sick.

And now, it had come for him.

Dwindling Profits, Rising Shadows

Thirteen months before the fever took hold, the currents of commerce had already begun to shift beneath him.

By the age of 24, he had spent his formative years at sea, navigating perilous waters, weathering storms, and learning the hard logic of trade. He had survived; but in a world like his, to survive was one thing; to thrive quite another.

Even so, in the eyes of his peers, Blundell was gradually becoming something more: a name of consequence.

Yet success was neither swift nor certain.

Blundell's final two voyages aboard the *Mulberry*, from late 1699 to mid-1701, were a test of endurance and diminishing returns.

His penultimate journey began in the autumn of 1699. The *Mulberry* slipped her moorings at 10 am on the morning of Friday, 9 November.

But before she had even cleared the Irish Sea, a gale forced her to take shelter at Milford Haven, a natural harbour on the southwest coast of Wales. Westerly storms continued for weeks, stalling their progress. Only at the end of the month did she finally round Cape Clear and strike out into the Atlantic.

By early in the new year, they were nearing the American coast, but the strain of constant sail in heavy weather had twisted their mainmast. Nevertheless, a week later they sounded 20 fathoms, then spotted anchor lights ahead. Not long after, land came into view.[2]

They had reached Virginia.

Over the next ten weeks, they worked the creeks and inlets of the Chesapeake, trading near Pungoteague. Trade was brisk. Blundell secured sixty-seven hogsheads of tobacco, paying between £14 and £16 apiece, including both regular and "sweet-scented" grades. By Friday, 12 April, he recorded simply: "out of the creek", homeward bound at last.

The storm-battered crossing to Virginia had been brutal, but the voyage home offered no reprieve. As they neared Newfoundland, thick fog rolled in, and the sea turned treacherous. Ice closed in again: vast slabs drifting south from the banks, some rising higher than the deck. Navigation slowed to a crawl.

Despite all their endeavours, they reached Liverpool in early June, only to find the tobacco market had collapsed.[3]

"This 4th voyage we came to a very sad market. 2¼d and 2½d was the price at the mast, but I cleared mine and believe made near 3 of it. I had by my own account aboard, 67 hogsheads and with wages and all, did not clear past £80 or £90."

He also held a quarter-share in the *Lever* and its cargo, but with tobacco selling so low, the investment had backfired. "It made the hull of the ship very dear to me," he added.

While Blundell struggled, others in Liverpool had already begun to look elsewhere.

In 1700, the *Liverpool Merchant* returned from the town's first recorded slaving venture.[4] At her helm on that voyage to Africa was William Webster, formerly captain of the *Reserve*, and once Bryan Blundell's commander, who, in recognition of his service to the town, was elected Mayor of Liverpool just five years later.[5]

For now, Blundell held his course. And in November, he set sail once again for Virginia.[6] But he was soon hemmed in by storms along the Irish coast and finally limped into Chesapeake waters in February 1701. He scoured every inlet he could find for cargo, from the dark, pine-fringed waters of Pickson's Harbour on the Western Shore to the marshy creeks of the Eastern Shore. The homeward crossing was swift, and by July, they were docked in Liverpool.[7] But the profit was meagre, just enough to cover costs. This would be Blundell's last voyage as master of the *Mulberry*.

That autumn, the fragile peace was coming to an end. In November, the War of the Spanish Succession broke out, a conflict sparked by the contested succession to the Spanish throne, with France and Spain on one side, and England, the Dutch Republic, and the Holy Roman Empire on the other.[8]

Although England would not formally join the war until 1702, for Liverpool's merchants, it marked the return of familiar risks: volatile markets, higher insurance premiums, and hazardous shipping routes. But war also brought opportunity, as trade shifted northward once again while southern ports came under threat.

Barrels and Barter

In September 1701, Bryan Blundell took command of the *Lever*, a 150-ton merchant ship he co-owned with three fellow investors – John Cleveland, William Bassnett, and John Pemberton.[9] She carried a crew of thirty-eight.[10]

In his journal, Blundell recorded his reluctance to displace the ship's former captain. But his partners, including future Mayor of Liverpool John Cleveland,[11] insisted his experience was essential to protect their investment.

Yet, one might question how unwilling he truly was. The language of hesitation may have served a purpose: a gesture of modesty, a nod to the displaced, or even a careful entry for the record. It is not impossible that the outcome had been quietly orchestrated from the start.

The *Lever* set sail at the end of September and soon cleared the Rock, the outcrop at the Mersey's mouth known as Perch Rock, where river gives way to sea. Leaving behind the smaller vessels of the estuary, she embarked on a carefully planned voyage to Dublin, Barbados, Nevis, and Virginia, each stop selected to maximise profit across the Atlantic economy.[12]

She reached Dublin the following day, where they unloaded their ballast and then rolled aboard hundreds of barrels of salted beef, soon packed tight against the sides of the hold. By the time the loading was done, 800 barrels were secured, and the *Lever* slipped away low in the water, bound for her next stop, Barbados.

They made swift progress across the Atlantic. In his journal, Blundell noted passing the *Leopard* of Bristol and a Bordeaux merchantman with ease.

Then, one day in the dark hours before dawn, a French privateer mistook the *Lever* for a pirate and fired six warning shots.[13] Only when the light rose did the truth become clear. It was a dangerous encounter, made more volatile by the fact that England and France were not yet officially at war. Without a formal declaration, or letters of marque to legitimise their actions, French privateers who attacked English ships risked being branded as pirates themselves. In the half-light of early morning, a misjudged volley could have sparked an international incident.

Barbados rose into view on the first day in December, but the *Lever* couldn't make the harbour before nightfall. By 6 pm, Blundell had taken in all but the mainsail and let the ship drift under minimal canvas until morning. The following day, they edged into Carlisle Bay and dropped anchor.[14]

But before any barrels could be landed, Blundell was obliged to visit the island's Powder Office, a colonial institution tasked with collecting the so-called "powder monies." The tax, intended to fund the island's defences, was calculated by tonnage and traditionally paid in gunpowder. According to Blundell's own record, he made the *Lever* out at 140 tons, paid 100 pounds of powder, and settled the rest in coin.

Once the formalities were complete, trade began in earnest. Over the next three days, he moved hundreds of barrels of beef, alongside smaller stocks of butter, cheese, soap, and candles. He even sold his own joiner, a shipboard servant, for £33.

But Blundell was already thinking ahead. When a sloop from Nevis arrived, he went aboard to enquire after local prices and conditions. The men told him that beef was fetching more there, and sugar was also moving at a decent price.[15]

He decided to sell no more in Barbados than was needed to buy rum for the next leg. That rum, 1,450 gallons in total, was split between trade and morale: 1,013 gallons for onward cargo, the rest kept aside "for myself and the men."

A ration of half a pint per man per day, by now a relatively common practice[16] among both merchant crews and naval vessels in the West Indies, would stretch Blundell's supply across roughly four to six months. For Blundell and his men, rum was one form of order at sea; religion was another on land.

In early seventeenth-century Barbados the Church of England was the established church, with Sunday services in principle compulsory at least once a month for free men, while masters were required to bring their households and servants.[17] Such rules were intended not only to enforce religious conformity but also to curb the drunkenness and profanity for which Barbados's planters had been notorious.[18] By 1701 enforcement was uneven, yet seafarers arriving in port appear to have fallen under the same expectation, as Blundell noted on 7 December: "this being a Sunday, it was all our business to go to church, and a very fine church it is."

Now, with both trade and worship attended to, Blundell had little reason to linger. Within days the *Lever* was ready to weigh anchor.

An Unyielding Island

They departed for Nevis on the following Friday,[19] navigating the Caribbean's fickle winds. Martinique and Dominica loomed in the distance, but calms and swells threatened to drive the ship ashore. A sudden shower brought relief, pushing the vessel clear. The journey continued past Marie-Galante and Guadeloupe, where shifting breezes again slowed their progress.

After a brief and disappointing stop for trade in Montserrat, they approached the island of Nevis the following Wednesday.

From the sea, this small island announced itself gradually: first the dark outline of its slopes, then the steep rise of its volcanic cone. At over 3,200 feet, Nevis Peak was often shrouded in cloud, its rainforest giving way to belts of acacia and, below them, plantations stepping down the hillsides toward the shore. The whole island seemed to climb like a vast amphitheatre facing the sea breeze. Rainfall was often plentiful, but in December the air would have been fresh, the trade winds steady.[20]

Once ashore, Blundell immediately paid his respects to the lieutenant-governor, Roger Elrington.[21] On Nevis, as in all the Leeward Islands, captains were expected to present themselves on arrival, be entered in the harbour books, lodge their manifests, and obtain leave to trade.

However, the market proved sluggish, though in truth Nevis was never an easy place to trade. One later visitor called the islanders "the most obstinate and particular-temper'd people I have ever convers'd with".[22]

Blundell quickly turned to others for guidance.

Chief among them was Solomon Israel,[23] a Jewish merchant who acted as attorney to planters, moneylenders, and brokers. By the early eighteenth century Israel had risen into the political elite,[24] and his counsel carried weight. He warned Blundell that large shipments of beef were expected daily, depressing prices and making buyers hesitant.

This advice ran against the assurances he had been given only days earlier in Barbados, yet Blundell acted on Israel's warning. He refused to sell his beef on Nevis and instead struck a deal to offload 100 barrels for trade in the nearby French islands.[25] Over the following days barrels were unloaded, while stones and sand were brought aboard as ballast to steady the ship.

However, amid the bustle of trade, sickness was spreading.

At first three of the crew fell ill. Within only a matter of days, Alexander Calinder was dead. No sooner was he buried than Blundell himself began to feel unwell.

The West Indies was thick with it: fevers, fluxes, infections that bred in the heat and struck without warning. Blundell knew the risks. Years earlier, he had watched disease ravage crews and settlements alike. On Montserrat, he had seen men sick for months put ashore and left behind: too ill to sail, too costly to save. He had written of it then with detachment.

Now, it was his turn.

Nevertheless, he followed the regimen he knew best – bloodletting and sweat.

It was a crude sequence born of the belief that illness could be expelled with the fluids it released. Physicians called this the antiphlogistic regimen: by letting blood and raising a fevered sweat, inflammation might be purged, the humours restored to balance, the body returned to health.[26]

In reality, it was rest, warmth, and water that did the healing, if healing came at all.[27]

Blundell was one of the lucky ones. By the time he returned to his journal, he wrote: "and bless the Lord I am better."[28]

In the midst of these disruptions, he searched the island for sugar, which was in short supply. Eventually he secured a small quantity, four hogsheads and five of molasses, barely enough to complete the cargo.[29]

On Christmas Day he went to the lieutenant-governor for sailing orders, but the governor refused his departure, as all official business was suspended for the holiday.

Finally on Boxing Day 1701, the *Lever* slipped her moorings.

The Caribbean faded astern as she turned toward Virginia.

Chapter 8

The Ledger and the Silence

"None ought to set what is private against the public, and prefer a little personal interest to that which is national and common. Everybody can see the reasonableness of this in another man's case — but most are loath to see it in their own, and that for this only reason, because it is their own."

Christopher Bassnett, 1711

Cape Hatteras, Off Virginia | Wednesday, 14 January 1702

At 5 am the crew rose early to find the ship sailing close to Smith's Island, a low-lying stretch of land off the entrance to Chesapeake Bay. A cold wind blew in from the north, thick with rain. Blundell kept near the shoreline, wary of the surf crashing along the outer banks. As they neared Cape Charles, the *Lever* briefly ran aground, but the sea was calm, and the ship drifted free without damage.

The wind freshened. Topsails were reefed. The ship creaked forward through the narrowing entrance of the Chesapeake.

By mid-morning, they anchored in 6 fathoms of water. The yards and topmasts were struck, and "a good scope of cable" was given out, letting the anchor line run long to ensure a firm hold in a rising sea.

Over the following weeks Blundell moved between Rappahannock, Occoquan, and Suggett's Point, selling off his rum and purchasing around 150 hogsheads of tobacco, as he threaded his way through Virginia's tangled networks of planters, factors, and merchants.[1]

Everything was going to plan, until the order came that changed everything.

No Permission, No Regret

In late May, an embargo was proclaimed, forbidding any vessel to sail without official convoy. With war with France looming, the Crown required all outward-bound ships to await protection.[2] As the weeks dragged on, Blundell petitioned for clearance, but his requests were denied, and the *Lever* remained trapped in the bay.

On Saturday, 11 June he was finally allowed to proceed, but only after posting a £2,000 bond, a legal guarantee that he would sail up the James River as ordered and not depart the colony without permission. But privately, Blundell had already decided otherwise.[3]

The disappointing returns from his final voyages aboard the *Mulberry* had taught him a hard truth: in a volatile Atlantic economy, profit belonged to those who moved quickly, took risks, and stayed ahead of their rivals. He had carefully considered his course and made his choice.

The next morning, he weighed anchor at first light. But trouble lay ahead. Two Royal Navy men-of-war now lay between the Capes, determined to prevent ships from slipping past the embargo.

Blundell waited. Off the Capes, the *Lever* lay still in open water, sails hauled in, her crew hushed and watchful. As the light gave way to dark, lanterns were extinguished, and the ship was slowly enveloped in shadow and silence. "We took in all our sails," he wrote, "lay off there till 6 in the evening".

As dusk gave way to full dark, they made their move. Canvas unfurled without a word. "Then set all our sails and ran out, keeping close to the Eastern Shore," he recorded.

The helmsman steered a careful line, hugging the shoreline while the Royal Navy ships stood blind in the night.

Under cover of darkness, the *Lever* slipped past the guards.

The gamble paid off. She gained a crucial two-week advantage over the rest of the tobacco fleet. It was a quiet act of defiance, calculated, and successful.

Despite the advantage gained, the return offered no relief – light winds, long calms, and a silence that seemed to stretch.

In early July, the sighting of the "Great Island of Aran" signalled their approach to British waters.[4] As the *Lever* passed the coast of Antrim, the crew spotted men on Sheep Island and sent a boat to shore to gather news.

The islanders fled at the sight of the ship, fearing it was a man-of-war come to press them into naval service. When contact was eventually made, the message was reassuring: peace still held.

But the calm proved deceptive.

Further along the coast, he encountered a Danish vessel. Blundell recorded the moment: "They told us that war was proclaimed between France and us the 15th May last, and that our men-of-war had taken abundance of French privateers and merchantmen."

It was true. War had officially been declared between Britain and France that May. From that point, he wrote, they "stood for the Scotch shore and kept along the Scotch shore, the wind at west," taking the more sheltered route home, close to the coast, to avoid open waters where enemy privateers were known to lurk.

It was a cautious decision, born of instinct and experience.

On the morning of Sunday, 12 July, the ship reached the mouth of the Mersey in heavy seas and strong winds. "It blowing very hard and a great sea going," he wrote. "We put two hands at the helm, and I stood upon the poop and conned."

Blundell was now high above the deck, issuing orders with the calm authority and seasoned judgement of a man who knew not just how to weather the sea, but how to command it.

Spray whipped across the deck as he charted his course through Liverpool's unsettled waters, his eyes fixed ahead, voice steady above the gale. Below, his men moved to his word as the town crept into view through the grey sea mist.

By 10 am, they had rounded the Rock and by 10.30 am, the *Lever* was safely moored at the town side, "when the people went in Church."

After nine months and eighteen days at sea, they were home – market strong, ahead of the fleet, and £600 to the good.

A Steady Hand

After just under three months ashore, Bryan Blundell set sail again from Liverpool aboard the *Lever*, bound once more for Virginia. His cargo, valued at £820, was shared among four investors, himself included.[5]

On the first Thursday in October, they slipped away at dawn. By afternoon they had past the Isle of Man and were heading north around Ireland.

The following day, fierce north-westerly gales forced the *Lever* to seek shelter in Londonderry, where she anchored as the winds howled through the night. Blundell attempted to resume the voyage the next morning, but shifting winds made progress difficult. Forced to navigate between the small island of Inishtrahull and the coast of County Donegal, Ireland, the crew battled high seas and squalls of hail for nearly a week before finally breaking into the Atlantic.

The crossing was fraught.

Towards the end of October, a great wave struck the ship broadside, nearly shifting the ballast and threatening disaster. Six days later, a large vessel appeared on the horizon, prompting Blundell to adjust course. By evening, the stranger had fallen 3 leagues astern, and the *Lever* continued on her way unchallenged.

At last, on 14 November, land was sighted. The "Table of Pines"[6] and the Capes of Virginia rose on the horizon, and by nightfall, the *Lever* had joined the *Lamb of Liverpool*, a vessel that had departed Londonderry three weeks earlier, yet arrived at the same time.

Upon reaching Rappahannock, Blundell faced difficulties. The tobacco crop had suffered from rain and sleet, and supplies were scarce. Securing a license to trade, he set up a store at Mrs Heales's tavern, purchasing what he could before winter set in.

Then on Christmas Eve, a naval sloop brought urgent orders: all ships were to depart for England by the end of February. With his own cargo incomplete, Blundell took on freight tobacco at £13 per ton, working through the bitter cold to prepare for departure.

Delayed by southerly winds, the *Lever* did not leave the James River until 19 March. The Atlantic crossing brought storms along with fears of French privateers, forcing the convoy to take a more easterly course for safety.

After six weeks and four days, the ship reached Ireland, passing Mizen Head in early May. Three weeks after that, the *Lever* cast anchor in Liverpool, her crew in good health and her cargo intact.[7]

With numerous successful voyages behind him, Blundell reflected on his good fortune at sea: "Blessed be the Lord did deliver us from dangers of the seas and out of the hands of our enemies. Who in his mercy hath promised and kept and prospered and directed me these 14 voyages to Virginia and West Indies."

He went on to write, "So as the Lord hath been bountiful in blessing my endeavours to the enlargement of a temporal estate, so I hope he hath, in his great mercy, caused me to grow in goodness, thriving in the knowledge of him, the Lord our God."

Line of Deception

In the spring of 1704, Bryan Blundell embarked on his third voyage aboard the *Lever*, once again bound for Virginia.

Stopping first in Dublin to take on victuals, food and provisions for the crew, the ship set sail across the Atlantic, enduring nine weeks of westerly winds before reaching Pungoteague to take on a cargo of tobacco.

Fully laden, the *Lever* departed Virginia in June to join a vast convoy for the journey home. The convoy, numbering around 160 merchant ships, sailed under the escort of 4 Royal Navy men-of-war: *Dreadnought*, *Oxford*, *Falkland*, and *Foy* (*Fowey*). The squadron was under the command of Captain John Evans of the 64-gun *Dreadnought*, a seasoned officer who took charge as commodore.

Tension remained high throughout the crossing. The escorts captured a French warship of 40 guns and 250 men bound for Canada with a cargo of dry goods.[8] Other enemy ships were sighted but proved too swift to intercept.

As the convoy neared European waters, the fleet's escort began to disperse. The *Foy* was ordered to accompany the North Channel ships, but in thick weather, she lost the main fleet.[9]

On Saturday, 2 August, seeking assurances of protection, Blundell and his fellow captains approached Commodore Evans, requesting escort to Ireland or at least a safe point along the coast. Evans refused, declaring that the fleet would proceed toward Plymouth.

With forty ships from Liverpool, Bristol, and Whitehaven now exposed, the merchants convened aboard the vessel of Blundell's brother-in-law, Ralph Williamson. They agreed that if southerly winds prevailed, they would sail independently without escort; if not, they would remain with the fleet.

At first light the following day, a large warship appeared on the horizon, in pursuit of a smaller vessel. As dawn broke, the ship fired six shots and quickly overtook its quarry. By 9 am, it was identified as the *Medway*, an English man-of-war, now joining the convoy.

But the relief was short-lived. Soon after, a squadron of ten large French vessels was spotted astern, bearing down under full sail.

Word spread that the French force was under the command of Admiral Jean-Baptiste du Casse, a feared and battle-hardened naval commander already renowned for his exploits during the Nine Years' War. Now a rising force in the War of the Spanish Succession, he was said to be hunting the English fleet with ruthless efficiency. Yet later evidence suggests it was in fact Captain Marc-Antoine de Saint-Pol Hécourt who led the French squadron that day.[10]

Commodore Evans gave the signal for battle, and his pre-planned defensive line was formed.

With the *Foy* lost, the British line now comprised just four men-of-war, *Dreadnought*, *Oxford*, *Falkland*, and *Medway*, supported by the fleet's best-armed merchantmen: six twenty-four-gun ships and several smaller vessels of sixteen guns. Together, they created a broadside wall of fire designed to deter or break up an enemy assault.

Many of the merchant ships had been newly scraped, their hulls cleaned of barnacles and marine growth that slowed a vessel at sea. The result was not just greater speed and manoeuvrability, but a deceptive gleam that made them look like freshly commissioned warships.

In the morning haze, and faced with what appeared to be a formidable line of battle, the French held back. Their mainsails were raised, smaller sails furled, as they hovered at a cautious distance, like a cat poised to pounce, measuring their odds.

After a tense stand-off, the French squadron turned away.

According to one French historian, a "lucky fog saved Saint-Pol from fifteen English men-of-war, which is a notable tribute to the Virginia merchantmen."[11]

Whether by design or good fortune, the illusion held, their scraped hulls and tight formation had masked how lightly armed they truly were.[12]

By evening, they had past Land's End, the coast obscured by thick weather. The next day, the fleet arrived at Plymouth, where unfavourable northerly winds delayed them for two months.

Safe Harbour, Silent House

While Blundell waited on the south coast, tragedy struck at home. On Saturday, 19 September, his wife, Samuela, died.

She had borne him four children, but only one, Hannah, born in 1697, had survived infancy. Now too Samuela was gone. The news likely reached him days later, carried by post or passing merchant, delivering a blow that distance could not soften. He was stranded and powerless, left to mourn from afar.

At last, in early October, the fleet departed. *Hector* and *Penzance* led the escort.

Off Land's End, a French privateer appeared but, wary of the convoy's strength, chose not to engage. Two weeks later, the *Lever* finally reached Liverpool, its cargo intact.

The tobacco market had weakened, with prices at 2¼ pence per pound at the mast, and merchants were now scrambling to redirect their shipments to Bristol in hope of better returns. Blundell had a fourth share in the ship and secured sixteen hogsheads in portage, but returns were modest.

Though he had once again defied the perils of war and sea, his safe return was bittersweet. The home he had left months before was now changed forever.

He gave thanks for his survival, but no triumph at sea could restore what had been lost.

Chapter 9

In the Shadow of the Privateers

"He that has delivered and does deliver, you may trust will deliver."
Christopher Bassnett, 1711

The Town of Liverpool | January 1705

The return of open conflict brought not only embargoes, but a more perilous threat: the rise of the privateer.

Armed with their letters of marque, these vessels now operated with royal sanction, preying on enemy shipping for reward. These were not pirates, but state-sponsored predators, who blurred the line between commerce and combat. Swift, aggressive, and highly motivated, they made their living off the misfortune of others.

For captains like Bryan Blundell, who relied on speed, timing, and careful risk management, their presence introduced a new level of uncertainty. Convoys offered some protection, but not enough. A change in the wind, a breakdown in communication, or a poor decision by a commodore could leave even the most experienced captains exposed.

This chapter follows Blundell through two final voyages aboard the *Lever*; the first uneventful, the second far from it.

The Calm Before the Storm

Blundell's fourth voyage as captain of the *Lever*, though successful, was marked more by patience than peril. Departing Liverpool in January 1705, he followed the familiar route north-about Ireland and made a steady six-week passage to the Chesapeake. After loading tobacco at Choptank in Maryland, he faced delays under an embargo that once again required another £2,000 bond and convoy clearance.

Seeking to improve his returns, Blundell invested in a small sloop, the *Phoenix*, placing his former mate George Duddall in command and dispatching it to Milford, Connecticut, with a mixed cargo. Meanwhile, the *Lever* waited in the "freshes" of the James River – the upper, freshwater reaches of the estuary, less affected by the tide and safely beyond the reach of the dreaded shipworm – lingering there until naval escorts arrived.

That August, the *Lever* joined a fleet of 90 ships, mostly from the North Channel ports, and sailed home under the protection of *Oxford* and *Hastings*, with Captain Moody as commodore. After a stopover in Kinsale and a fortnight's wait, the *Lever* returned to Liverpool in early October, its voyage completed without incident.

In Blundell's words: "All things well with us. Blessed be the Lord for it."

From Cargo to Keel: A New Venture Begins

Blundell's final voyage with the *Lever* began in early 1706, departing Liverpool that January alongside the *Indian Queen*, the *Endeavour*, and his sloop the *Phoenix*. The route north about Ireland was familiar, and true to form, Blundell outpaced his companions, reaching Virginia in just six weeks. The others followed two weeks later.

Upon arrival in the Chesapeake, the Royal Navy's *Woolwich* lay at anchor, awaiting further orders from England.

Ever the opportunist, Blundell quickly offloaded part of his cargo into a sloop and sailed up the bay to the Wye River. He was chasing market intelligence, hoping to learn what goods were most in demand.

His timing proved perfect, as tobacco was plentiful but imported goods were scarce. Within 3 weeks, he had successfully secured 400 hogsheads.

He then set his sights on Philadelphia, the colony's principal town and a thriving port.

He rode north on horseback,[1] across forests and tidal marshes, following rough colonial tracks that linked the upper Chesapeake to the Delaware River. The journey was slow and rutted, the path winding through scattered settlements and dense woodland, ending at a town scarcely 30 years old.[2]

Founded by William Penn in 1682 as a "greene country towne," Philadelphia had grown from a riverside settlement of wooden houses and wharves into one of the fastest-rising ports in the English colonies. Now, wagons rumbled through its narrow streets, and out along the waterfront past the growing shipyards and warehouses stacked with hides and tobacco.[3]

Its quays hummed with carpenters, caulkers, rope-makers, and sawyers; pine masts from the forests of New Jersey rose like a second skyline above the sheds. Quaker merchants, many of them émigrés from Bristol and London's Southwark shipyards, had brought with them the skills of the Thames. Their yards now lined the riverfront, where the smell of tar and oakum hung in the air and hammers rang from dawn until dusk.[4]

Blundell arrived in Philadelphia to find that, while his goods were in demand, money to pay for them was in short supply. Rather than force poor sales, he took a bolder path: he commissioned the construction of a new ship, which he would later name the *Cleveland*.[5] In early colonial markets, goods often moved faster than hard currency, and for a merchant with Blundell's experience, Philadelphia was the perfect place to turn goods into planks, and planks into profit (see Plate 7).[6]

The region offered cheap labour, and deep inland waterways, both advantages that made its vessels sought after across the colonies, even if their workmanship did not always match the standards of the Thames. The surrounding forests provided the timber: hundreds of mature oaks for keels and frames, and tall, straight pines for masts and spars. These were resources that England's shipyards were already beginning to lack.[7]

The terms were clear: £15 12s per ton for a vessel 74 feet in keel, 26 feet across the beam (the ship's widest point, critical to stability and internal volume), 10½ feet deep in the hold, and 5½ feet between the decks. Blundell himself would supply the ironwork.

Over seventeen days, he sold £650 worth of goods to finance the build.

Returning to the *Lever*, he joined fellow Liverpool traders in the Potomac to take on tobacco, including his brother-in-law Ralph Williamson[8] aboard the *Indian Queen*, and his cousin Edward Tarleton on the *Endeavour*.

Ever resourceful, he scoured the countryside for iron, eventually collecting 7 hundredweight (roughly 784 pounds) and acquiring a full set of smith's tools. One of Williamson's crew was a smith; Blundell paired him with one of his own servants and sent them, along with the tools and iron, to Philadelphia in a sloop to begin outfitting the new ship.

We will return to the story of the *Cleveland* in the next chapter. Its launch would mark a new phase in Blundell's maritime aspirations.

The Largest Fleet and Its Fatal Flaws

By late August, Blundell and the *Lever* had moved down the James River.

In early September, they joined what Blundell described as "the greatest fleet that ever went out of Virginia": 230 merchant vessels gathered from across the colony, their hulls packed with tobacco, rum, and raw American goods bound for Britain.

This vast armada sailed under the command of Commodore Jameson, escorted by four Royal Navy warships: the *Greenwich*, *Woolwich*, *Advice*, and *Hazardous*, a captured French prize.[9]

Chief among the escorts was the *Greenwich*, a fourth-rate ship of the line carrying around fifty guns. Under the Royal Navy's rating system, ships were classified from first to sixth rate, based on their firepower. First-rates, floating fortresses, carried over a hundred guns. Fourth-rates like the *Greenwich* bore between forty-six and sixty: powerful enough for the line of battle, yet nimble and versatile, often favoured for convoy duty, colonial policing, and distant station service.[10]

The scene on the morning of departure would have been breathtaking: masts crowding the horizon, sails furled in the light, flags snapping in the breeze, and decks bustling with final preparations. Some vessels were sleek and swift, others broad and heavy with cargo. Many flew the colours of Liverpool, Bristol, or London; others hailed from Ireland, Scotland, or the American colonies.

Then came the signal.

Cannon fire cracked across the water, a thunderous command to weigh anchor. Decks heaved with motion. Sails unfurled in unison, snapping taut in the wind. The ships began to move, slowly at first, then gathering rhythm as tide and canvas took hold. Timber groaned, ropes strained, and the fleet began its uncertain journey across the Atlantic.

Blundell watched the procession with a calculating eye. Amid the grandeur, he saw a problem. With twenty-five Liverpool ships in the fleet, "Tobacco could not be worth much at Liverpool".

So, he recalibrated.

He would remain with the convoy as far as Harwich, then break away. His aim was twofold: first, to sell his finest tobacco on the Dutch market, where prices remained strong; second, to reach Hull, where rigging, sails, anchors, and cables could be purchased far more cheaply than in Liverpool. Outfitting the *Cleveland*, his newly commissioned ship, would cost significantly less there.

It was a careful, calculated pivot. For now, Blundell remained within the formation, watching and waiting.

But scale, under poor command, turned from strength to liability.

Formation broke down. Ships drifted apart, fell behind, or foundered in isolation. A few were rescued by fellow merchants; others vanished into the distance, abandoned to their fate.

Then, in early November, a violent storm struck the convoy.[11] Of the original 230 ships, only 85 remained in sight; by the following day, just 55 had regrouped. Commodore Jameson, commanding from the *Greenwich*, pressed on, leaving the scattered ships to fend for themselves.

By nightfall, Blundell was sailing about a mile to the south, accompanied by a loose cluster of twenty vessels. The wind had dropped, but visibility was poor. Around them, darkness closed in. Sailors doused lanterns and muffled orders; any glimmer of light could betray their position to French privateers prowling the open sea.

Blundell expected the commodore to maintain course until morning. Jameson had never tacked after dark; it was too dangerous to attempt a coordinated manoeuvre in pitch black seas. More importantly, he had promised to signal any such manoeuvre with a series of gunshots and lights.

That night, there were no guns. No lights.

Trusting that the formation was still intact, Blundell and the others held their line. By morning, the truth became clear: Jameson had altered course, and Blundell's southern group had been left behind.

Then came the worst turn of all: the wind died.

The great Atlantic heave – the long, rolling swell of the open ocean – rose and fell, but there was no breeze. The ships' sails collapsed against the masts, limp and useless. "As if I must be bound hand and foot," Blundell wrote, "and go no further."

For hours, they drifted – silent, motionless and exposed. The sea no longer raged. It didn't need to. It had taken something far subtler to undo Bryan Blundell – stillness.

Then, out of the haze, a French privateer appeared under full sail, cutting swiftly through the calm.

Blundell and the others scrambled to raise sail as a faint breeze returned, but it was too late. The privateer seized five ships in rapid succession, including the *Lever*. Together, they carried 2,300 hogsheads of tobacco, a staggering prize worth over £50,000 at the time.

It was one of the most significant single hauls taken by a privateer in the war to date. The audacious raid not only stunned the convoy but also dealt a heavy blow to Britain's trading houses.

No shot was fired. No escape was possible. The calm had sealed their fate.

Captivity and Conviction

Seized without a shot and stripped of their ship, Blundell and his nineteen-man crew were landed at St Malo.[12] The *Lever* was taken to nearby Morlaix. Both ship and cargo alike lost to the enemy.

Any expectation of gentlemanly treatment quickly evaporated. Under armed guard, the English seamen were marched through cobbled streets and into what Blundell called a "nasty stinking prison and there shut the doors upon us." It was a grim welcome to wartime captivity.

The stay was short, but the shock was lasting. St Malo's prisons were notorious for poor air, damp straw, and the press of bodies. Blundell's account is restrained, but his reflection is telling: "some of us began to think how we had abused our former liberty… a just rebuke… by giving up our labours into the hands of the enemies."

After just one night in St Malo, the prisoners were moved inland to Dinan, a quieter Breton town. There, Blundell was permitted to rent private quarters, not only for himself, but for all nineteen of his crew.

Many of the men had been stripped of their belongings during capture, but Blundell had been spared. With access to credit and the freedom to move within the town, he took full responsibility for their care. He paid for beds at 4 pence per night, supplied meat, drink, and new clothes, and ensured that all of them were housed together. "I had credit at large," he wrote, "so that I did not want anything that was reasonable fitting." Even in captivity, he remained both master and caretaker, shouldering the cost of dignity.

Though deprived of his ship and cargo, Blundell's spiritual clarity never wavered. He wrote that while "the enemy was permitted to take our outward enjoyments," he and his men still had "free recourse unto God," whose "comforts refreshed my soul."

Stranded in a Catholic country, he found unexpected inspiration in the devoutness of local religious life. He observed how frequently and fervently the French attended church, noting with quiet admiration that their piety "far exceeded us that profess ourselves before them."

For many, captivity might have meant bitterness. But for Blundell, it became an opportunity for reflection. He turned loss into humility and hardship into conviction. His concern for his crew, and his openness to different forms of devotion, revealed a man who understood the burdens and responsibilities of command.

The circumstances of his release are unclear in his journal, but Blundell left France in mid-January aboard a crowded 80-ton boat with 540 aboard, landing at Weymouth 2 days later.[13] He reached Bristol four days after that and arrived in Liverpool towards the end of January.

The capture had cost him £800 in profit and another £68 in expenses. Yet he closed the episode without bitterness: "Instead of complaining, I bless the Lord for his goodness and mercies to me."

But more than money had been lost, and more than fortune had been gained. His time in captivity had tested not only his endurance but his sense of purpose.

As he stepped ashore once more, Blundell was no longer just a trader navigating markets and winds. He was a man beginning to understand the weight of leadership, both aboard ship and ashore.

The *Cleveland*, still under construction in the yards of Philadelphia, would soon be launched.

For nearly a decade, she would carry his fortunes forward. It was a ship shaped as much by conviction as by commerce, and a symbol of his growing reach in transatlantic trade, and all it would come to bear.

Chapter 10

The Making of the *Cleveland*

"We say that a soldier carries his life in his hand – but it is just as true that a sailor bears his life upon the waves. Each moment at sea is a moment of risk. A vessel may be but an inch or two from destruction."

Christopher Bassnett, 1711

The *Endeavour*, Mid-Atlantic | Monday, 12 May 1707

Somewhere aloft, canvas had fouled. Orders rang out above the din of wind and spray. A young sailor, Thomas Haddock, was told to climb and clear the toggles on the topsail yard: a horizontal spar high on the mast, where the upper sail strained against the gale.

It was his first time at sea.

He climbed carefully, his coat streaming, the ropes slick with salt and rain. Then, without warning, the *Endeavour* rolled sharply to starboard. A sudden pitch wrenched the ship sideways and hurled him from the maintop into the ocean below.

Blundell, walking the deck, saw it happen and instinctively seized the main-brace, a thick line used to steady the mainsail, and flung it toward the struggling figure. But the boy was stunned from the fall. He could not grasp the rope.

The ship surged ahead. No boat could be launched in time. The crew stood powerless, watching the sea close over him.

"All we could do," Blundell later recorded, "was to implore God's mercy."

To Cross and to Build

Blundell's destination was Philadelphia, where his new ship, the *Cleveland*, was taking shape on the stocks.

The vessel was named after his close friend and business partner John Cleveland, a prominent tobacco and sugar trader. Cleveland had served as Mayor of Liverpool[1] and would later represent the town in Parliament.[2] Commissioned before Blundell's capture, the ship now carried a deeper meaning, reflecting a renewed sense of purpose after a difficult year.

The Atlantic routes demanded vessels that were swift enough to evade privateers, robust enough to endure harsh seas, and versatile enough to navigate both open oceans and colonial rivers. Recognising these demands, Blundell sought greater control over the design and construction of his ships. From early in his career, his journal reveals a careful attention to the mechanics of seafaring, including drawings of sails and spars, rigging configurations, wind charts, and observations on ship handling.[3]

His decision to build the *Cleveland* in Philadelphia was both pragmatic and ambitious. English shipyards were struggling with rising prices and dwindling supplies, while across the Atlantic, skilled craftsmen and plentiful timber kept colonial costs low. Blundell saw the advantage and moved quickly.[4]

Some materials, though, could not be sourced locally. Quality canvas, cable, and iron fittings were harder to come by in the colonies,[5] so Blundell sent these components out in advance aboard his sloop, the *Phoenix*, ensuring the new vessel would be built to his exact specifications.

The *Cleveland* was conceived with adaptability in mind. Designed to carry twenty guns and a crew of up to fifty, it could transition swiftly from merchantman to privateer; a valuable trait in an era where the lines between commerce and conflict were often blurred.

Passage Through Storms

Blundell and the *Endeavour* departed Liverpool on the last day of March, bound for Philadelphia to supervise the *Cleveland's* final fitting-out.

They sailed in company with at least three ships: the *Indian Queen*,[6] the *Oak* of Virginia and the *Barbados Merchant*. Blundell's journal charts the passage in his usual clipped precision: fair weather through the North Channel, the Tory Island sighted to the south, a favourable breeze from the SSW, and a sharp westerly to push them into the Atlantic.

As ever though, speed was on his side. Within days, the *Endeavour* overtook the *Oak*, sailing "much better" than her companion. Other vessels appeared across the horizon, some a comfort, others a threat.

On Friday, 3 May, off the Banks of Newfoundland, Blundell recorded a tense moment when a ship came rapidly astern in fading light. "He came very fast up with us," he noted, fearing a hostile encounter. But as night fell, a fresh gale and a rising sea obscured the stranger, and the *Endeavour* altered course under cover of darkness.

By the following week, the sea had turned heavy. Waves pounded the hull in long, thudding intervals, and the ship groaned under the weight of the weather. Rain came in bursts, carried sideways by the wind. The shrouds and stays thrummed under pressure, the masts trembling with the strain.

It was in these conditions that tragedy struck: the loss of young Thomas Haddock, sent aloft to clear the fouled canvas and swept to his death. The grief lingered as the ship pressed on, every creak of the timbers and shudder of the sails a reminder of how close each sailor lived to the edge.

Five days later, the *Endeavour* crossed paths with the *Loyalty*, captained by Blundell's former mate George Duddall. For more than a week, the two ships sailed together before parting ways, with Duddall bound for Virginia, Blundell for Philadelphia.

By early June, they reached the Delaware Capes, navigating the tricky, shifting soundings into Delaware Bay. Cape Henlopen, Cape May, and at last the town of New Castle came into view, each a signpost along the narrowing channel. The Bay could be deceptive: broad and calm at first glance, yet filled with hidden bars and shifting sands that tested even seasoned pilots. Many ships never made it past the Capes.[7]

On Monday, 9 June, they arrived in Philadelphia, where Blundell found his advance supply vessel, the sloop *Phoenix*, already safely docked.

To Finish What Was Begun

When Bryan Blundell stepped ashore, he expected to find the *Cleveland* rigged, painted, and afloat. Instead, he found her still on the stocks – silent, skeletal, unmoving – her hull resting on timber cradles that creaked in the humid June heat.

Construction had begun months earlier. But materials ran short. Deadlines drifted. For Blundell, fresh from the Atlantic and impatient to begin, the delay was intolerable. He brought in his own men and set them to work, lashing rigging, trimming sails, tightening every knot by hand. No excuses. No wasted time. This was more than a ship. It was a statement.

Ten days later, they launched her.

Just after 11 am, the hull slid stern-first toward the water. For a moment, all seemed well… then came a jolt. The keel scraped the riverbed with a hard, grinding thud. She settled awkwardly but held. Blundell inspected her form, measuring trim and draught. She sat 9 feet at the stern, 6 at the bow: balanced, he judged, and ready.[8]

But something wasn't right.

Below deck, the hull was leaking. Blundell ordered the vessel hauled out again, slowly and painfully, by winch and horse, dragging the sodden hull back up the slipway.

The repairs would take days. To make use of the delay, he decided to divide his crew: half were sent aboard the *Phoenix*, now ready to sail down to the Chesapeake to collect tobacco and provisions from scattered plantations. Blundell himself travelled overland to Maryland, sourcing tobacco and critical supplies.

The others stayed behind to finish the ship.

Both crew and tradesmen swarmed over the vessel – carpenters, a carver, a joiner, caulkers, sailmakers – each adding their piece to the intricate wooden-and-canvas puzzle.

Chisels reopened the seams; caulkers packed them tight with oakum. Then came the pitch, boiled thick and dark, brushed deep into every joint. Weak spots were patched, rough edges trimmed. Blundell had expected flaws, but not this many. Early colonial shipyards, it seemed, were rich in timber but uneven in quality. In England, he could have demanded better. In the colonies, he now had to make do.

The ship's joiner and carver shaped the main mast by hand, fitting it with careful precision before it was raised and stepped into place.

At last, the crew returned to their tasks: lashing down cables, setting blocks, trimming spars, and aligning the sails.

In early August, he recorded the result in his journal with satisfaction: "I had the ship rigged, careened, and painted and completely finished, ballasted, and all her provisions on board." Every spar was set. Every shroud drawn taut. The hold was packed. The decks, newly caulked, gleamed in the summer light.

One final obstacle remained. The ship's sheet cable, ordered from England months before, had never arrived. It was no minor detail. Without it, the *Cleveland* could not anchor in deep water. A storm would tear her loose. There was no time to wait.

Blundell scoured the docks and found a replacement: "by chance…in ye town." A thicker line, originally meant for a brigantine. He bartered for it, matched it with a second spare, and declared it fit. "It must serve," he noted. And it did.

A World of Warehouses and Wharf Talk

On Friday, 8 August, the *Cleveland* finally left Philadelphia, bound for the Chesapeake to load tobacco.

The wind was contrary, and for several days she made slow progress down the Delaware Bay, tacking against headwinds, anchoring by night, and seizing every favourable tide. "The ship works very well," Blundell noted, quietly pleased with her performance under pressure.

By Wednesday they were off the Capes of Virginia, where the *Cleveland* crossed paths with ten ships outward bound. Among them were the *Loyalty*, the *True Love*, and the *Catherine* of London, a heavily armed man-of-war commanded by the convoy's redheaded commodore. Blundell sent letters aboard, exchanged news, and pressed on into the Chesapeake.

Early the next morning, he took a boat to procure what freight he could on the Eastern Shore. On Friday, Blundell noted simply "this day I rested amongst my old friends." This was likely at Hungars, where he had long-standing ties through men like his cousin Thomas Preeson who inherited[9] a plantation there in 1705. Preeson's own grandson, Thomas Preeson Junior, would later become a supporter of the local church.[10]

Over the following week, he crossed between Maryland and Virginia by boat and horseback, posting men at key locations such as Nanjemoy, Rappahannock, and Coan's Landing to gather more tobacco.

Trade, in the absence of formal marketplaces, relied on names, favours, and handshakes. Blundell, by now well known on both sides of the Atlantic, navigated this world with ease.

At one plantation he might inspect bales for mould or shortweight. These were goods delivered below their declared weight, whether by accident or deceit. At another, he might discuss prices over cider at a kitchen hearth. He was not just securing a cargo; he was managing a chain of risk, cost, and obligation that stretched from rural Maryland to the counting houses of Liverpool.

Rowing up the Potomac River, he found the *Elinor* and *Indian Queen* at anchor, both crewed by his two brothers-in-laws, John and Ralph Williamson.[11] The men were still recovering from the fevers that often struck crews in the humid summer months.

Tobacco purchases were steady and Blundell pushed to complete loading quickly. The *Cleveland* waited offshore, while his sloop, *Phoenix*, ranged the coast. It was a model he would return to, both effective and efficient.

Labour Beneath the Barrels

Yet while Blundell's records tracked cargo and cost with precision, they make no mention of the people whose labour underpinned every hogshead of tobacco he loaded.

But they were there, visible at every landing and in every field. Whether clearing ground, curing leaf, or rolling barrels to the riverbank, their presence would have been impossible to ignore. It is hard to imagine that a man as observant and exacting as Blundell could have failed to notice how the colonial economy was built, and who was made to bear its weight.

By now, the old system of indentured servitude was largely a thing of the past. In the early years of his career, Blundell had occasionally carried them, one or two per voyage, but by the early 1700s, the numbers had dwindled dramatically. In 1698, more than 400 indentured servants had departed from Liverpool. By 1707, just 16 were recorded. The collapse reflected deeper changes in both Britain and the colonies.[12]

Across the Chesapeake, freed servants once expected land, freedom, and opportunity. Now, land was increasingly fenced off by powerful planter elites. What had once been a society of contracts was hardening into one of inheritance and ownership.

Enslaved Africans had replaced them almost entirely, their bondage permanent, hereditary, and sanctioned by law.[13] The shift was not only economic but ideological: race had become the defining line between freedom and captivity.

The Sinking That Saved Her

On Saturday, 23 August, Blundell rejoined the *Cleveland* at Wye River. Her hold was nearly ready.

However, by now Blundell had begun to harbour doubts about colonial workmanship, particularly the timber framing, which he feared might not withstand the pressures of the Atlantic. With the long crossing ahead, he wanted to inspect the *Cleveland's* hull for himself and ensure she was truly sound. He ordered the ship heaved down, a process used to expose the lower hull for cleaning and repair.

The operation began six days later. The crew removed her rigging and emptied the ballast, then used a system of ropes and pulleys rigged between two sloops to slowly tilt her onto her side.

As the *Cleveland* leaned and her keel rose clear of the water, Blundell noticed something wasn't right. The ship was settling awkwardly, and her weight felt unbalanced. He called to the men: "was water coming in?"

"No," came the reply. "We think not."

But Blundell remained uneasy. Something felt off, an imbalance he could sense, even if no one else yet saw it.

He "ran up the post, looking in at one of the ports," and, to his horror, saw "an abundance of water in the ship."

He immediately ordered the toggles trimmed, release pins in the pulley system, hoping to let the ship rebalance and float free.

All hands went to work at once.

But then, all of a sudden, the toggles gave way. "Down went the ship."

"Gunwale-under," Blundell wrote: the top of the hull now submerged. The *Cleveland* had capsized, her upper deck plunging beneath the river.

"All we could do was to cut our spare cables and haul her ashore."

By the next day, the *Cleveland* lay hard over in the shallows, her stern in 14 feet of water, her bow in 9.

A sloop was lashed beneath her main shrouds to keep her from slipping deeper. She had rolled with such force that much of her remaining ballast shifted, the deck tilted at an impossible angle, and the coamings (the raised edges of the hatches) were level with the waterline.

"A sad sight to me it was," Blundell wrote, as he surveyed the damage.

But there was little time for reflection. He hired ten carpenters and put them to work immediately, patching and caulking her exposed hull. The unexpected immersion had revealed a multitude of weak spots, "many ill places," he called them, that might otherwise have gone unnoticed. In his view, providence had intervened. Had the ship not capsized in the river, she might have come apart at sea.

On Monday, 30 September, after a month of labour, Blundell prepared to raise her. He fixed lines from the masts to shore, reinforced the toggles, and tied additional stays to two sloops and a brigantine positioned on the far side. He spread the word for help.

By sunset, more than 300 people – labourers, sailors, carpenters, and townsfolk from nearby settlements – crowded the riverbank.

The price of their help was typical for the time: a slaughtered bullock, 50 gallons of rum, barrels of beer, sugar, and whatever else could be spared. It was a noisy, crowded affair: casks rolled ashore, ropes coiled and checked, men shouting orders across the mudflats.

Working by torchlight, they hauled the lines taut. Slowly, the *Cleveland* began to move. Encouraged, they pulled harder. By 11 pm, she finally came upright.

Cheers must have followed, but the job wasn't done.

Two days later, Blundell ordered her heaved down again to inspect the opposite side. By the following afternoon, she was upright, tight, and floating clean.

Loading began immediately. Over the next 10 days, 300 hogsheads of tobacco were brought aboard. Two sloops were sent upriver to collect more, but one returned empty-handed after losing her anchor in a storm. The other, worm-eaten after a summer's hard use, had to be hauled out, careened, and sheathed, delaying her for nearly three weeks. Blundell, travelling by boat, continued to secure freight along the Rappahannock.

But winter was closing in, and the *Cleveland* would soon face her greatest test, this time not on a quiet riverbank, but in the open Atlantic.

The Longest Twenty-Five Days

By early December, the *Cleveland* was finally ready. Her seams were sealed, her ballast reset, and her hold packed tight with tobacco. Blundell had waited nearly a month for a break in the weather.

On Monday, 8 December 1707, with the last safe window of the season narrowing and the winds still uncooperative, he made the call. The ship and her companions, the *Phoenix* and Edgar Bassnett's brigantine, set out from the Rappahannock.

But the wind was fickle, the skies grey. Progress was slow. The *Cleveland*, heavily laden, struggled against contrary winds for much of the run down the bay. As they tacked slowly through shifting waters, Blundell noted with quiet pride that even under half sail, the *Cleveland* outpaced her companions.

That Saturday they were near Cape Henry when the weather started to turn. The wind veered suddenly to the northwest and grew stronger by the hour.

By morning, it was clear something was wrong.

The ship had sprung a leak. At first, the crew manned the pumps every two hours. By the second night, it was every hour. By the third, the work was constant, day and night, without pause.

"The men kept the pumps going," Blundell recorded.

As seawater sloshed in the bilge, the men hauled at long wooden pump handles linked to iron-bound cylinders below deck. The clattering chain pump heaved cold, briny water up through narrow pipes and spilled it overboard in rhythmic surges. When the pump faltered, the work grew worse still: bailing with barrels and ropes, their hands raw and chapped from salt water and the friction of sandy fibres.[14]

It was back-breaking work: exhausting, relentless, and vital. The carpenter eventually traced the leak to the run of the ship, low and far aft, where the hull narrowed near the stern, but it was impossible to reach. They were barely holding their own. The ship was heavy with cargo, and without the pumps, she would not stay afloat.

Then came the gale.

The Saturday before Christmas, the wind roared in. "A very hard gale of wind," Blundell called it, and it came near to breaking them.[15] It took two men striking the pumps continuously just to keep the water from rising. Sometimes, both pumps had to be worked at once. The ship was deeply laden with cargo. Too deeply.

Blundell made the difficult call to jettison some of it. Fifteen hogsheads of tobacco went over the side. It helped, "she was some little better," but the crew were exhausted, and the leak continued.

His cousin, Thomas Preeson, travelling as a passenger, urged him to go further: strip out the between-decks, jettison the rest, save the ship.

But Blundell refused. "I was not for doing that," he wrote, "whilst we could keep her free with our pumps." So they continued, striking the pumps in shifts. Day after day. Night after night.

In one final storm, on Sunday, 4 January, it took four men at once to keep the water down. The pump-leather, used to seal the valves, was wearing out.

They were running out of time.

And then, a break.

The following Wednesday, after twenty-five days in the open sea, the coast of Ireland came into view. Later that day they limped into Kinsale, exhausted, soaked, but intact.

Blundell later reflected that had the voyage lasted even a little longer, they might not have survived. The ship was leaking constantly, the crew exhausted, and their pumps were on the verge of failure.[16]

But they were not yet home. For three weeks, the wind kept them in port. In the harbour, they encountered a familiar face: Blundell's cousin, John Green, recently arrived from Virginia. He, too, had endured a long wait. There was no convoy, and winter gales continued to batter the coast.

Eventually, Blundell made the decision to press on. Without naval escort, they set course for Waterford, hoping to join other ships for the final crossing. But the weather did not improve. Even after a convoy arrived from Virginia, they remained storm-bound, and then fog-bound, off the Irish coast.

The delays mounted. After a month-long passage, the *Phoenix*, which had become separated during the crossing, finally rejoined them at Waterford.

At last, the man-of-war *Arundel* was appointed as their escort, the convoy assembled and departed.

On Thursday, 20 March 1708 the *Cleveland* came into Liverpool for the first time.

Fine Margins

Blundell immediately took her ashore for a full inspection. She had taken damage, but far less than expected.

Had the *Cleveland* not been hauled over and inspected in Virginia, had her seams not been resealed, her toggles re-rigged, or her ballast reset, there is little doubt she would have been lost.

Blundell didn't dwell on it. His journal offered no self-congratulation. Only quiet thanks. But the facts speak for themselves: twenty-five days under storm and strain, leaking steadily, with pumps manned round the clock. And yet, she made it.

Many ships did not. Mortality among transatlantic crews was high. Sickness, shipwreck, and enemy capture claimed thousands each year. That the *Cleveland* reached Kinsale at all was not luck, but method. That she reached Liverpool was a measure of the man who had built her, tested her, and refused to let her go under.

He soon got to work. New trunnels (wooden pegs used to fasten planks) were driven into her hull, her bottom re-sheathed, and her fittings reinforced.

Twenty-six guns were mounted aboard, and she was made ready, not only to carry goods, but to fight if need be. Blundell had been captured once, and he had no intention of letting it happen again.

This ship had been designed with both commerce and caution in mind, its hold built for cargo, its decks prepared for resistance.

The refit cost £1,400. The voyage had earned £1,750 in freight. The profit was slim, but it was enough.

By the spring of 1708, Bryan Blundell had weathered more Atlantic crossings than many sailors of his generation would survive. He had sailed as cabin boy, second mate, captain, and now shipowner – through war, wreck, and winter.

The first voyage of the *Cleveland* had tested everything he'd learned and demanded all he had to give.

What came next would test him in other ways, but his ship had held. And so had he.

Chapter 11

Among Fire and Ice

"It is wonderful to think how a ship will work upon the tempestuous sea, and how strangely sometimes it will ride a storm — at a time when you would really think that in the nature of the thing it were impossible: when the very frame of nature seems as if it were dissolving and falling into pieces."

Christopher Bassnett, 1711

Archangel, Russia | Saturday, 13 August 1709

A fog hung low over the White Sea as Bryan Blundell anchored the *Cleveland* in 7 fathoms of water. The Northern Dvina's channel ahead was narrow, twisting, unnavigable at low tide. For now, the ship sat idle, waiting on wind, waiting on water, waiting on permission.[1]

This was not Barbados. This was not Virginia. This was Russia: distant, ceremonious, and slow.

He was far from Liverpool, and farther still from the familiar rhythms of tobacco and tide. Yet here, on the edge of empire, amid fire and ice, Bryan Blundell saw not exile, but opportunity.

It hadn't always been this way. A year earlier, he had stood on the banks of the Mersey, preparing to remarry and resume more familiar voyages.

Between Winds and Waters

In 1708, war still raged across Europe, but for Bryan Blundell, the waters had briefly calmed. His ship was home, his ledgers in the black, and after four years as a widower, he decided it was time to remarry.

At the age of 34 he took Elizabeth Livesley[2] as his new wife. His diary, however, records the event in the same dry tone he reserved for his contracts and cargo. "Staying long at home, and my former wife being dead near four years, I thought it time to take another, so married Elizabeth Livesley, oldest daughter of John Livesley."

There is no mention of love or ceremony, and in fact, no detail beyond her lineage. It reads more like a transaction than a turning point in a personal life. Like many of Blundell's choices, the marriage appears, at least on the surface, to have been shaped by pragmatism rather than sentiment.

Yet the union brought a degree of stability. Bryan Blundell and Elizabeth would go on to have at least eight children, anchoring his domestic life even as his ventures at sea continued to expand.[3] With a growing household and a flourishing maritime career, Blundell's future seemed increasingly secure.

With his new household established and the *Cleveland* once again readied, Blundell resumed his maritime ventures.

In early September 1708,[4] he set sail for Virginia. This was a now-familiar route, marked more by efficiency than discovery.

The *Cleveland* sailed in company with the *Prince Eugen* and several smaller ships. They soon reached Belfast, where Blundell provisioned the vessel and took on a group of Quaker passengers, likely hopeful settlers bound for the Chesapeake. From there, they passed the Aran Islands and made steady progress across the Atlantic, encountering only one other ship along the way.

After arriving in Chesapeake Bay, he chose to load in Rappahannock rather than risk winter delays further north at the Wye River.

Yet one moment of tragedy broke through the routine: At 11 am, one bitter December morning, Frank Ward, a young apprentice, was sent aloft to haul out the outer part of the foresheet. Suddenly, he "missed his hold and tumbled overboard" without a sound. The crew rushed to launch a boat, but it was already too late. "Before we could get one [boat] out," Blundell wrote, "he was drowned."[5]

Despite the human loss, the voyage was a financial success. Tobacco was purchased, new freight secured, and Blundell even commissioned the construction of a brigantine in Philadelphia. By March 1709, the *Cleveland* was homeward bound, arriving back in Liverpool by mid-April. On his return he simply wrote, "All well with us."

Around this time, perhaps moved by his experience of loss at sea and a growing sense of providence, Blundell began making modest donations to Liverpool's fledgling charity school – which would become the Blue Coat

School, originally established to care for the orphaned children of sailors and the town's poor. In a later account, he recalled giving £25 from "passengers and saved by insurance… in acknowledgement of God's goodness and mercy to me in succeeding me on my voyages."

What began as a quiet act of thanksgiving would, over the years, become one of his most enduring legacies.

For the time being, though, Blundell's next journey would take him far from Liverpool, and from the warmth of the Chesapeake, into truly unfamiliar waters.

To the Edge of Empire: A Cold Reckoning at Archangel

At the turn of the eighteenth century, Russia was both a frontier and a promise – distant, austere, and increasingly essential.

The Arctic port of Archangel, today known as Arkhangelsk, was locked in ice for much of the year, hibernating through its long winters but bursting to life each summer when the "fair" transformed it into the Tsar's northern gateway to Europe.

Although Peter the Great's newly founded St Petersburg was already drawing investment and prestige, Archangel remained vital. In 1709, it was still a key entrepôt for British merchants seeking hemp, flax, tallow, hides, and timber. These were the raw materials of every navy and merchant fleet.[6]

Hemp and flax made ropes and sails; tallow served for candles and lubrication; hides became leather for rigging, pumps, and sailor's gear; and Russian timber, especially tall pines, was essential for shipbuilding and masts.

The War of the Spanish Succession had thrown much of Europe's seaborne trade into uncertainty. The Mediterranean was risky, the Atlantic competitive, and privateers patrolled the western approaches. For enterprising Liverpool merchants, new routes meant new security.

That summer, Rochdale merchant Josiah Gartside had commissioned Bryan Blundell and the *Cleveland* for a voyage to this remote Arctic outpost. For a man whose fortune had been built in warmer waters, Archangel posed a very different trial. This was a world of cold margins and colder diplomacy, but it paid. And for someone like Blundell, that was reason enough.

The venture promised freight of £17 per ton, a lucrative rate by any standard, but it began with delays. Westerly winds stalled cargo in Liverpool, and the *Cleveland* did not finally clear the Mersey until mid-July.[7]

Blundell sailed north past Belfast, through the Minch,[8] and out across the Norwegian Sea. Two weeks later, he joined the London fleet, sixty-two merchant ships escorted by four men-of-war, off the North Cape. From there, the fleet scattered, and Blundell: "Outsailed every one of them," he wrote with quiet satisfaction.

The White Sea offered a final, frozen gauntlet. Shrouded in fog and swept by contrary winds, its waters narrowed into the winding mouth of the Northern Dvina, a long, silted artery leading to Archangel. Near its entrance lay a treacherous sandbar, known to English mariners simply as "the Bar."

By the middle of August, the *Cleveland* had reached the edge of the Bar, anchoring in 7 fathoms.[9]

Pilots from nearby Kholmogory, once the principal trading town of the region, rowed out to guide ships across the Bar and through the 30 miles of shifting channel that led upriver to Archangel. Navigable only at high tide, it offered little room to turn, and the relentless downriver winds made progress treacherous. Even with pilotage the dangers were real: sandbanks shifted with every season, and more than one vessel had been lost here, cargo and crew swallowed together. At peak season the river could be crowded with vessels, their masts stretching upriver towards the nearby monastery, a procession of ships all waiting their turn to run the gauntlet of the Dvina River.[10]

For nearly two weeks the *Cleveland* lay at anchor, waiting passage. From the deck, the crew may have glimpsed what other contemporary travellers described along the Dvina: backwaters filled with perch and pike, forests and marshes alive with hares, and great "teetars", birds as large as turkeys. Overhead, ducks called "gagares" wheeled and cried in voices "not unlike the human."[11] To foreign eyes, it was a landscape both strange and bountiful.

When at last the *Cleveland* attempted to cross, the danger became plain. Her keel rode at times barely 2 feet above the sand, the water so thin beneath her that any sudden shift of wind or tide might have stranded her on the Bar.[12]

Crosses and Calculations

Blundell himself entered Archangel ahead of his crew arriving on Wednesday, 17 August. He had travelled by boat and entered the city later that day.

For a Protestant mariner from Liverpool, Archangel must have been bewildering.

The physical city reflected its dual role as both marketplace and fortress. At its centre stood the so-called "Russian palace," encircled by stout walls nearly 900 metres in length, with 3 gates and 6 towers. These defences reminded visitors that this was still a frontier outpost as much as a port. Within those walls lay the courts and customs houses, the governor's seat, and a scattering of churches (see Plate 8).

But the real business took place outside. Along the river stretched the *posad*, where the Russian guesthouse and the "German yard" for foreigners housed more than a hundred warehouses and shops. It was here that trade flourished, downstream from the fortress, in a district that pulsed each summer with the noise of wagons, barges, and haggling merchants.

Wooden houses lined the banks. They were often rough and uneven on the outside, but inside, the wealthier traders furnished them with boarded walls, painted icons, and vast stoves that heated entire rooms. The streets themselves were less forgiving: "covered with broken timbers," one traveller observed, so uneven that a man might stumble and lame himself crossing them.[13]

For most of the year Archangel hibernated, its river frozen, its streets half-deserted. When Blundell arrived, the city was at its busiest. The *iarmarka*, the great annual fair, was not just any event but the city's raison d'être.

Thousands descended, including Russians from as far as Moscow, Dutch and English factors, even Tatars bringing hemp and hides from the steppe. Transactions ran from dawn till dusk, a frenzy compressed into the brief northern season before ice returned to lock the White Sea. Here, a year's fortunes were made or lost in weeks.[14]

The fair drew traders, porters, and pilgrims into the narrow streets. Blundell found the people numerous but unrefined: the women "hard-favoured and not well dressed," the men "all wear chin beards except the gentry."

The markets flowed with provisions as much as people. Another traveller noted that "all the necessities of life abound in this city": the best beef in the world for a penny a pound, plenty of fowl, partridges and woodcocks for 2 or 3 pence, even turkeys and geese for 7 or 8 pence. Hares, too, were sold cheaply, while stalls offered salted fish from the Dvina, including the prized *karotes*, small and delicate. Beer was also plentiful and of good quality, though it could not be brewed or sold without a licence from the Tsar's officials.[15]

Yet within that chaos stood structures of quiet solemnity. Wooden churches with onion domes leaned into the skyline, their gilded crosses glowing in the low Arctic sun. Icons of saints adorned church doors and street-side chapels, and townspeople crossed themselves and bowed deeply as they passed.[16]

Blundell observed it all with a merchant's detachment. "They are as ceremonious in their services as the Roman Catholic," he noted, marking the rites of the Russian Orthodox Church with a mixture of curiosity and disdain. The local devotion was intense, frequent, and performative – entirely alien to his own brisk, Calvinist piety.

That evening, as the bustle of the fair quietened and lamps flickered in the merchant quarter, Blundell retired to his lodgings with Josiah Gartside.

But just as he settled down for the night, fire struck.

The Day the City Burned

From his lodgings in the merchant quarter, Blundell woke at 1 am to a red sky.[17] At first it seemed distant, an orange flicker behind rooftops. But by dawn the fire had swept into the heart of Archangel. Fuelled by its wooden buildings and pine-board streets, the blaze moved fast.

Blundell watched helplessly as more than a hundred homes were consumed by the fire. The acrid smoke of burning resin filled the river air. "Had not the factories been built of brick," he wrote, "it had consumed all the town."

His comment was grounded in precedent. A great fire in 1667 had destroyed every guesthouse, warehouse, and customs office in the city. In its wake, Moscow ordered that new trading posts for foreign merchants be built of stone and brick. By the 1680s, a new complex had risen on the Dvina's bank: the so-called "Stone City," flanked by the German yard for foreign factors to the north and the Russian yard to the south. Together, these guesthouses and warehouses formed the fortified heart of Archangel's commerce, over 200 rooms and storage chambers in all. In 1709, that brick quarter halted the flames, barely.[18]

The blaze revealed the city's fragility, a medieval city in a modernising empire. Its churches stood untouched, but its houses smouldered.

Commerce and Cunning

Yet business resumed almost immediately. As church bells tolled for the dead, pontoon bridges were reopened, barges continued unloading flax onto the *Cleveland*, and merchants haggled over the price of hemp.

To Blundell, the merchants themselves proved the greater trial: "Very active and cunning and knavishly false," he wrote, lamenting the artful evasions and calculated delays of the Russian merchant class. Honesty was not a prized virtue in the Archangel marketplace – wit and deception were. Among Russian traders, a successful deal was one in which the other man lost. Prices were fluid, promises vague, and every agreement a negotiation in disguise. Deceit, he observed, was "reckoned a great qualification," an admiring, if begrudging, nod to the cultural premium placed on commercial cunning.

In Liverpool, Blundell was used to a different kind of economy, one built on familiarity, kinship, and reciprocal trust. His world was bound together by overlapping networks of family, faith, and favours: transactions were often mutually beneficial, shaped by long-standing relationships and shared reputations, many of them generations deep and sealed over chapel pews or tavern ledgers.

Here in Archangel, none of that held. Every exchange was transactional in the bluntest sense, stripped of context, driven by gain.

Nevertheless, Blundell admired the people's physical resilience, "lusty, strong people," but had little patience for their duplicity. He quickly learned that business here required sharp elbows and a thick skin. Deals shifted mid-sentence, prices danced, and no promise came without a shadow.

The bureaucracy moved at a glacial pace, and the harbour choked with waiting barges. Since 1687, a new checkpoint had tightened control: officials boarded ships at the estuary and accompanied them upriver to ensure nothing was unloaded along the way.

Every manifest was scrutinised, captains interrogated about wars and epidemics, and cargo inspected again at the harbour. The customs staff – headed by a *gost*,[19] assisted by "heads of customs" and sworn *tseloval'niki* drawn from merchant guilds and northern towns – were relentless in their tallying.[20] Blundell learned quickly that here nothing moved without payment. He noted, even the pontoon bridge that spanned the Dvina charged a fee each time it opened.[21]

Still, he conducted business with characteristic precision. At Solombala,[22] a fortified trading island just across the river from Archangel, the *Cleveland* discharged her cargo and took on "flaxes", sixty bales of hemp, twenty bales of linen and some rolls of hides. These were the standard staples of the northern trade.[23]

Blundell noted that the warm weather, "very common in that country at that time of the year," was a great help to the ship's dispatching and in loading "hemp and flaxes which is brought down the river in great barques that will carry 500 tons."[24] Barges and punts were loaded by hand in the long northern light, while the sound of bells carried from the churches beyond.

Here, the sacred and the cynical coexisted without tension. Archangel, he found, was a city of contradictions. Of faith and fraud. Icons and invoices. The same hands that crossed themselves at a shrine or doorway might cheat you on the quayside an hour later.

To Blundell, this duality seemed peculiarly Russian. Yet he came from a world where piety and profit, too, often shared the same dockside.

Tempest in the White Sea

The *Cleveland* departed Archangel on Saturday, 10 September, her hold fully laden. By noon, they had anchored at Sea Island, waiting for the tide before crossing the Bar.

At 5 pm, with a gentle southeast wind and the tide nearing "half flood," they weighed anchor. Two boats from a nearby man-of-war assisted in towing them over the shallows. They struck ground a few times and were stopped for around a quarter of an hour, but with the tide coming in and waters calm, they scraped clear by 8 pm. That night, after saluting the warship, they slipped into open sea, steering northwest for Kanin Nos. The homeward voyage had begun.

But almost at once, the weather turned.

The following morning, the wind backed easterly, then to the northeast, cutting across their path and forcing them to veer westward. All that day and through the night, they tacked against it, beating into rising seas. At 2 am, with the wind building, they reefed their courses. Two hours later, they struck their topsails, driven backwards up the White Sea.

By dawn, they were facing a tempest.

The gale howled and billows roared. "It was the most terrible gale I ever was in," Blundell wrote. The *Cleveland* lay with her lee side buried beneath waves. Water surged across her hatches. Under bare poles, with all sails struck to avoid capsizing, she drifted helplessly, nearly foundering. They cast their poles and loose timber overboard, followed by two of their guns. Even the water casks were hauled up onto the deck in a desperate attempt to lighten and steady the ship.

Still, she would not wear. The crew tried to bring her round by turning the stern through the wind, a last resort in heavy weather when tacking was too dangerous, but she would not respond.

Only after lashing a cable astern and sending men into the icy rigging did she finally begin to answer the helm. They struck the main-topmast. Then, as she steadied, the fore-topmast snapped and went overboard.

Snow began to fall.

The *Cleveland* drifted helplessly all that day. The crew could do nothing but wait as the gale blew her northwards, toward the narrowing throat of the White Sea. Only twelve leagues wide at its mouth, the sea had become a trap. Had the wind turned from any other quarter, they would have been dashed upon its frozen, desolate shore.

"Blessed be the Lord," Blundell wrote, "for his great mercies to us."

By nightfall, the storm began to ease. The crew scrambled to raise a staysail, a small triangular sail rigged between the masts. It was just enough to steady the ship and give her headway once more.

With the wind mercifully abating, the *Cleveland* clawed her way westward down the White Sea, still under reduced sail.

The following day,[25] they passed Kanin Nos, the stark headland receding behind them in sleet and silence. The weather offered no reprieve. Day after day, snow fell and winds battered the ship from the northern quarter.

The *Cleveland* tacked constantly, wearing every few leagues in the endless grey. Ice crusted the rigging. Hands froze at the lines. For days they were unable to re-rig the broken fore-topmast, the salvaged spars lashed on deck.

With reefed topsails finally aloft, the ship picked up speed and bore northwest, rounding Seventy Nos, a cluster of islands in the White Sea, on 21 September. Three days later, they cleared the North Cape.

With the dangers of the White Sea behind them, the crew now faced the long haul through the Norwegian and North Seas, waters no less unpredictable than the Atlantic.

In early October, the *Cleveland* made sight of the Faroes, high and broken against the sky. Near Loch Stornoway, anchoring proved too risky, and they pressed on. Off the Shiant Isles, rugged islets off Scotland's northwest coast, the wind shifted southerly. By middle of the month, they had passed Tiree,[26] an Inner Hebridean island, battered but making way.

More threats lingered. The next day, near Lough Swilly, a deep inlet on Ireland's north coast, two ships appeared to the westward. Suspecting privateers, the *Cleveland* prepared for action, but the strange vessels failed to approach. The following night they passed the Copeland Islands, and by the next morning they were in sight of the familiar outline of the Isle of Man.

At last, on Tuesday, 18 October, Bryan Blundell stepped ashore at Hoylake. They had been gone three months and two days. The venture earned £1,100 in freight, against £150 in wages, a handsome return for a journey that had nearly cost them everything.

Where the Ledgers Froze

The voyage to Archangel had been, in every sense, a passage through fire and ice: one day a burning city, the next seas lashed with snow and sleet. It was a world apart from the familiar latitudes of the Chesapeake, where tobacco weighed heavy in the hold, but the winds, at least, were known.

There is no triumphalism in Blundell's tone, only a steady conviction that survival came through faith, diligence, and the hard calculus of trade.

1. Bryan Blundell (1674–1756). (*Courtesy of the Liverpool Blue Coat Foundation*)

2. Liverpool Castle, by William Gawin Herdman, from Pictorial Relics of Ancient Liverpool (1878). Painting of Liverpool Castle showing the arrival of William III's army. (*Public domain*)

3. Harbor at Sunset, follower of Claude Lorrain, late seventeenth century. The close of a trading day – ships at rest, the light fading, the ledgers still open. (*Public domain*)

4. Moonrise by the Sea, Caspar David Friedrich, 1822. The sea at night, as a boy in a Liverpool port town might have imagined it – vast, luminous, and full of promise. (*Staatliche Museen zu Berlin, Nationalgalerie / Jörg P. Different. Public Domain Mark*)

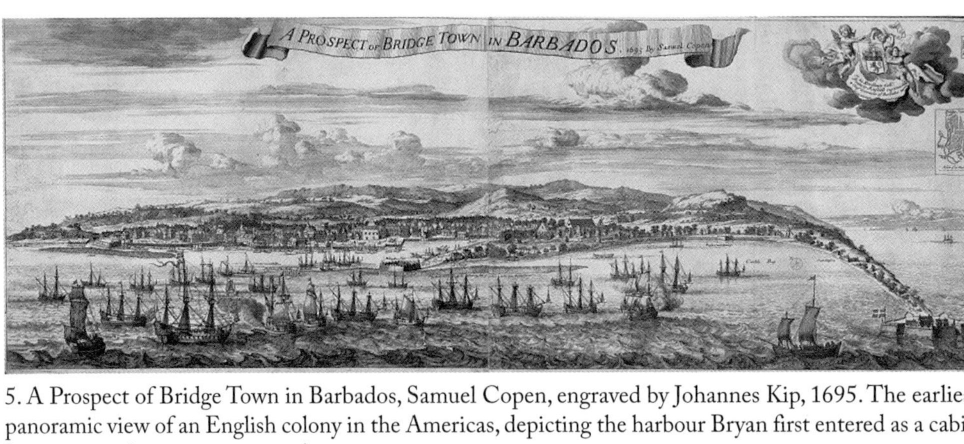

5. A Prospect of Bridge Town in Barbados, Samuel Copen, engraved by Johannes Kip, 1695. The earliest panoramic view of an English colony in the Americas, depicting the harbour Bryan first entered as a cabin boy in 1688. (*Library of Congress*)

6. Enslaved Africans working in Virginia, 1670. Artist unknown. (*Public domain*)

7. The bustling Philadelphia waterfront at the close of the eighteenth century, with shipyards, warehouses, and merchant vessels preparing for naval defence during the Quasi-War with France. See: W. Birch & Son, "Preparation for War to Defend Commerce," Plate 29 in The City of Philadelphia, in the State of Pennsylvania North America; as it appeared in the Year 1800. (*Public domain*)

8. View of Archangel (Arkhangelsk) in 1701, Russia. (From Bruyn, Cornelis de. Travels into Muscovy, Persia, and part of the East-Indies, vol. 1. (*London: A. Betteswortb and C. Hitch, et al., 1737, public domain*)

9. Willem van de Velde the Younger, A Ship on the High Seas Caught by a Squall (The Gust), c.1680. Oil on canvas. (*Rijksmuseum, Amsterdam (SK A 1848), public domain*)

10. Ships in Distress off a Rocky Coast, Ludolf Bakhuizen, 1667. In August 1718, the *Cleveland* – Bryan Blundell's beloved ship of ten voyages – was lost off the coast of Madagascar. (*Public domain*)

11. Recollections of the Blue-Coat Hospital, Liverpool, St George's Day, 1843. Lithograph by Thomas Picken (c.1818–1870), after a painting by Henry Travis (1805–1853), published 1850. (*Courtesy of the Liverpool Blue Coat Foundation*)

12. The Boardroom of the Liverpool Blue Coat Hospital, 1844. Oil on canvas by Richard Ansdell (1815–1885), a former pupil of the Blue Coat School. (*Courtesy of the Liverpool Blue Coat Foundation*)

13. Jonathan Blundell (1717–1800), treasurer of Blue Coat School from 1760–1796. (*Courtesy of the Liverpool Blue Coat Foundation*)

14. William Roscoe (1753–1831). (*Public domain, Artvee*)

15. London Road and the Gallows Field, site of the 1715 Jacobite executions. From a drawing by W.G. Herdman, based on a work in the possession of John Rankin, Esq. As noted by Ramsay Muir, this site (later known as Gallows Mills) was where Jacobite prisoners were hanged and quartered following the failed uprising of 1715.

16. The Slave Trade, George Morland, c. 1788. (*Collection of the Smithsonian National Museum of African American History and Culture*)

17. *Dale Street, Liverpool.* Drawing by W. G. Herdman (1805–1882), after an original drawing by George Perry. Reproduced in Ramsay Muir, *Bygone Liverpool* (1913). (*Public domain*)

18. Photograph of shackles used in the trans-Atlantic slave trade. (*Creative Commons Attribution–ShareAlike 4.0 International* (*CC BY-SA 4.0*), *ZekethePhotographer*)

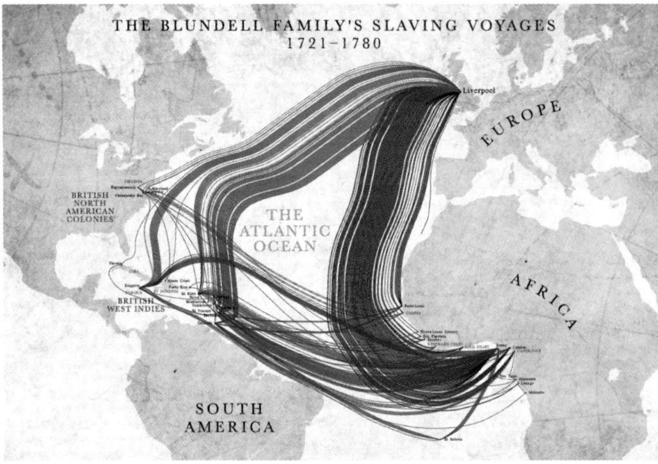

19. The Blundell Family's Slaving Voyages (1721–1780). A pictorial representation produced by The Bluecoat as part of its Echoes and Origins heritage participation project (2020–22), created in collaboration with local young people to interrogate the building's colonial legacies and connections to transatlantic slavery. Michelle Girvan researched the data for the map which was designed by Naomi Waite. (*Courtesy of the Bluecoat, Liverpool*)

20. *The Hunted Slaves*, 1861. Oil on canvas by Richard Ansdell (1815–1885), a former pupil of the Blue Coat School, Liverpool. (*Collection of the Smithsonian National Museum of African American History and Culture, public domain*)

21. The Bluecoat today is a contemporary arts centre. (*Image courtesy of The Bluecoat*)

Yet beneath that piety lies another truth: he had outsailed the London fleet, bargained in a foreign tongue, and weathered a storm that might have ended him. For Blundell, God's mercy was written not only in church pews but in the margins of his ledger.

The voyage had tested him. He returned richer, and perhaps more certain of his place in a widening mercantile world. He would not forget what the White Sea had cost him, and neither would those who knew him.

Two years later, preaching to Blundell in Liverpool, the Reverend Christopher Bassnett would recall that voyage:

> *And this is a Mercy that I must call upon you this Day, to commemorate; when you went before to Archangel, God spoke to you in a Storm, and a very terrible one too; and blessed be God, that delivered you from so great a Death.*
>
> Christopher Bassnett, 1711

Part III

A Precarious Balance

Chapter 12

Powder and Providence

"The Race is not to the Swift, nor the Battle to the Strong."[1]

Christopher Bassnett, 1711

The Town of Liverpool | Saturday, 16 December 1709

In the final weeks of 1709, Liverpool's waterfront bristled with masts. Dozens of merchant ships were preparing to cross the Atlantic: brigs, galleys, and pinks, their holds heavy. Most were armed with little more than hope and a few small guns. But among them, one ship was different.

The *Cleveland*, Blundell's own, had been built not only for profit, but for survival. She carried sixteen guns, her hull broad and fortified, her rigging cut for speed. Below deck, she was braced to withstand a broadside, because in these waters, trade and war were no longer separate pursuits.

The War of the Spanish Succession had turned the Atlantic into a battleground, and privateers flew false colours on every horizon. Blundell had no intention of sailing unarmed.

Powder in the Wind

He set sail, noting with typical precision that it was "at 12 o'clock… being the last quarter of the ebb tide," the outgoing tide that carried ships seaward.

The *Cleveland* was "towed down" the Formby Channel, accompanied by the *Indian Queen*, and by 5 pm had cleared the banks and reached open water. But the wind was already turning against them.

They beat past the Calf of Man and struggled along the Irish coast, eventually making the Bay of Dublin. There, while the *Indian Queen* bore away for Carlingford, Blundell anchored for two days and went ashore to buy beef.

But the weather worsened. By Christmas they lay weather-bound in Milford Haven, where storms hemmed them in for the next twelve days.

From there they pressed on to Cork, where the *Cleveland* was provisioned and loaded. At the end of January, they joined a convoy of twenty-six ships under the escort of the *Hastings*, a 44-gun fifth rate.[2]

"We sailed as well as most of them," Blundell noted with pride.[3]

Yet the protection did not last. Just five days out, the *Hastings* turned back. The convoy scattered. The *Cleveland* held company with the *Lyon* and a handful of others, but by the time they reached the Azores, only a ship belonging to a Captain Brownbill remained nearby. Eventually the *Cleveland* and Brownbill parted company. One stood west, the other southwest.

Blundell was alone.

At 9 am on Saturday, 4 March, a sail appeared to the west-southwest. At first it seemed to be passing, a harmless shadow on the horizon.

But then, suddenly, it tacked and turned into their wake. Blundell observed that the stranger "bore away after us. Came up fast."

He responded with caution. The *Cleveland* reduced sail, and as the ship drew closer, Blundell furled the mainsail entirely and swung the helm around to allow it to approach more easily, testing its intent.

But the pursuer held off. That hesitation told him everything. This was no passing merchant.

The game was on.

So Blundell reset every sail and resumed his course. By nightfall, the stranger was still following, never quite gaining, but never letting go. When the sun rose, it was clear: they were being hunted.

Blundell recorded the vessel as a brigantine, flying neutral colours, but he had little doubt of its purpose. Privateers were rarely what they claimed to be. As the wind stiffened and visibility grew patchy, he made preparations for a fight.

The *Cleveland*'s crew were, almost certainly, a capable body of men. As with other merchant crews of the period, they were expected to both sail and shoot, and to be ready at a moment's notice to go to quarters.[4]

At Blundell's order, practice turned to reality. The men sprang into action.

First, they cleared the decks. Every cask, plank, or coil of rope that wasn't stowed could become a killer once the cannons opened. When enemy fire struck, it was often the ship itself that turned deadly. Splinters of oak, torn loose by shot, could rip through a man's body like shrapnel.[5]

To blunt that danger, hammocks were often lashed along the bulwarks, pumps rigged in case shot pierced the hull, and tubs of water set by the guns to smother stray sparks. The decks were then sanded, ready to absorb blood and provide better footing in combat.[6]

Only then did the heavier work begin. They ran out the guns, loaded shot, and set powder kegs ready near the magazines – sponges, rammers, handspikes, and gun tackles[7] all laid ready. Cutlasses were brought up from the chest.

Blundell would have given the orders in calm, measured tones. Methodical even under pressure.[8] They waited.

And still the brigantine came on.

At around 2 pm, the stranger opened fire. A chase began, the sea erupting behind the *Cleveland*, with spray, smoke, and shot. Blundell returned fire with his stern guns, holding his course. Within moments, the ships had closed to musket range.

Then the brigantine made its move.

She clapped alongside the *Cleveland*, hard to starboard, and attempted to board, shattering one of the ship's quarter galleries in the process.

But Blundell's crew were ready. They met the assault with furious resistance.

"We plied him so well with our small arms," Blundell wrote, "that we prevented him from entering any man."

The fight was brutal and close. The enemy could not board.

In the end, it was the brigantine who pulled away, bloodied and beaten. Blundell did not follow.

One of his men was killed; no others were wounded.

In Barbados, he later noted a report, said to have come from Martinique, that the French had lost thirty men, dead or injured. Whether true or inflated, it spoke to the violence of the clash.

That night, the *Cleveland* sighted land. Four days later, on Thursday, 9 February, battered and scraped, she dropped anchor in Carlisle Bay.

Whatever damage she had taken in the fight was patched swiftly. In his journal, Blundell recorded the sale of beef at 30d per pound, and butter and cheese at 7½d. Sugar cost between 13d and 16d per pound.

But not every ship was so fortunate at sea. Blundell noted that the *Lyon*, one of the Liverpool vessels that had sailed with him from Cork, was "overset and lost" in Barbados at the end of March.

A Sea Full of Shadows

Blundell and his crew departed Barbados in the last week of April, bound for Liverpool.[9] Their course was set to go north about Ireland, avoiding the Azores and French patrol routes further south. The *Cleveland* sailed in the company of several other vessels, including the frigate *Boyle* and a few small sloops.

Their escort was the *Hector*, a Royal Navy man-of-war under a Captain Clark, who agreed to accompany them partway, though not without a gratuity, which Blundell paid.

A few days later, the *Hector* parted company bearing away for Antigua. The sloops, bound for the American colonies, veered westward. The *Boyle*, for once the faster ship, gradually outpaced the *Cleveland* and was soon lost from sight. Blundell found himself alone again.

Calms and unfavourable winds hampered progress. But as they reached the latitude of Antigua, the wind shifted at last, allowing the *Cleveland* to make better headway. However, with every gain came new risk.

A week later, a sail appeared to the southeast.[10] The vessel was larger than Blundell's and stood to the westward, mirroring his course at a distance.

Blundell held to windward, sailing upwind to preserve the tactical advantage, and by nightfall, he had slipped past her. Yet the stranger did not disappear.

As the sun rose, he could just make out "its topgallant sails above the horizon from our poop."

Then the wind changed.

By noon, the stranger had the advantage; Blundell could now see "his hull from the poop, a large ship, a seeker, to be shunned." The breeze was fresh and westerly, favouring the chase.

The ship began to close the gap. Blundell prepared for the worst: he cleared the decks, "got out all our great guns and small arms, loaded them all", drove out the mast wedges, and soaked the sails with seawater to tighten them, a technique used to improve their hold on the wind and gain speed in a chase.

At 2 pm, the ship was barely a league off.

Then came more sails. First two. Then fourteen.

From among them, a much larger ship broke out: a great warship flying English colours. It fired a warning shot. Blundell returned the signal. Moments later, the vessel struck the Union Jack and raised the French ensign. She again opened fire.

Blundell and his crew, believing capture imminent, changed their clothes, preparing, as he wrote, for prison. Blundell noted that he and his men "despaired of escaping."

Then the original shadowing ship, the one that had paced them through the night, closed from the lee side, pressing in with the wind on their beam. To gain speed and lighten the bow, Blundell ordered two of the forward guns thrown overboard. The shadowing ship fell back.

However, the great ship kept coming, firing sporadically while flying the French flag. At pistol-shot range, the flag dropped.

And up went the red ensign.

This second attacker was not French. It was British: the *Bedford*, man-of-war of sixty guns. She had pursued the *Cleveland* so far and fast that she'd lost sight of the very convoy she was meant to protect, merchant ships bound for Virginia.

Once the mistake was clear the crew "rejoiced and brought to". Signals were exchanged, and at close range they recognised one another. Blundell, shaken but unharmed, resumed his course alone.

The real French ship had vanished in the confusion.

Landfall and Profit

After more than six weeks at sea, the *Cleveland* made Hoylake on Monday, 5 June. Eight days later, she rounded the Rock and returned to Liverpool. Blundell's journal noted it without flourish: "We made £2,400."

Behind the ledger lay the story: storms endured, a privateer repelled, a man-of-war mistaken for the enemy. He had brought his ship home intact, turned a profit, and lived to sail again.

In that season of false colours and shifting winds, survival itself was a kind of mastery. In a world ruled by powder, providence had brought him home.

Chapter 13

The Price of Reputation

"However great and agreeable it may sound in a worldly trader's ear, that such a one died worth so many thousands — his stock so great, his goods and lands so highly valued — yet these things should make but little impression upon a Christian."

Christopher Bassnett, 1711

Carrickfergus Lough, Northern Ireland | Monday, 16 October 1710

For nearly a month Blundell had waited here, wind-bound and working the lighters hard.

The *Cleveland* had first discharged her burden of Liverpool coal, around 120 tons ferried ashore load by load, and then set about taking in her freight for Barbados. By now her hold was crammed with 1,650 barrels of beef and herring, 1,200 firkins of butter, 160 barrels of tongues, pork, tallow, and "groots".[1]

But the cargo was not just provisions. It was obligation: a cousin to convoy, a network to maintain, a reputation to uphold.

Two days later, Blundell cleared out of the bay, sailing in the company of his cousin William Everard, who commanded his own vessel, also bound for Jamaica. To keep company, and to command: these were as much the cargo as anything in the hold.

Though bound for different ports, they kept company across the Atlantic, watching each other's lights through the dark and sharing the burden of command. Everard was kin, but also a kind of mirror: another provincial captain trying to rise in a world ruled by credit, caution, and colonial spirit.

"We were very good company all our passage," Blundell noted. "Being little or no difference in our sailing when blowing strong." In lighter winds, Everard had the edge. But Blundell's *Cleveland* was the more aggressive ship, better with canvas, stronger under pressure.

They finally parted ways on 19 November, deep in the tropics. Everard bore away westward; Blundell held course for Barbados.

Moonrise and Thunder

Now sailing alone and knowing these waters swarmed with French privateers, he once again made ready. The decks were cleared. The guns loaded. "Fixed all our men in their quarters," Blundell recorded. Five men were stationed in the fore-top, one in the mizzen.

After five days, a sail appeared to the west-southwest. They lost sight of her at dusk. Then, at 2 am, just as the moon rose, Blundell's crew sighted land. Moments later, a second sail closed on their broadside. Blundell fired three shots. The stranger sheered off, then turned to follow.

A running fight ensued.

Soon, Blundell brought his chase guns to bear: long-barrelled cannons at the stern, meant to cripple sails, rigging, or rudder. He fired from the cabin and roundhouse, trying to slow his attacker.

The enemy replied from its bow guns. Within moments, musket fire crackled across the sea. Then the enemy closed and clapped aboard on the larboard side getting ready to board.

As the hulls collided, Blundell met the assault with grenades and small shot. His men, stationed in the fighting tops, raised platforms on the masts, fired down with muskets and rained explosives onto the deck below.

It was brutal, close-quarter fighting. The tops, high above the fray, became crucibles of smoke and sweat, their occupants gripping the rigging with powder-blackened hands, delivering death from above with a butcher's precision.

The musket balls, small but deadly, lodged deep. Some killed instantly; others tore through flesh, leaving wounds that festered, crippled, and killed days later. The grenades followed: a brutal rain of fire and steel, some igniting on impact, others rolling before they burst, scattering jagged fragments into bare arms and open faces.

Amid the chaos, one of Blundell's men took a shot through the arm. Posted in the maintop, he dropped his musket and slumped against the shrouds, blood soaking through his sleeve as the fight raged on beneath him.

Then a thunderous crack. One of the enemy's great guns had struck true. The shot landed directly between two of *Cleveland*'s cannons, shattering a quarterdeck brace and sending wood splinters and iron shards flying. It broke one man's legs. Others were thrown back, stunned or bleeding. As Blundell later wrote, "It was great providence did not kill many of us."

Every brace had been cut by enemy fire; Blundell's sails hung slack. But he held his nerve.

When the enemy shifted to *Cleveland*'s weather quarter – laying his boom sail across her stern, "by which he thought himself hid from us," Blundell wrote – his men responded with precision. Shot tore through his canvas from below, while from aloft the tops raked his decks with iron and fire.

Soon the enemy's cheers turned to "mumbles and groans, so that their extreme firing ceased and most of them who could get off the deck, did."

For the first time, Blundell had the advantage.

For a moment, *Cleveland* had him fast: a grappling iron locked into his rigging, Blundell's men ready to haul him in. Then the enemy sheered hard to the wind; the chain snapped under the strain. With every brace shot away, *Cleveland* could not give chase.

It had been close. One man was killed outright. The man with broken legs died days later. Four more were wounded.

And yet, *Cleveland* survived. She reached Carlisle Bay by 9 am: battle-worn, scarred, but intact.

Blundell sold his beef at 30 pounds per scoreweight. Butter, candles, cheese, and soap all fetched fair prices, though the market was already crowded. The old sugar crop had not yet all gone; the new had not yet come. He took what he could. The rest would wait.

The Weight of Return

The *Cleveland* departed Barbados at the end of January, bound for Liverpool.[2]

Among her passengers were Colonel Thomas Maycock, his family, and Major Howe, a British officer returning home after years in the Caribbean trade.

Maycock had recently acquired Redland Court in Gloucestershire, but his fortune lay in Barbados.[3] Howe's did too.[4] Both men had profited from sugar, land and enslaved labour. They were the sort of passengers whose presence lent weight to a captain's name, and whose comfort had to be safeguarded at all costs.

Blundell ensured their departure was conducted with symbolic pomp. He arranged for every fort on the island to fire a round in farewell. As the *Cleveland* sailed from Spickles Road, the coastal cannons fired in salute. Blundell responded in kind, expending two barrels of powder in return. This was a ship of trade, but now also one of diplomacy and decorum. Such performances mattered, especially when reputation was currency.

Concerned for his passengers' safety and comfort, Blundell also arranged for a naval escort. For £20, the *Guernsey* man-of-war accompanied the *Cleveland* out to sea. He had, as he put it, "no wish to disturb the passengers." In 1711, a Royal Navy escort offered more than protection; it was a signal of confidence and status, reassuring those aboard and those who watched from shore.

Not long after clearing the coast, a sloop was sighted in open waters. "We gave her chase and came up with her," Blundell noted in his journal. She had, he recorded, "been trading amongst the French." The vessel was handed off to the *Chester*, a nearby man-of-war.

As Blundell and his crew waited, they chanced upon several casks the sloop had hove overboard in a vain attempt to lighten her and make an escape. On recovering the barrels, they discovered they "had brandy in." What became of them, Blundell does not say, but it is fair to assume the crew saw to their safe and proper disposal.

The following evening, the captain of the *Guernsey* dined aboard the *Cleveland*.[5]

Colonel Maycock and Major Howe were almost certainly present. All of them would have gathered in the *Cleveland*'s great cabin, where Blundell set before his guests the best the ship could muster: fresh meat, fruit, and vegetables newly loaded in Barbados, perhaps even turtle or fish bought in the market a few days before. To this he might have added punch, a measure of wine, or even some of the recently captured brandy.

Conversation most likely turned to business and the fortunes of Barbados's plantation economy, matters of land, labour, and wealth. The captain of the *Guernsey* might have reflected on the navy's role in protecting the trade that sustained the island. For Maycock and Howe though, the prospect of home after years in the Caribbean must have loomed large. And beneath it all lay the unspoken subject: the long voyage still ahead, and the ever-present dangers of the Atlantic.

By the following Monday Blundell had parted company with the *Guernsey*, which, as he later noted, "would have gone further had we desired it." Instead, the man-of-war turned back, and the *Cleveland* was left to make her long passage home.

Alone now, the *Cleveland* pressed north into open water. For a time, the winds held steady.

But on the night of Friday, 23 February, the weather turned.

The storm gathered slowly, then broke suddenly. At first, only a shift in the wind, then a groan in the timbers, a tremble in the sails. Within moments, the sea rose and the ship was in chaos.[6]

Orders rang out: sails had to be struck, yards brought down, everything that could be lashed was lashed, including the men. Tied to the rigging to keep them from being swept overboard, they clung to soaked ropes as the gale drove cold salt into their eyes and mouths.

The *Cleveland* pitched and rolled as if gripped by a vast, invisible hand. The ship was cloaked in pitchy darkness, broken only by flashes of lightning that darted across the sky.[7]

Waves reared like walls crashing down with such force that the vessel seemed to vanish beneath them, only to rise again, as if climbing the back of some immense beast. It mounted wave after wave, the prow tilting skyward before plunging into troughs so deep the masts seemed to pierce the sea itself.[8]

The winds roared. The sea foamed. Thunder cracked.

Now the vessel lurched from one side to the other, staggering under the weight of each blow. A heavy sea rolled over the deck. Below, the miserable inhabitants clung on, their hearts failing them for fear, unsure whether they would sink or survive[9] (see Plate 10).

There was no sleep, no sense of time: only noise, motion, and the cold that found every joint.

Hearts pounded. Hands bled.

A single bolt working loose, or a plank giving way, could have meant death. But the ship held. Somehow.

Major Howe, staying in Blundell's roundhouse, never came up on deck. A former officer, used to hardship, he remained in his cabin. Perhaps it was fear. Perhaps pressure. The storm passed, but something inside him had already broken.

Blundell later wrote, with uncharacteristic softness, that "he was never rightly himself afterwards." He was still breathing. But some part of him had not survived the night.

Outside, a different stillness settled. The wind grew colder with each degree. As the *Cleveland* neared Ireland, she passed Islay, Rathlin, and Copeland Island.

They encountered no enemy ships. Just cold. Fog. Silence.

On Friday, 9 March, they anchored near Hoylake. Howe, gravely ill, was carried ashore and taken to Thomas Ansdell's house. He died eight days later.

Blundell buried him "very handsomely" in Liverpool and paid for the funeral himself. He acted as executor, managing Howe's goods, settling accounts, and handling the freight. The estate, he noted carefully, was considerable: plantations in Barbados "well stocked with negroes and cattle," as well as houses in London. It was worth, he estimated, £10,000.

These were the quiet burdens of command: not just to sail, but to represent, protect, and account – for the living, and for the dead. Blundell said little. But he buried Howe with care. In death, as in life, he handled the estate like a ship: methodically, carefully, and with all possible exactness.

As for the *Cleveland*, she had made "a tolerable freight out and home," bringing in £2,070 for her voyage, with £200 paid in wages. It was a satisfactory return for her owners, duly recorded in Blundell's journal. Figures balanced against loss, entered without flourish, the business of the sea reduced to bare numbers once more.

A Cold Calculation

By July 1711, the *Cleveland* was at sea again, this time not westward but north, bound for Archangel once again. She sailed together with the *Norris*, and later the *Content* of Lancaster.[10]

After five days, she anchored in Carrickfergus Lough to take on provisions from Belfast.[11]

She was then swiftly on her way.

Off Islay the ships were forced into Lough Swilly, where they lay weather-bound for a full week before pressing north again. By early August they were near Tromsø in Norway, and at Vardø,[12] Blundell recorded they caught cod: fifty in just one morning.

When they reached Cross Island in the White Sea, the wind failed altogether, and for a time the *Cleveland* drifted beneath slate skies, her sails limp. Still, they soon pressed on.

By the end of August, the wind still worked against them. Then, on the morning of Sunday, 2 September, off Kanin Nos, they met a fleet of London ships already homeward bound from Archangel. The sight must have been sobering. Those merchants had loaded, traded, and turned for home, while Blundell and his company were still beating northward. Time was slipping; the season was closing. And if they delayed much longer, the ice would trap them in Russia all winter.

That evening they reached the Bar of the Dvina River, the narrow, shifting gateway to Archangel. On his last voyage, Blundell had been forced to wait nearly two weeks for a pilot to lead them across the treacherous channel.

He knew the dangers ahead, yet this time there was no waiting.

Blundell and the other merchants resolved to cross without a pilot, gambling their ships against the sand.

At first light, he gave the order. Crews scrambled to shift their goods, trimming weight and bringing their "ships on an even keel," so they might ride higher in the water. With the tide beneath them, the merchants advanced together across the Bar.

As they did, the *Cleveland*, drawing 13.5 feet, struck ground as she went over. She was dangerously close to ruin. But she scraped through.

It was a high-risk decision, one Blundell must have felt was born of necessity. To linger meant not just delay and lost profit, but the danger of being trapped for months.

It would not be the last time Blundell ignored a warning. But this one, at least, paid off.

At Solombala, they worked the quays night and day, moving hemp, flax, yarn, oil. They loaded by the barrel, signed papers by candlelight, and were ready to sail just over a week after arrival.[13]

But bureaucracy and weather intervened. Gartside's papers, Blundell's agent, were not in order, and then the Arctic winds turned against them. Departure was delayed nearly a fortnight.

At last, on Sunday, 23 September, they crossed the Bar again, with the *Norris* in company. They soon fell in with a Dutch fleet and sailed together, but Blundell quickly grew impatient at their pace. The *Cleveland* and the *Norris* pressed on ahead.

On their voyage home they battled contrary winds, snow, and heavy seas for over three weeks. Yet by mid-October, Blundell was safely anchored at Hoylake.[14]

"We made £860 freight or near £900. Was three months on our voyage – £146 wages."

He logged the numbers. Nothing more.

But the silence was its own kind of record: he had, once again, reached the edge of Europe and made it back.

Chapter 14

Stillness Before the Storm

"If your Consciences reproach you secretly for the Way that you are in…In the Name of God quit it, and betake yourself to some other Way that you are better satisfied about."

Christopher Bassnett, 1711

Key Street Meeting House, Liverpool | Thursday, 13 December 1711

The year of 1711 finished not with cannon or convoy, but with silence. After long seasons of Atlantic crossings and battles fought in open water, Bryan Blundell was at home. For once, the *Cleveland* remained moored, her timbers resting, her guns unfired.

Recent voyages had tested every part of her, from her brace-splintered quarterdeck to the men who fought to keep her afloat, and the judgement of the man who commanded her.

Now, as frost lay across the Mersey shore and salt air mingled with chimney smoke, Blundell stepped back.

A Sermon of Salt and Soul

That morning, the streets of Liverpool stirred with an unusual sense of ceremony. Blundell had gathered his crew, not in the counting-house or on the docks, but in a meeting house.

The preacher was Christopher Bassnett,[1] a prominent nonconformist minister and the first pastor of the New Meeting House on Key Street. The subject of his sermon was both timely and intimate: *The Seaman's Character and Calling Consider'd and Improv'd.*[2]

It was, in part, a tribute. Dedicated to Blundell himself, it acknowledged not only his seamanship but his steadiness of spirit. "It was upon your account, my good friend, that I preached this sermon," Bassnett wrote. "Could I allege no other reason, I should reckon it very sufficient, that hereby I have an opportunity of showing to men of your profession the rare and singular good pattern that you have set 'em".[3]

In the preacher's own words, they had weathered "a very gloomy dispensation" together: not a physical voyage, but a season of shared difficulty. The phrase may have referred to the recent death of Major Howe, or to a broader darkness: grief, illness, or spiritual strain. Bassnett himself had been incapacitated by illness that year, a period that overlapped precisely with these trials.[4]

Bassnett went on to praise the discipline and industry of Blundell's men, contrasting them with the "idle sailors" who made poor ballast, "bad company, but that is the best thing you can make of 'em at sea."

He marvelled at shipping itself, "a great and noble invention… the riches and ornament of a nation… a shovel-ful of Earth thrown up in the midst of the Sea."

But his tone grew heavier when he turned to the trade which loomed increasingly over Liverpool's future.

"For though 'tis a trade that the laws of our country allow us to follow," Bassnett cautioned, "yet it carries considerable difficulties along with it, to which it is not easy to return clear and satisfactory answers."

He meant, of course, the slave trade.

Blundell had not yet directly entered it. But the sermon made its unease plain.

"Supposing the calling should be in itself lawful, in order to render it innocent to those that are engaged in it," Bassnett continued, "such should see that they treat these poor miserable people with humanity; they should at least take care, that they don't deal unmercifully by 'em… They should not be cruel to, nor hide themselves from their own flesh".

It was not a denunciation. But it was a warning.

In choosing to preach this message to a ship's company, Bassnett risked more than theological debate. Liverpool's merchants were watching. The port was stirring with enterprise, and some among them were already financing ventures to the African coast.

But in this moment, in this sermon, the pulpit offered a stillness, a warning, and a quiet reflection on what it meant to carry power over other lives.

Blundell sat among his crew, the men who had fought beside him and seen death come close more than once.

Whether the words stung or comforted, we do not know. But the decision to print the sermon and distribute it in Liverpool and London, at Blundell's own expense, suggests a degree of assent.

Crowded Waters

In the three years that followed Bassnett's sermon, Blundell remained a man of the sea.

In January 1712, the *Cleveland* sailed again, bound for Cork, then Barbados.[5] The route was familiar; the cargo routine: barrels of beef, pork, herrings, butter.

By late March, they were nearing Barbados and the crew were on alert once more. "We made a clear ship and loaded all our guns, but saw not a sail in the latitude," he wrote.[6]

In the early evening of the first of April, their destination appeared on the horizon. Blundell recorded, "could see Needham's Fort,[7] but no flag hoisted so brought to and stood off and on all night."

When he entered Carlisle Bay the following morning, he found dozens of ships already at anchor. Prices were low. Freight was scarce.

He considered pressing on to the Leeward Islands, but news from a man-of-war warned of oversupply there too. With herrings spoiling and Barbados still hungry for beef, he chose to stay. He sold what he could and while beef, herrings, and butter moved steadily enough, his dry goods stagnated and sugar remained costly. Still, with persistence, he secured a modest return cargo: 400 casks of sugar, with bags of cotton, ginger, and freight for London.

Two months later, the *Cleveland* cleared out,[8] sailing under the protection of the *Panther*,[9] a 50-gun man-of-war, alongside vessels from London, Bristol, Glasgow, and Liverpool. Winds were fair but tempers short: one Bristol captain quarrelled with the commodore, and the fleet splintered within days.

Blundell, with his brother-in-law, Thomas Lace,[10] who commanded his own galley, the *Clayton*, and two Bristol cutters, kept closest company with the man-of-war, pushing hard through weather and sail.

On 6 July, one of Lace's men slipped while climbing the ratlines. He "missed his hold and tumbled overboard. We were going at the rate of six or seven knots…so that we could not save him," Blundell recorded.

A broken yard followed soon after, adding further delay.

By mid-July, they reached the Mersey.[11]

Twelve weeks out; £2,077 in freight earned; £300 in wages paid. Another voyage behind him.

Frayed Lines

In late November 1712,[12] Blundell sailed for Cork and the West Indies once again. On the first night, the foreyard snapped, forcing a return to Hoylake. Having secured a new yard, the *Cleveland* was out again three days later, snow in the air, but the wind at her back.

At Cork, Blundell reloaded with beef, pork, herring, and butter. While the lighters worked, he rode on horseback into the town to buy rock salt. Within two weeks the *Cleveland* was ready to depart. He was meant to be travelling with the *Norris* and her captain John Tunstall, but when the weather turned, Tunstall dared not sail.

Blundell, unwilling to wait, slipped out alone, as he briskly recorded: "he durst not turn out, so I went and left him there."

Cape Clear fell away astern.

Two days later, they sighted a small English galley out of Lisbon, limping westward after being plundered by a Frenchman. She had been six weeks at sea, short of provisions. Blundell noted simply that "it blowed so hard we could not well help them." In such seas, to linger was to hazard his own ship. Yet for the galley, left adrift in winter waters, want of food and water often led to only one end.

Christmas brought a storm. Heavy weather forced the ship to wear under reefed sails. For days, the wind stayed foul.

They finally reached Carlisle Bay at the end of January.[13] But Barbados's market was already flooded with goods. Dry goods fetched little. Blundell stayed anyway. He found space for sugar, cotton, ginger, and lime juice, and booked freight for London, not Liverpool.

In early April, with eight passengers aboard at £10 each, the *Cleveland* cleared for home.[14]

The winds favoured them, and soon the Leeward Islands slipped astern. They passed French and English ships with ease, sailed past the *Stokes* man-of-war, and overtook all but the tide. Blundell landed at Greenwich on Sunday, 17 May. By 7 am, he was in London. That night, the *Cleveland* was moored at Deptford.

The sugar market had cooled. Prices fell from 40d to 30d per pound. Cotton dropped too. Still, Blundell made do: £1,850 earned out and home; £231 in wages; £1,360 in costs. Enough profit. A new charter waiting.

The Last Strands

In late June 1713, the *Cleveland* cleared Deptford once more. This time, she was bound for Archangel, sailing alongside the *Norris* and Captain Tunstall.

Both winds and moods were foul from the start.

Battling headwinds, they took nearly a month to reach the North Cape, approaching the Bar of the Dvina River at the end of July.[15]

No pilot came out to meet them. In fair weather, they again took the risk, crossing without assistance. *Cleveland*, heavy with freight, scraped the bottom but made it through.

This was Blundell's third voyage to Archangel, but the trade winds were shifting. Peter the Great's new city on the Neva, St Petersburg, was rising fast. Within a generation, the Tsar would decree that the northern port should receive no more goods than were needed for local consumption. Voyages like Blundell's marked the fading edge of a once-vital route.

But in the summer of 1713, trade still flowed.

Cleveland was soon alongside the quay at Solombala.[16] "The next day got a scow or lighter on board and got our goods all out and in 2 days were ready to take in our loading," Blundell wrote.

But their factor was absent. "Find only his man, Mr. Booker: Mr. Gartside being not come from Moscow."

Blundell had come earlier in the season than before, seemingly to allow more time to load and discharge before the White Sea closed with ice. On his second voyage in 1711, he had cut it close, and the risk of being trapped for winter was never far from mind. But arriving early also carried its own hazard: the English Russia Company's agents often wintered in Moscow, nearer to the Tsar's court and inland markets that governed supply.[17] Without Gartside's authority, the process stalled.

Blundell had expected to reload swiftly, and his irritation showed: "He was not so ready with his goods as I expected or as he ought to have been."

With the threat of demurrage, a financial penalty for delays beyond the agreed time for loading or unloading, tempers frayed: "We threatened him very hard that we would protest as soon as our days were out, which was nearly 20 days." The pressure worked. "He did all he could to get the goods for us," and by 25 August, the *Cleveland* was nearly ready to sail.

Yet even then, bureaucracy frustrated him further. "We are all obliged to come to anchor and show our passes before we can be admitted to pass the Fort," Blundell noted.

A week later, they crossed the Bar again, outbound in convoy with several English ships and three Dutch galleys. Blundell, ever watchful, took quiet pride in their performance: "We outsail all the English ships, that is the *Norris* and we, being very nearly equally yoked as to sailing."[18] The Dutch had the edge in daylight, he admitted, "but we bear more sail than they in the night so that we got to the North Cape as soon as any of them."

Then the weather turned. Westerlies rose. Near the island of Sanina,[19] hard seas drove them toward shore. "But it pleased God to moderate the weather," Blundell wrote, and they held their course. It was 21 September before they sighted the Scottish Isles. On the first Sunday of October, they reached Formby Channel, but a gale forced them to anchor offshore, yards struck, topsails reefed.[20] By the following morning, they were safely in port.

The voyage had taken over three months. They earned £667 freight, with £50 lost to damaged flax and £120 in wages paid. Blundell recorded just one line of reflection: "We bless the Lord for his great mercies shown unto us."

But he was not yet finished. Blundell and the *Cleveland* would sail together one final time.

Stillness at the Edge

In early 1714, Bryan Blundell undertook his final voyage as master of the *Cleveland*. It was one last crossing to Barbados and back.

In mid-January, they slipped from Formby Channel, the Mersey behind them, the wind easterly and the skies cold. The *Elizabeth* and *Ann* sailed alongside in company.

The days ahead were marked not by drama but delay. They waited on tides at Holyhead, drifted in calms off St David's Head, and edged slowly past the coast of Ireland.

At Passage West, near Cork, they discharged their outbound salt and took on beef, butter, and biscuit for the West Indies. The winds remained uncertain, and it was February before they caught a fair breeze.

They pressed on slowly south and west, catching the Trade Winds. They passed Madeira, caught sight of Foyal and the Canaries,[21] and made Barbados after a month at sea. There they exchanged their cargo and loaded sugar for the return leg.

The outward trade had been modest: "250 tons," Blundell noted, "and the same cargo under the *Providence*." The return was no richer.

By the last week of June, they had reached Deptford. The "24th, being a holiday," Blundell wrote, "I got a grant from the Commissioners to discharge the ship, being deep loaded, had not water to ride afloat in, so discharged and eased the ship in 9 or 10 days."

"All our loading in good order," he wrote. "And by the 10th, went down – by land – to Liverpool."[22]

His final crossing complete, his seafaring career quietly closed.

* * *

Back in December 1711, Bryan Blundell stood at the edge of something, not death (he had faced that already), but reflection.

Years at sea had honed his caution, his judgement, his instinct for weather and risk.

But it was the stillness of that morning ashore: the meeting house, the sermon.

A moment between voyages, between callings, that asked something deeper. What kind of man was he becoming?

Chapter 15

Not for Oneself but for All

"Men insure their cargo with one another when they venture to sea – but no man insures as God insures. Charity may seem lost, but it is the best venture you can make."

Christopher Bassnett, 1711

The Town of Liverpool | Wednesday, 14 July 1714

The coach reached Liverpool late in the day, the wheels grinding to a halt as the bells of St Nicholas Church struck six. Blundell stepped down stiffly, adjusting his coat. He had travelled overland from London by post chaise, a four-day journey in a hired carriage with horses changed at inns along the way.[1]

He returned home with a quiet resolution, writing, "I now purpose to leave off going to sea; not to quit all business, but rather to change my employment." For Blundell, it marked the close of a remarkable twenty-seven-year seafaring career.

His future as a merchant-investor would soon gather pace, but before commerce took hold, another cause demanded his attention.

Almost at once, he turned to the town's faltering charity school, a refuge for orphans and the children of destitute seafarers. He had been at sea when the town's first charity school was planned, but he had supported it from the start.

Now the school was adrift. The Reverend Robert Styth,[2] its rector and treasurer, had died the year before, and his successor was "much afflicted with a disorder in his senses." Funds were low, attendance patchy, the schoolhouse opposite St Peter's Church neglected.[3]

Blundell resolved to act. He set out his ambition "to find 60 boys meat and drink and clothes; to take them wholly from their parents at 8 years old and keep them till fourteen." In other words, he envisioned a true boarding school, where poor boys would live as well as learn, removed from the uncertainty of their homes. "I think it will not be time lost," he concluded, "but may serve as encouragement for others that may come after me."

When he put this proposal before the mayor and "other gentlemen of the town," he explained that if they would "excuse me of all other offices," he would "undertake to promote that School all I could." They agreed, though not, as he noted wryly, to excuse him from the mayoralty.

And so, in August 1714, Bryan Blundell took up a new helm: trustee and treasurer of Liverpool's Blue Coat School.[4]

A Great Work Begins: A School in the Shadow of the Waterfront

The early eighteenth century was an age of reform: political, religious, and educational. Following the Glorious Revolution the Society for Promoting Christian Knowledge (SPCK) had been founded in 1699 by the Reverend Thomas Bray. The SPCK soon emerged as a powerful force in efforts to expand access to education under the banner of Anglican orthodoxy.[5]

Charity schools were central to its vision: institutions that would instruct the poor not merely in reading and writing, but obedience, piety, and work discipline. Often located near docks and slums, these schools were intended to rescue children "from idleness and irreligion" and prepare them for lives of usefulness and faith.[6]

Such ventures also reflected wider thinking of the age. Philosophers like John Locke had argued that the mind was a *tabula rasa*, a blank slate shaped by experience. Train the poor in discipline and obedience during childhood, and they might grow into productive citizens rather than burdens on the parish.[7]

In Lancashire, a region marked by widespread poverty and fears of lingering Catholic resurgence, these efforts took on a special urgency.[8] Among the region's SPCK leaders was the Reverend Styth. It was in partnership with him that Blundell emerged not only as a merchant of growing stature but as a key lay ally of the SPCK. Elected a corresponding member in 1703, he became a recognised organiser and donor.[9]

In 1708, while Blundell was in the Chesapeake, Styth had proposed establishing a charity school for Liverpool's poor. The town council approved his proposal, and upon his return, Blundell funded the original schoolhouse within the yard of St Peter's Church with a £25 donation.[10]

Its children were admitted at 8, apprenticed out at 14, and clothed in coarse blue uniforms. Blue was the colour of almsgiving, long associated with charity, and it gave this institution, and others like it across England, their name: the Blue Coat School.[11] The coats were typically worn with knee breeches and yellow stockings. According to one account, the stockings were dyed with saffron and onion peel to deter rats and fleas from biting the children's ankles.[12]

Over the next six years, Blundell contributed more than £250 to the cause. In his journal he noted, "the more I parted with to charitable services, the more I had still – the one much like the increase of the Widow's Oil; the more vessels she got, the more oil she had."[13]

However, by 1716, Blundell found himself "under great discouragement in the children's improving." Some of the poorest parents could not even supply meat; others sent their children out "a'begging for it in the School habit by which they got such habits of idleness."[14]

As treasurer, he now raised a subscription fund for a new boarding school. Beginning with £500 of his own and calling on the merchant networks he had cultivated as a trusted sea captain for Liverpool's leading figures – men like John Hughes, Nathaniel Bassnett, James Tarleton, and Thomas Earle – all prominent in shipping, West Indian trade, and local politics.[15]

Blundell described the effort with characteristic precision: "got a parchment and went about with it," and soon "a great many gentlemen subscribed handsome sums." With those pledges in hand, he "employed workmen to build a large building with two wings," at a cost of £2,100, designed "for convenience to accommodate and recover the children's lodgings and diet."[16]

By 1717, a new boarding school had been constructed on School Lane: symmetrical, imposing, and distinctively Anglican in its Queen Anne style (see Figure 13). It contained wings for boys and girls, dormitories, workshops, and a hall for public catechism. This was a structured form of religious instruction based on set questions and answers, covering the Ten Commandments, the Lord's Prayer, and core Anglican doctrine.[17]
Above the entrance, the Latin inscription still survives, translated as:

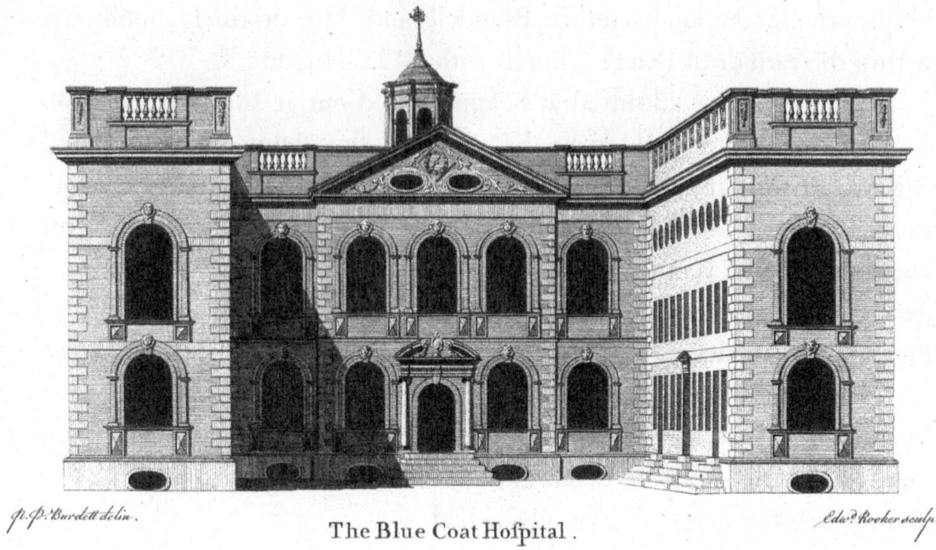

Figure 13. *The Blue Coat School*, Liverpool. Line engraving by E. Rooker after P.P. Burdett. (*Wellcome Collection*)

> Dedicated to the promotion of Christian charity and the training of poor children in the principles of the Anglican Church. Founded in the year of salvation 1717.[18]

A cupola crowned the roof, once topped with a ship-shaped weathervane: a subtle but pointed reminder that this building, for all its piety, was built by trade and tied to the sea.

Inside those walls, boys and girls now lived the life that Blundell and the SPCK had imagined.

Disciplined Lives, Ordered Days

Each morning at the Blue Coat School began with a bell.

At dawn, the children rose from narrow wooden bedsteads, their dormitories lit by low, leaded windows. They got dressed in long blue coats, yellow stockings, and caps, then assembled for prayers, reciting the Lord's Prayer and selected psalms before breakfast. The meals were simple: porridge or bread, sometimes with a little cheese. On Sundays and feast days, meat.[19]

The day was divided neatly into lessons and labour. Mornings were spent in reading, writing, arithmetic, and religious instruction. Scripture was central. Catechism was not just recited: it was rehearsed aloud in chapel and in front of visiting patrons. Singing was also taught; the pupils performed metrical psalms on Sundays and were expected to master hymns that reinforced obedience and gratitude.[20]

In the afternoons, the curriculum turned vocational.

The boys learned practical trades: spinning cotton, picking oakum (a tar-soaked fibre made from old ropes, used to seal the seams of ships), winding twine, mending sails. "They be made seamen or clerks," Blundell wrote, "and not idle." The girls were trained in sewing, cotton spinning, and domestic skills, preparing them for a future in a merchant's household, or in one of the town's textile yards.[21]

Evenings brought prayers again, then supper and lights out by candle curfew. The rhythm of the day, like the school itself, was designed to mould the child: not simply to educate, but to shape moral character, piety, and useful labour.

In 1717, Blundell received approval from the Consistory Court of Chester, an ecclesiastical body responsible for church property and faculty permissions, to construct a dedicated gallery in St Peter's Church, where the schoolchildren could "stand, sit, kneel, and listen to divine service."[22]

The school's walls offered shelter. But its timetables offered something else: order in a world of chaos. In a port town where poverty loomed large and temptation beckoned from every tavern and quay, the Blue Coat offered a doctrine of discipline: by day, by prayer, by hour.

A Beacon for the Town

Blundell's success in establishing and expanding his Blue Coat School was not an isolated act of civic virtue, but part of a broader movement sweeping early eighteenth-century England. Between 1700 and 1723, the number of charity schools rose from just 112 to more than 1,300.[23]

Yet among them, Blundell's stood out. In 1723, the SPCK commended its efficient integration of labour, instruction, and economy in a letter to its

London trustees, proposing his school as "an example to be practiced in other places." He remained in correspondence with the society as late as 1744.

Blundell expanded the school further, adding two wings for almshouse residents. In 1739, he obtained a Chancery decree that formally secured the school's governance and enabled legacy giving.[24] Donations followed. One benefactor, Madam Clayton,[25] gave £1,500. By 1748, the school supported 100 young children.[26]

At least thirty of the boys would go on to be apprenticed to Blundell's own vessels or those of his family.[27] Some, after completing early voyages, returned to the school to study navigation at the school's expense. It was a programme Blundell personally endorsed. "Many of them that proved good and industrious attained to be mates and masters of ships," he wrote, "and some supercargoes and merchants."[28] The school, in this way, became both sanctuary and supply chain.

The school adopted the motto *Non sibi sed omnibus*: "Not for oneself, but for all."

It was more than a guiding principle for its pupils: it cast the institution as a civic beacon, where religious piety, social order, and commercial ambition converged.

Family, Faith and Stone

The school also linked Blundell more deeply to the Anglican reform network that underpinned the SPCK. One of its leading northern figures, the Reverend Samuel Shaw, had long championed educational and spiritual reform across Lancashire.[29]

In 1717, the connection became personal. Shaw's son, also named Samuel,[30] married Hannah, Blundell's only surviving child from his first marriage. Samuel and Hannah's union joined not just two families, but two strands of Anglican purpose.

The joy, however, was short-lived. Within a year, Samuel the younger had died, leaving Hannah widowed with their infant son, another Samuel. Hannah took Samuel to live with her in the Blundell household. There, under his grandfather's roof the boy would be raised for the next fourteen years.

In Liverpool, such ties mattered. Faith, business and family were not separate spheres they were part of a system which carried across generations.

For Bryan Blundell, the Blue Coat School became one of his lasting legacies. His sons took up the cause, expanding its reach and reputation.

By 1769, 16-year-old William Roscoe (See Plate 14)[31] would reflect on the institution's enduring role in his poem, *Mount Pleasant*:

> Yon calm retreat, where screened from every ill;
> The helpless orphan's throbbing heart lies still;
> And finds delighted, in the peaceful dome,
> A better parent, and a happier home.[32]

Chapter 16

Between the Tides

"And thus, I fear, it is with too many of you that go to sea. While you are out upon the ocean, in the midst of great dangers, you may have some sense and impression of God upon your souls. But once you find yourselves safe again on land, you throw off all such thoughts and become, it may be, the same bad men you were before – perhaps even worse."

Christopher Bassnett, 1711

London Road, Liverpool | Tuesday, 25 February 1716

The rope creaked.

A hush fell over the crowd, packed shoulder to shoulder in the chill morning air. They watched intently.

Beneath the scaffold, a soldier read aloud the charges: high treason against His Majesty King George I. The condemned man was stripped to his shirt, soaked in sweat. He swayed slightly in the breeze, lips moving in silent prayer or defiance.

He stood atop a cart, the rope already fastened tight.[1]

Then the signal came.

The cart lurched forward. A crack. A gasp.

It should have ended there. But this was not mercy: it was justice, seen to be done.

The body was cut down, laid upon a block. An axe rose, then fell, once, twice. The hangman worked methodically, limbs severed, entrails pulled from the cavity and tossed into the fire. Smoke curled skyward.[2]

By month's end, four men had been executed, quartered and dismembered for the sake of a rebellion that had never even reached the town.[3] Their remains were dispatched to Manchester, Lancaster, and beyond. Liverpool kept the heads.[4]

The Jacobite rebellion had failed.

In the autumn of 1715, supporters of the deposed Stuart line had risen in arms to restore James Francis Edward Stuart, styled James III, to the throne. The rebellion swept through Scotland and northern England, culminating in a brief but dramatic occupation of Preston. Liverpool, however, stood firm in its loyalty to the Hanoverian king, George I.[5]

Business Before Blood

Eighteen months earlier, Blundell had retired from the sea, but his ships had not.

The *Cleveland*, under Josiah Atherton, left London in July 1714. She first crossed to Norway for timber, then loaded sugar in Barbados, before heading back to Liverpool.[6]

By the spring of 1715, she was sailing again. This time ballasted from Liverpool to Cork and onward across the Atlantic. The plan was simple enough: to load salt and supplies at Cork, sell timber and flour in New York, and return via Barbados with a cargo of sugar for London. Salt, lumber, flour, and sugar.[7]

But while the *Cleveland* traced familiar routes abroad, the tides at home were anything but steady. By that summer, change was coming: across oceans and through the streets of Liverpool itself.

The wars with France were over. The Treaty of Utrecht, signed in stages between 1713 and 1715, had reconfigured Europe's empires – and with them, the flow of Atlantic commerce. New permissions, new privileges, and new markets were opening up in the Caribbean and the American colonies. Ships now sailed with fewer guns and greater ambition.

Yet for Liverpool, opportunity alone was not enough.

New Dock, New Beginnings

For centuries, Liverpool's trade moved with the tide. Larger ships anchoring in the river could only unload by means of flat-bottomed lighters, which ferried cargo to shore.[8]

The River Mersey, with the second highest tidal range in the UK, rising up to 10 metres between neap and spring tides, made this work particularly unpredictable and dangerous.[9] Its vast vertical shift meant that cargo could only be moved during brief, fleeting windows of time.

Trade lagged. Capital was stalled by current and clock.

And yet, Liverpool's geography held promise. The Mersey widened as it approached the town, offering a natural harbour sheltered from the Irish Sea and ideally placed for access to the expanding trade of the Atlantic world. It just needed the right infrastructure to unlock it.

In 1709 Liverpool's Town Council made the decision to build the world's first commercial wet dock: an enclosed harbour with lock gates to maintain constant water levels, allowing ships to remain afloat while loading and unloading, regardless of the tide. Its site was to be the Pool: the liver-coloured tidal inlet from which Liverpool takes its name. On contemporary maps, it is clear how the town formed around it, its roads converging on this watery centre. In time, people would speak of it not just as a dock, but as "the heart of Liverpool."[10]

The project was led by Thomas Steers, a former army engineer who had served under the Duke of Marlborough during the War of the Spanish Succession. Trained in the fortification methods of continental Europe, Steers now applied his skills to civilian infrastructure.[11]

By the summer of 1715, Steers's masterpiece was complete: an enclosed dock covering 3.5 acres, with brick-lined walls, timber quaysides, and lock gates engineered to hold the tide in, rather than waiting for it to return. It was not just a feat of engineering; it was a reinvention. And it changed the town forever.

The opening of the New Dock was rightly a moment of immense pride for the town. Nicholas Blundell,[12] the diarist, had a keen interest in maritime affairs and recorded the atmosphere of celebration. He wrote that the New Dock opened in August 1715 "with great rejoicings".[13] He went on to write, "I rode to the Old Dock and saw *Mulberry [Marlborough]*, *Bachelor*, and *Robert*, the first ships ever to enter it."[14]

This was a new era. Now, ships no longer waited on spring tides. Merchants could now plan to the hour. Trade quickened. Predictability, once elusive on a tidal river, became part of the port's promise. And for men like Blundell, predictability meant profit.

"This is of so great a benefit," wrote Daniel Defoe a few years later, "and its like is not to be seen anywhere in England."[15]

Seams of Empire

The New Dock had barely opened when a new opportunity arose for Bryan Blundell.

William Clayton,[16] six times MP for Liverpool, a towering figure in the maritime supply trade, and the town's earliest known slave trader died. Clayton left behind a thriving tar business, he was nicknamed the "Old Tar Barrel."

Blundell, a close associate and trusted member of the same merchant circle, stepped in. He assumed control and made it his own.[17]

With all his experience, Blundell understood what few in Liverpool did. Britain's victory in the Atlantic, or a merchant's survival in the tropics, might hinge not on a broadside, but on a substance so ordinary it rarely earned mention in dispatches: tar.

Poured hot and packed in barrels, it coated the wooden world at sea: hulls, masts, cables, rudders, spars. It sealed seams. It stiffened rigging. It kept out water, held off rot, and kept ships afloat long enough to return with profit. Without it, no vessel, merchant or man-of-war, could survive a season.

But its true value revealed itself in tropical waters. In Virginia and the Caribbean, teredo navalis, the shipworm, could bore deep into planking, weakening a hull until it became dangerously unsound. Blundell himself referred to the threat, a constant concern on return voyages from Barbados and beyond. Tar was their shield. Without it, a ship was defenceless.

His journals record over 120,000 barrels of tar shipped across the Atlantic in more than a hundred vessels over three decades.[18] Few in Liverpool saw it. Fewer understood its reach. But it mattered.

"I had two or three ships in the tar trade in which I was wholly concerned and kept in that trade, in the which I had good success," he wrote. "And from the year 1720 I was concerned generally in eight or ten ships yearly, four in the tar trade…"[19]

In peace and war, Britain's naval reach relied on a wooden fleet: frigates, brigs, sloops, merchantmen, each one hungry for maintenance. Contractors scrambled for access to colonial tar markets, especially from the Baltic and the pine-rich coasts of North Carolina. Every barrel that landed in Liverpool fed the global supply chain.

Blundell moved those barrels, steadily, silently, and at scale.

But in the autumn of 1715, before his hold on the tar trade was complete, the town faced a different kind of threat.

The 1715 Jacobite Rebellion was underway.

A Town Alone

September saw the Earl of Mar raise the Stuart standard in Scotland; by November, Jacobite forces had crossed into England and taken Preston, barely 30 miles from Liverpool.[20]

Across Lancashire, "eager mobs everywhere cheered for the Stuarts; bells were rung to celebrate King James III's birthday; and in Manchester the mob took possession of the town, organised a force, and sent out emissaries to stir up similar movements elsewhere."[21]

All of the north was aflame; except that is Liverpool.

The reason lay in politics and profit. Since the Glorious Revolution, Liverpool's Corporation had been dominated by Protestant Whigs, many of them merchants. Their loyalty to the Hanoverian succession was not only ideological, but commercial: stability meant shipping, insurance, and credit. Disruption threatened everything.

In November, when Lord Derwentwater's Jacobite army occupied Lancaster and proclaimed James III king, Liverpool, now the only major town in the county to remain loyal, faced the real possibility of siege.

But the townsmen, Blundell almost certainly among them, were ready to resist.

A ditch was cut, deep and fast, along the old Civil War ramparts, running from the upper reaches of the river to the Pool and New Dock. Guns were hauled into place, seventy in all, mounted across the embankments and along the quays. The Pool itself was dammed to create a defensive floodplain. Ships were repositioned mid-river, ready to fire on any advance. Seamen drilled in the streets. Merchants took up arms.[22]

In the end, the rebels never reached Liverpool. Lord Derwentwater's army stalled at Preston, trapped in narrow streets and caught between loyalist forces. Surrender came within days.

But Liverpool had proved its mettle.

In the aftermath, the government turned to the town. Its tower overflowed with prisoners.[23] Four were hanged on the Gallows Field. Dozens more were transported across the Atlantic, some aboard ships owned or insured by men who had helped dig the ditch and mount the guns.

The rebellion failed. Liverpool profited. Trade resumed.

The Tide Turns

As the gallows fell silent and Jacobites were shipped overseas, Liverpool's merchants tightened their hold.

With their loyalty rewarded, rivals removed, and a new dock open, they moved with even greater confidence. Liverpool was changing fast, and Bryan Blundell had already seized his next opportunity.

But the path ahead would be measured not only in pounds, shillings and pence, but in lives shaped – some for better, many for worse.

Part IV

The Slave Trader

Chapter 17

A Ship in the Dock: A Line in the Ledger

"There are callings men may abide with God in – and others so doubtful that few can be satisfied about them. To this class belongs the Guinea Trade."
Christopher Bassnett, 1711

Blundell's Counting House, Liverpool | July 1717

The wood-panelled walls of his counting house carried the familiar smells of ink, tobacco, and strong coffee. Here, among ledgers and low voices, Bryan Blundell's future was quietly taking shape.[1]

He sat at one of the long tables, papers spread before him. He carefully read the figures again. The *Cleveland* had returned from Lisbon with "a few pipes of wine and some corkwood," and nothing to show for it but a loss.[2]

Eight hundred pounds gone. "A bad voyage".[3]

By now, his name carried weight across the town – none more visibly than through the Blue Coat School, which he had helped to found and generously endowed. He embodied the ideal of a godly businessman: one whose piety matched his profit.

But mercantile and civic success depended on more than faith or charity. It demanded discernment, a tolerance for risk, and a readiness to navigate uncertain waters.

Blundell stood at a crossroads. And soon, he would choose his course.

A Ship in the Dock

The *Cleveland* sat quietly in the New Dock that summer, battered by nearly a decade of Atlantic crossings. Her ageing wooden timbers creaked quietly while Blundell and his business partners weighed their next move.[4]

With peace came both opportunity and complexity. French and Dutch shipping, once strangled by wartime blockades, returned to the seas with vigour, their vessels undercutting English prices in Lisbon, Oporto, and the Caribbean. Sugar prices dropped in Jamaica and Barbados as shipments surged. Chesapeake tobacco flooded English warehouses, driving down margins for middling merchants.[5]

Returns were shrinking. Ledgers told stories no sermon could soothe.

Blundell was far from alone. Across England, rising prices, unpaid debts and tightening credit squeezed merchants from every direction. Meanwhile former privateers, stripped of their wartime commissions, increasingly preyed upon merchant shipping in the Caribbean and off the West African coast, driving up marine insurance premiums and ushering in what would later become known as the "Golden Age of Piracy."[6]

Merchants in Liverpool, Bristol, and Whitehaven tightened their belts. Some pulled out of shipping entirely. Others sold vessels or sought new partners. Most watched and waited, cautious of risk, wary of missing the turn.

In Liverpool, the New Dock had changed the rhythm of trade. Ships turned around faster. At first cargoes flowed with less loss, but these improvements only intensified competition. The dock had freed trade from the tide; it had also seemingly untethered it from patience. As the drive for returns intensified, profits soon began to outrun principles.

For Blundell, the loss on the *Cleveland* was not ruinous, but it was humbling.

A single voyage, gone sour, had exposed the fragility beneath the success he had so carefully built. Behind the veneer of stability – the school, the syndicates, the pew at St Nicholas Church – was a balance sheet that now needed correcting. His rising civic status now depended not just on reputation, but on solvency.

The arithmetic was harder now. Margins narrower. Each mistake more costly. If this voyage had been repeated, another season of corkwood and spoilt wine, he could not have absorbed the loss so easily. And with the demands of the Blue Coat School growing by the month, even the appearance of decline carried risk.

So, they deliberated.

"We put the ship in dock," he wrote, "and then consulted…"[7]

There is no list of attendees. No agenda or transcript. But we can imagine the meeting. Men at a merchant's table, ledgers open, wine poured, weathered hands pointing at columns of figures and costs.

They must have considered their alternatives with quiet calculation.

The prospect of returning to Lisbon seemed out of the question. What was left to stake their hopes on?

Could they expand their tar trade, increasing shipments from the Baltic or the American colonies? Or perhaps the *Cleveland* could be chartered, even converted for local trade, short coastal runs that offered safety, but little reward.

What about selling her? It could have been the rational choice. But, Blundell had built her from scratch. He knew every creak of her timbers. She had carried him across oceans, through storms, and safely home again, when others had not.

Or what about taking a different course, one others were already charting?

The African route had its allure: higher risk, yes, but the returns were well known.

The African Option

Liverpool had not yet become Britain's slaving capital, but the door was open.

In 1698, Parliament stripped the Royal African Company of its exclusive rights to the British slave trade, opening the way for independent traders from London, Bristol, and, increasingly, Liverpool.[8]

In 1700, the *Liverpool Merchant*, owned by Blundell's close associate William Clayton, was among the earliest recorded slave ships to sail from the town.[9] Within two years, four more followed. Then came a hiatus, likely caused by the War of the Spanish Succession.

Voyages resumed slowly. In 1710 and 1711, the *Patience* sailed twice under Clayton's ownership. That same year, John Cleveland's *Indian Queen* was converted for the slave trade. One ship cleared for Africa in 1713. Four followed in 1714.[10]

Now, with the war ended and the New Dock in operation, Liverpool's slaving activity was beginning to scale. Eleven ships left for Africa in 1715. Seven more in 1716. As always, there was safety in numbers, each new voyage helped legitimise the next. The tide had turned.

From the waterfront, and from the numbers, Blundell would have seen it.

The arguments against the trade? They existed, but they were faint, and rarely louder than the sound of commerce.

As we have seen, one of the earliest recorded expressions of local unease came from the dissenting minister Christopher Bassnett. In 1711, he delivered a sermon specifically for Bryan Blundell and the crew of the *Cleveland*, recognising the trade's legality but warning of its troubling moral dimensions.

Yet even this was cautiously framed. Bassnett stopped short of outright condemnation; his warnings were hedged in scripture and deference, as though even conscience had to tread carefully in Liverpool.

The sermon held the warning. The ledger held the numbers.

A Line in the Ledger

By now, Bryan Blundell was no stranger to slavery and the plantation economies of the West Indies and Virginia. For nearly thirty years, he had dealt directly with colonial landowners, first as a mariner trading sugar and tobacco, later as a shipowner and investor. His circle now included some of the wealthiest planters in Virginia. Amongst these was Robert "King" Carter, a man who controlled over 300,000 acres and more than 700 enslaved people.[11]

Nor was Blundell's involvement restricted to colonial goods alone. As early as 1701, he had carried enslaved people aboard his ship, the *Lever*. On 26 December that year, he wrote: "This day I got the Governor's seal to our pass and cleared at the fort. I filled some water (casks) and sailed in the afternoon. We carried a passenger, one Thomas Creasey and his negroes, with us to Virginia."[12]

By 1716, he would have known that the East India Company had begun issuing a limited number of licences for slaving voyages from Madagascar to the colonies.[13] The route was considered speculative: less regulated than the West African coast, less crowded, and potentially more profitable. Slaves from Madagascar were cheaper. Licences fewer. Competition thinner. Margins could be high.

Nine slave voyages had already cleared Liverpool's port in 1717 alone.[14] If he opted for caution, the opportunity would pass. The ship would sit idle. His rivals would profit. His influence would fade. The Blue Coat accounts, still reliant on merchant subscriptions, might falter. His name, carefully built over decades, might slip in its standing.

And then came the decision.

It appeared, as so many of Blundell's most consequential choices did, not with fanfare or reflection, but with the clipped neutrality of a businessman accustomed to weighing risk and making decisions.

He wrote it flatly: "Consulted and determined her to go to the Madagascar for slaves, in order to which we procured us a licence from the East India Company, which cost us £25."[15]

The record is chilling in its sparseness. No moral reckoning. Just a plan, concluded and set into motion.

The *Cleveland*, once a tobacco trader and colonial cargo hauler, would now become a slave ship.

As a mariner, Blundell had long understood the pull of the tide, when to wait for it, when to follow it in. And now, like so many of his peers, he was following it once more, into the slave trade.

It was the course others were already charting: familiar names, men he knew well. William Clayton. John Cleveland. Now, it was his turn.

Blundell and his partners moved quickly.

His trusted vessel of ten prosperous voyages was rearmed, re-crewed and readied for dispatch to Madagascar.[16]

The refit would have been comprehensive. Though no full manifest survives, the requirements of such a voyage can be inferred from common practice. The lower deck would have been scraped and re-laid with slatted wooden platforms to increase capacity and facilitate waste drainage. Bulkheads were often removed or repositioned to force more bodies into confined spaces. Iron shackles, typically in pairs or chains, were ordered in batches, some forged locally by Liverpool smiths, others shipped from London.[17]

Water casks were cleaned, re-hooped, and increased in number. Provisions such as rice, biscuit, and dried pulses were probably stacked high, rationed for a crossing that could last up to four months.[18]

She was fitted out for the purchase of hundreds of enslaved people: a grim arithmetic of tonnage, mortality, and return.

Then the cargo was carefully assembled.

It was worth more than £1,400 in total. It was almost certainly a rich inventory of beads, firearms, textiles, and iron bars, calculated to match the known preferences of slave merchants along the East African coast.[19]

Though Blundell initially held a quarter-share in the venture, the scale of the costs led him to sell it: "Mr Ogden being desirous to buy it I let him have it." Even so, Blundell remained financially exposed to the voyage, having helped outfit the vessel at Cork and insured £500 of goods under his own name.[20]

A new master was appointed: Robert Gardner. Fifty men were hired to crew the vessel. Twenty guns were mounted.[21]

Finally, by June 1718, the ship was ready to depart.

A quarter-century at sea. A reputation in the port. A school bearing his leadership. His beloved *Cleveland* would sail again. But this time, its final cargo would be human.

No argument. No unease.

Only: "Consulted and determined."[22]

A Storm Foretold

In 1711, from the pulpit of Liverpool's First Presbyterian Chapel, minister Christopher Bassnett had preached directly to Bryan Blundell and the crew of the *Cleveland*.

His sermon recalled the Apostle Paul's voyage to Rome, a ship pressing forward against all counsel, into a storm that would destroy her. Paul, though a mere passenger, had warned the officers plainly: "Sirs, I perceive that this voyage will be with hurt…" (Acts 27:10). They did not listen. The ship was lost.

Bassnett drew the lesson carefully. He noted that Paul "humbly represented to 'em the Danger of their Voyage…But when they would not receive it, he sat down and said no more." The warning had been given. What followed was on those who ignored it.[23]

Beneath the parable lay something more direct. Turning to the trade that loomed largest over Liverpool's future, Bassnett chose his words with care. The Guinea Trade, he said, was one of those callings that carried "considerable Difficulties along with it, to which it is not easie to return clear and satisfactory Answers." He urged those who entered it to treat the enslaved "with Humanity" and not to "hide themselves from their own Flesh."[24]

It was framed as spiritual counsel. But for those who knew the sea, and its costs, it was more than that. It was a warning.

Years earlier, the preacher had spoken.

But in Liverpool, the profit spoke louder.

Chapter 18
All Souls Lost

"There is one Test that you should have always upon your Minds;
You are Sailors, should have it engraven upon the Decks and Sterns of your Ships;
You that are Merchants shou'd have it writ in fair and legible Characters upon your Counting Houses and Bills of Exchange: It is Mat 16.26.
What shall it profit a Man, if he gain the whole World and lose his own Soul?"
Christopher Bassnett, 1711

The Equator, off West Africa | August 1718

The *Cleveland* crossed the equator that month, the line that marked the start of both a new hemisphere and a new kind of voyage, slipping into the deep waters of the southern Atlantic.[1]

From there, she continued southward, rounded the Cape of Good Hope, and entered the Indian Ocean. It was a long and hazardous route, used by a small but growing number of British slavers seeking profit in Madagascar's markets.

According to letters brought back by the *Elizabeth* she arrived at the island in October. She had called at one part of the coast to take on wood and water, before setting out again for another region to begin purchasing captives. The captain hoped to secure 500 enslaved people; the *Elizabeth*, he wrote, had already acquired 600.[2]

That was the last anyone heard.

Months later, a London brigantine passed through the waters where the *Cleveland* had last been seen. Her crew made enquiries at the intended slaving port. No one there had sighted the ship. It had never arrived.[3]

Word spread that she must have struck rocks or foul ground somewhere along the uncharted coast, lost between the bay where she had watered and the place where she had planned to slave.[4]

Blundell later recorded the loss with chilling detachment: "Believe all the men was lost, for never heard more of ship or men. So ended the ship *Cleveland*, in the which providence had blessed me wonderfully ten prosperous voyages. And at last I did not lose by her, being fully insured."[5]

The ship was gone. The men were gone. The enslaved never embarked. Blundell, shielded by insurance, emerged whole. If he mourned anything, it was not the crew. It was the vessel.

One ship sent for human lives. One ship lost. All souls claimed by the sea.

Blundell had crossed a line. He did not retreat. He re-entered the trade with sharper intent.

Within a few years, his name would reappear in slaving manifests, listed among owners and underwriters, his capital bound to ships sailing for Africa, the Caribbean and the American South.

What had begun as a single decision had become a pattern. And soon, it would become a family trade.

After the Wreck

The voyage to Madagascar had failed, yet the logic behind it had not. Across the Atlantic world, demand for enslaved labour was only growing. Sugar and tobacco plantations devoured human lives. Men who supplied them grew rich.

The road back for Bryan Blundell was not immediate. In 1720, the South Sea Bubble burst, wrecking fortunes across Britain, including those tied to the Atlantic trade. The South Sea Company, granted a monopoly on British trade with Spanish America, had become a vehicle for fevered speculation, its share price soaring, then collapsing in a matter of months. What had begun as a promise of rich returns from Spanish America ended in financial ruin, shaking the very foundations of trust and commerce.[6]

The collapse not only devastated investors but narrowed Britain's access to South American markets. Confidence in maritime speculation faltered. Credit contracted. Ventures were postponed. In Liverpool, the effect was stark: ten slaving ships returned in 1719, five in 1720, and none whatsoever in 1721.[7]

But the tide did not stay slack for long. As financial markets recovered and confidence slowly returned, so too did ambition. The port of Liverpool, once tentative in its reach, was beginning to find its rhythm.

Among those returning to the trade was Bryan Blundell. In his journal, he described himself as "concerned in several ships," a phrase that, in typical fashion, blurred the line between investment and implication.

Some of those vessels were engaged in what he called "the Guinea and West India trades," a common euphemism for slaving voyages.[8] Cross-referencing Blundell's journal with shipping records and entries from the Transatlantic Slave Voyages Database reveals a stark pattern.[9]

What follows is not merely a list of ships. It is a call to understand the story behind the entries. A journey not of profit, but of loss – measured in human lives.

To understand what Blundell was "concerned" in, one must follow the journey to the deck, and then one must understand what happened below.

In Command, Without Mercy

Bryan Blundell's name reappears in the records with the *Martha*, and a slaving voyage he financed with two fellow investors in 1721.[10]

The first task facing Blundell and his fellow investors was to appoint a captain, and it was no small decision. A captain's conduct shaped the fate of hundreds. But in the world they were entering, cruelty was not a failing; it was an expectation.

One young recruit later described a captain who was "all condescension, politeness, and civility" before the voyage, only to reveal himself at sea as "morose, peevish, and tyrannical…an unlimited despot." Too inexperienced to recognise the trap during his recruitment, he later concluded: "we became an easy prey to these dealers in human flesh."[11]

At sea, a slave ship captain had a daunting task. He had to maintain control over a resentful crew, whilst securing a hold full of captives whose desperation could spark rebellion. He needed to preserve human cargo in saleable condition while suppressing any signs of resistance. To achieve their task, it was not uncommon for captains to beat their men, starve unruly crew members, or kill enslaved people they viewed as threats.[12]

In short, they were often bullies, men who ruled by violence, sustained by fear, their success measured not in humanity, but in returns. The cat-o'-

nine-tails, a rope whip with nine knotted cords, was standard issue aboard many ships, its strokes recorded in the log as punishment and ritual.[13]

This was the machinery behind the "concern" Blundell recorded in his diary. For his investment to succeed, the captain had to prevail.

Template for a Trade

The *Martha* sailed from Liverpool on Wednesday, 17 May 1721, under the command of Captain Thomas Lady, an experienced master with at least one slaving voyage already behind him.[14]

As they closed in on the West African coast, the transformation of the *Martha* into a slave ship intensified.

The work now was rough and immediate. Carpenters and seamen set about reinforcing the lower deck, fixing temporary partitions and rough bulkheads to create the final spaces where captives would be confined. Timber for the barricado, the stout wooden barrier erected on deck to divide the crew from the enslaved, was cut and fitted near the mainmast, its height and thickness providing both segregation and defence.[15]

The men worked in heavy heat, their voices echoing across the timbers as they lashed spars, tightened rigging, and raised a ridge-pole for the shelter they called the "house," a crude awning of canvas to protect the crew from the sun and prevent the captives from jumping overboard. They wove rush matting between the trellised spars, fastening it with rope-yarn, and cut a small trapdoor through the lattice for hoisting water casks.[16]

The ship's gunner inspected and cleaned the vessel's small arsenal: muskets, pistols, and swivel guns mounted on deck. Meanwhile below, the tools of restraint were readied: shackles and chains sorted, oiled and stacked with cold precision, their iron links rattling against the planks in the half-dark.[17]

Every task, from lashing down casks of provisions to ensuring the ventilation grilles were passably clear, contributed to the ship's conversion into what was, in effect, a floating prison designed for maximum confinement and minimum resistance.[18]

After more than four months at sea, the *Martha* reached the African coast, likely Sierra Leone, on the last day of September.[19] There, the bartering began. Cargo for captives.

The Shore of No Return

The enslaved did not arrive all at once. They came in increments, bartered one by one.

Those brought from the interior were shackled wrist to wrist. Some were taken in the chaos of local wars. Others were handed over to repay debts. Many were simply stolen.

The journey to the coast had already claimed many. Historians estimate that between 15 and 30 per cent of captives died during forced marches from the interior to the coast, with an additional 5 to 10 per cent perishing while held in coastal forts awaiting embarkation. These figures varied by region and over time, but for every hundred who boarded a slave ship, as many as forty had already died.[20]

Those who survived often arrived at British coastal forts – Bunce Island in Sierra Leone, Cape Coast Castle on the Gold Coast – where they were held in darkness, branded, confined, and renamed in ledgers.

Bunce Island, operated by private British companies under royal licence (including Liverpool merchants), was among the most significant slave-trading posts in West Africa. Cape Coast Castle, the largest British fortification in the region and headquarters of the Royal African Company, stood on the coast of present-day Ghana. From these strongholds, thousands were dispatched to the West Indies and the American South – commodified, recorded, and shipped like goods.

Yet not all captives passed through such stone enclosures. Many Liverpool captains conducted their trade directly from the decks of their ships at rivers and beachheads.[21] (See Figure 15.)

Figure 14. Olaudah Equiano, also known as Gustavus Vassa. Frontispiece portrait from *The Interesting Narrative of the Life of Olaudah Equiano, or Gustavus Vassa, the African* (London, 1789). (*Public domain*)

People were brought in small groups or in coffles, lines of captives chained together lurching forward step by step. Women clutching infants. Boys too young for the work that lay ahead.

Figure 15. *On Board a Slave-Ship*, engraving by Joseph Swain, c. 1835. (*Public domain*)

All were stripped, branded, renamed in chalk or ink – converted from person to price.[22]

And then came the moment that many would later describe as the deepest break: not the capture, not the march, but the sea.

Forced into canoes and paddled out to the waiting ships, they left behind not only land but language, memory, and self.

English captain Thomas Phillips later wrote:

> When our slaves were come to the seaside, our canoes were ready to carry them off to the longboat, if the sea permitted, and she conveyed them aboard ship. The men were all put in irons, two and two shackled together, to prevent their mutiny or swimming ashore.[23]

Then, more starkly:

> The Negroes were so loath to leave their own country that they have often leapt out of canoes, boat, and ship into the sea, and kept themselves under water till they were drowned, choosing death rather than slavery.[24]

Olaudah Equiano (Figure 14), kidnapped as a child and sold into slavery, later recalled the terror of first boarding a slave ship. To his young eyes, it seemed a floating furnace, built to roast its captives.

> When I looked round the ship too, and saw a large furnace of copper boiling, and a multitude of black people of every description chained together [...] I no longer doubted of my fate; and, quite overpowered with horror and anguish, I fell motionless on the deck and fainted.[25]

He went on to write of the moment he was forced below deck: "I was soon put down under the decks, and there I received such a salutation in my nostrils as I had never experienced in my life; so that, with the loathsomeness of the stench, and crying together, I became so sick and low that I was not able to eat...I now wished for the last friend, Death, to relieve me."[26]

The interior of a slave ship was typically divided into three compartments: the men confined to the fore part of the vessel, the boys in the middle, and the women and girls aft.[27] Each captive had less space than a hogshead – 5 feet to lie flat, less than 2 in height. They lay "in two rows, one above the other like books upon a shelf."[28] These cramped decks, scarcely tall enough to kneel beneath, were designed not for comfort but capacity.

In the dark, airless hold, the stench of waste and sweat was suffocating. Fever spread. So did fear. So did death.

It could take weeks, sometimes months, to fill the hold. During that time, the crew waited. And they, too, died.

Conditions aboard were grim even before departure, during the long anchorage on the African coast, crew mortality surged. Exposure to tropical disease, especially malaria and yellow fever, claimed life after life. Water supplies turned stagnant. Rations spoiled in the humid air. Crewmen, already weakened by months at sea, sickened quickly. Some died in their hammocks, too weak to rise. They were committed to the sea, wrapped in sailcloth and slipped over the side, their names recorded only as "dead" in the muster roll. These deaths were not exceptional, they were expected.[29]

There were other dangers too. "The article of Women, likewise, contributes largely to the loss of our Seamen," one officer wrote. "When they are on shore, they often, from their known thoughtless imprudence, involve themselves,

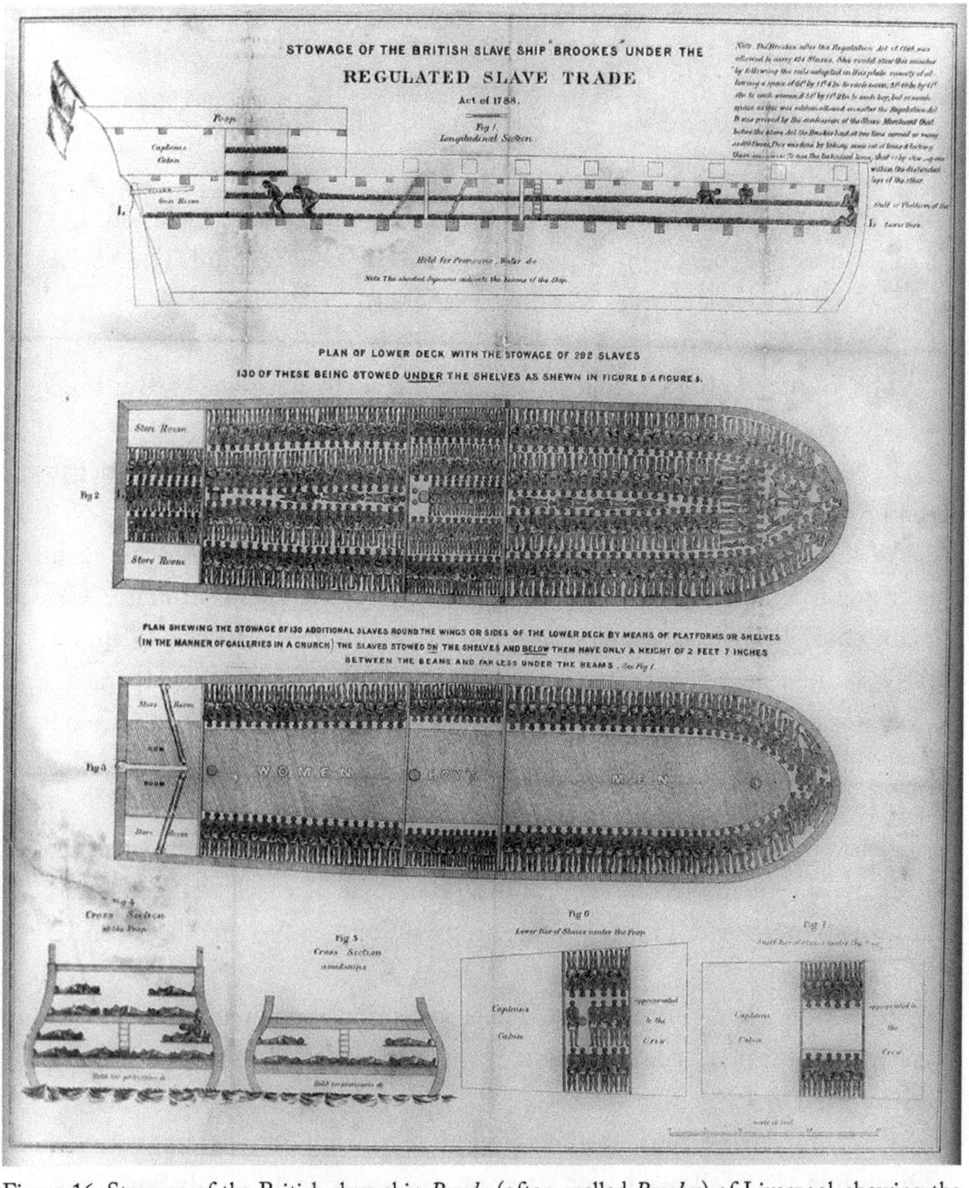

Figure 16. Stowage of the British slave ship *Brooks* (often spelled *Brookes*) of Liverpool, showing the regulated capacity for enslaved Africans under the Slave Trade Act of 1788. (*Library of Congress, public domain*)

on this account, in quarrels with the Natives; and, if not killed upon the spot, are frequently poisoned."[30]

On some voyages, one in five sailors died before the ship ever left Africa. The fewer who remained, the harder the labour became.[31]

All the while, the ship slowly filled. Its hold growing heavier with every human life dragged aboard.

The Middle Passage

Then, after weeks off the coast, Captain Lady made his calculation. He had secured 142 men, women, and children. The hold was full. The books balanced. He gave the order to raise the anchor.

And the *Martha* turned west into the Atlantic.

The journey to the Caribbean took around six to eight weeks. But time aboard was measured less by distance than by ordeal.

Food came in rations, boiled beans, millet, water thickened with vinegar to prevent scurvy. Not enough to sustain. Just enough to sell.[32]

When weather allowed, the captives were brought above deck each morning to gasp fresh air and undertake the forced ritual of "exercise." On many ships, this meant being dragged upright and driven to "dance" under the lash, their movements governed by shouted commands and whipcracks. Captains believed it preserved muscle tone, and market value. Yet, once on deck suicide attempts were common, and many slave ships installed netting over the rails to prevent captives from leaping into the sea.[33]

Below deck, others were left to rot in their chains, lying in their own filth. Lack of movement bred sores, atrophy, and despair. The sick were separated or thrown overboard. The death rate on these voyages averaged between 12 and 20 per cent.[34]

Rebellion was a constant fear. The air was thick with tension and with one wrong move all could be lost. Some captives tried to rush the deck; others tried to starve themselves.

Captains carried irons, muskets, and cat-o'-nine-tails to deter resistance. Discipline that followed any attempt was swift and brutal: floggings, confinement, withdrawal of rations. One device used was the thumbscrew; "a dreadful engine." It could twist bone and flesh with unbearable force. Prisoners were sometimes left bound in this way "agonising for hours", even days.[35]

The *Martha* saw no documented revolt. But her silence tells its own story: twenty-eight captives died during the crossing, nearly one in five.[36] They died of fever, of dysentery, of dehydration, of despair. They died in chains, in darkness, in isolation.

Their bodies were dragged from the hold and cast into the Atlantic, unmarked, unburied, unnamed.

The sharks followed.

Lured by the scent
Of steaming crowds, of rank disease, and death,
Behold! he rushing cuts the briny flood,
Swift as the gale can bear the ship along;
And from the partners of that cruel trade
Which spoils unhappy Guinea of her sons
Demands his share of prey – demands themselves.

Excerpt from "Summer" by
James Thomson – *The Seasons* (1730)

The names of those who perished went unrecorded. Their deaths were reduced to tallies in a logbook, their absence noted only in profit margins and mortality tables.

This was not an aberration. It was a pattern.

Sold on Arrival

Those who survived the Middle Passage found no mercy, only another kind of bondage, shaped by cane and lash.

Forced ashore, 114 souls were washed, oiled, and made to stretch and dance. These were rituals Blundell had seen since the age of 13.[37] Some were children. Some were pregnant. Rows of barefoot bodies, silent, their names replaced with prices.

A healthy man in his twenties might fetch £50, a child perhaps £10, a woman with child less. All of it recorded in margins.[38]

Sugar plantations in Nevis were among the harshest in the Caribbean. One of the earliest and most intensively cultivated sugar islands in the British West Indies, Nevis ran on enslaved labourers who endured gruelling work routines, high mortality rates, and frequent violence. Cane was cut with curved blades, heavy, repetitive work under a punishing sun, then fed to the boiling pans. The labour driven by the lash from first light to nightfall.[39]

Blundell knew all this. He didn't need to be there. He had seen it before, the blistering heat, the sugar, the salt, and the sound of the drums.

The only difference now was that the profit was his.

The *Martha* returned to Liverpool on Thursday, 26 April 1722.[40] Its cargo had been delivered. Its profits calculated, its losses written off.

Its owners, Bryan Blundell, Robert Armitage, and Owen Pritchard, all prominent merchants, all future mayors of Liverpool, were no doubt satisfied.[41]

This was Blundell's first successful slaving voyage. It would not be his last. What began with the *Martha* would not end there. He had found the template.

The Ships That Followed

Two years later, another vessel followed.

The *Jane and Ellen*[42] departed Liverpool in July 1723, once again bound for the West African coast and the sugar islands beyond. Its owners included Blundell, William Cleveland, John Morton, and Blundell's cousin, Ralph Williamson.[43] The ship reached Nevis in early April 1724, having embarked 153 enslaved people in West Africa. Only 131 survived to be sold on land, a mortality rate of just under 15 per cent.

Over the next five years, more ships left the Mersey under Blundell's name. The *Good Intention*,[44] despite its name, made two voyages between 1726 and 1728, carrying more than 400 captives in total; close to 1 in 10 died at sea. Another, the *Tarleton Gally*,[45] was owned jointly by Blundell, Robert Armitage, and Foster Cunliffe. She carried more than 200 enslaved Africans across the Atlantic, with mortality again approaching 15 per cent.

Blundell's connections stretched beyond the Middle Passage. The Intra-American Slave Trade Database links him to at least one additional vessel, the *Jonathan*,[46] which in 1733 embarked forty enslaved Africans in Jamaica. Thirty-nine were disembarked in the Lower James River region of Virginia, where Blundell had long maintained commercial ties with local plantation owners, including "King" Carter.

These voyages were no isolated ventures but part of a deliberate system. They formed a network of merchants, mayors, and mariners bound together by profit. Blundell was both participant and architect, his name recurring across the ledgers and cargo lists of a trade he helped to build.

These were his initial slaving voyages that left a paper trail, manifested, insured, and eventually recorded. But there were others. Many early slaving ventures lack full ownership records, particularly in the 1730s, when documentation from Liverpool-based voyages is often incomplete. A significant number of slave ships list no identifiable owners. Between 1733 and 1744 Bryan Blundell's name and those of his close family vanish from surviving lists.

Yet what is clear is this: he had never truly stepped away. Twenty years later, in 1752, his own journal records his direct involvement in two slave ships.[47]

The Human Cost

These early grim ventures tell a story of collaboration among Liverpool's rising elite, of calculated risk and of profit extracted from human lives.

Taken together, these 6 voyages alone embarked 1,033 enslaved Africans. Only 904 survived. That is a known death toll of 129, drawn from just 6 entries in a database that spans tens of thousands.[48]

These initial investments helped set the framework: family capital, civic power, and a network of kin and colleagues that bound public piety to private gain.

And it began with ships like the *Martha*, the *Good Intention*, the *Tarleton Gally*, and the *Jane and Ellen*. His children, grandchildren, and great-grandchildren would continue the work.[49] But this is where it began.

Blundell was not coerced. He made a choice. He was not merely carried by the current. He helped shape the tide, ledger by ledger, ship by ship.

The logic of the trade may have been financial. But what amount of money could ever account for the souls that were lost?

Chapter 19

To Govern This Town With Order

"There is also the business of authority and command. This is no small burden. It is a very hard province – and many times difficult to govern well."

Christopher Bassnett, 1711

The New Dock, Liverpool | November 1721

The woman's screams echoed off the brick walls of the New Dock. A crowd had gathered at the water's edge, jeering, shoving, some clambering onto barrels for a better view. Children were hoisted onto shoulders, their eyes wide, their mouths open in laughter or fear. At the centre loomed the ducking chair: a long wooden beam, roughly sawn and water-stained, balanced on a heavy post. At its far end sat an iron-ringed seat, bolted and slick with salt spray off the dock.[1]

The woman – soaked, shivering, still shrieking from her last descent – was lashed into the chair. A constable raised his hand. The crowd hushed. Then, another swing, another plunge. Wood creaked. Rope groaned. She hit the water with a slap and vanished beneath the surface. For a moment, nothing. Then she burst upward, gasping, only to be hoisted again, her skirt clinging, hair plastered to her face. Each drop drew a cheer.[2]

Among the crowds, the new Mayor of Liverpool likely looked on with quiet satisfaction.

This was a punishment for "scolds," for "common strumpets," for disorder, sin, and female defiance.[3] Though women were most often its victims – those accused of gossiping, slander, or selling themselves – records also show it used on men, and even on quarrelsome couples tied back-to-back. Elsewhere, even dishonest traders and unruly paupers met the same fate.[4]

The ducking stool had been restored at his order. It was to be a tool of discipline, deterrence, and moral reform.

And for Mayor Blundell, it worked.

Public Order by Public Humiliation

Liverpool in 1721 was bawdy, growing, and brimming with vice. "The lack of piety and religion," Blundell lamented, "and the increase of sin and vice were so visible... that no additional help ought to be omitted."[5]

Blundell claimed he had not sought the mayoralty. Yet he accepted it, "thinking I might be much more serviceable and beneficial to the School in a public capacity than a private one." That October, he was elected without opposition, and, as he proudly noted, "over the heads of many in the Council."

As mayor, he pledged to make his town not only prosperous, but pious. He was, in his own words, "willing to govern this town with order."

He was a man on a mission. On his first day in office, he increased the number of constables from just one to six and instructed them to "go their rounds" nightly, ensuring that "good hours and order was kept through the whole town." He praised them as "very diligent in their watch in the night in finding out ill houses and persons and taking the strolling persons into custody till they could be brought before the Mayor."

He summoned innkeepers and landlords, warning that "if they continued such practices they should be punished as the law directs." Night-time drinking, "unseasonable hours," and the presence of "disorderly persons" were no longer to be tolerated.

His war on vice spread to the printed page. He ordered 2,000 royal proclamations pasted across Liverpool: stern warnings against "excessive drinking, blasphemy, profane swearing and cursing, lewdness, [and] profanation of the Lord's Day." The fines, he recorded, "I gave to the Overseers of the Poor to distribute to the poor of the Parish."

Words and fines alone were not enough. "The instruction and admonition either from the pulpit or by word of mouth, by the mercy of God and all those means," he wrote, could bring the people "into tolerable order and into a more regular way of living." But when sermons and proclamations failed to change behaviour, Blundell turned to what he called "terror amongst them."

Figure 17. Illustration of a ducking stool from an eighteenth-century chapbook. Reproduced in *Chap-Books of the Eighteenth Century* by John Ashton (1834). (*Public domain*)

The ducking chair became its emblem. He commissioned it himself: mounted on wheels, fitted with iron rings, designed to be paraded through the streets. Offenders were wheeled from the Exchange to the New Dock, strapped into the chair, and lowered, at least three times, into the Mersey as townspeople looked on.[6]

The stool was not unique to Liverpool. Used across Britain, it had long served as punishment for those accused of scolding, slander, or disorder. New stocks also appeared. A twelve-person "cage" was erected for public shaming. Offenders, Blundell wrote, "were put into the cage for two, three or four hours… hauled above and exposed to their greater shame."

This was governance through fear. The message was clear: under Blundell's stewardship, Liverpool was to be a godly town, not a godless one.

By his own account, the measures had effect. "Many of these common strumpets," he noted with satisfaction, "quitted the town." Some, it seems, simply crossed the Mersey. Soon after he noted that butchers were fined for "going over the water on Sunday about needless business."

It was just one small episode, but it revealed the shape of his reforms, and the resolve behind them.

Political Order

When he returned to the mayoral office in 1728, it was into political tumult.

Liverpool's parliamentary contests had become theatres of corruption, drunkenness, and factional strife. "All in a manner do what they please without control," Blundell lamented, "for fear they should be disobliged" on polling day.[7]

He was now at the centre of it. As mayor, he was tasked with overseeing the fiercely contested vote between Sir Thomas Ashton and Thomas Brereton, a Walpolian loyalist.[8] It was a duty made more difficult when Brereton demanded the late admission of forty questionable voters. Blundell refused, citing ineligibility and the formal close of the polls. Brereton protested to Westminster.

Summoned to London, Blundell travelled with allies to defend his conduct before the House of Commons. Witnesses were called, accusations levelled. "Grievous things were laid to our charge," he wrote, "very falsely that could not be proved."[9]

Sir Robert Walpole, the prime minister, attempted to adjourn proceedings. But when the vote was called, the motion failed by 120 to 99.

Ashton then gave his evidence, followed by what Blundell called a "very handsome" speech.

And with that the question was put: "Whether Sir Thomas [Ashton] was duly elected or not?"

"It was carried," he recorded simply, "that Sir Thomas was duly elected." His stance held. His judgement, vindicated.

And Mr Brereton, he added with satisfaction, was "damned as base and unjust."

Bryan Blundell's two terms as Mayor of Liverpool were not simply a matter of civic duty. They were also an instrument of strategy, allowing him to consolidate influence at a time when commerce, politics, and the transatlantic slave trade were becoming increasingly entwined.

In an era when many of the town's most prominent slave merchants also served as mayors, Blundell was no exception: a man whose public piety and philanthropic image masked more worldly pursuits. Over the next century, at least ten of his relatives and close allies – including Crosbies, Tarletons, Blundells, and Shaws – would hold the same office.[10] The mayoralty became not just a mark of service, but of succession.

His time as mayor was now over, yet his reach in Liverpool's civic world was only beginning. His next concern was the parish poor.

Charity and Control

Under the Old Poor Law, Liverpool's parish was responsible for caring for its poor. This was done through a mixture of alms, "outdoor relief" in money or food, and, where possible, accommodation in a parish poor house. By the 1720s, demand had "outstripped the capacity" of the existing institution. Overseers scrambled to find space, procuring lodgings across the town. They soon turned to Blundell, who provided thirty-six cottages of his own.[11]

Then in 1732, as part of the Vestry's retreat from outdoor relief, Liverpool sought a more permanent solution. Blundell was on hand once again: his Blue Coat Charity School agreed to build the town's first workhouse on land leased from the Corporation. The trustees financed it in return for a steady rent.[12]

Inmates of the new workhouse, meanwhile, found their labour channelled into the same economy that defined the town: spinning cotton and wool, picking oakum for caulking ships, or apprenticed into Lancashire's mills.[13]

Yet the workhouse was, by now, only part of a broader system, one in which charity, commerce, and control were closely entwined. Back at the Blue Coat School, the boundaries between charity and personal interest had become just as blurred.

In 1734, Blundell reported that the school had taken in sixty children, with half set to labour in the afternoons, while the others studied. They earned "near £50 per annum" by also picking oakum and knotting yarns. Spinning cotton alone, he noted, brought the school's net costs down to "very little more than £300 per annum."

Then, at the age of 14, the children were apprenticed "to all sorts of trades, but mostly to sea." Some eventually became "mates and masters of ships"; others found work in domestic trades, becoming "useful men in the World's" wider economy.

This was not simply Christian charity but economic preparation, feeding labour into the very industries that powered Liverpool's rise.

Private Order

Perhaps the clearest measure of his influence among Liverpool's elite was this: by the time of his death, he had been named executor under twenty wills. This was a remarkable figure in a period without formal probate institutions.[14]

Being named executor was not simply an administrative task. In the eighteenth century, it meant managing estates, settling debts, ensuring provisions for widows and orphans, and, in many cases, adjudicating family disputes. Executors were legal stewards of the dead, and few were asked to do it so often.

In Blundell's case, it reflected both his meticulousness and his reputation. He was known not only as a successful merchant, but as a man who could be trusted with the most personal of responsibilities: final wishes.

Blundell's public rectitude was mirrored, sometimes painfully, in his private life. He was married three times, each union marked by devotion and, ultimately, by loss. His first wife, Samuela, died while he was at sea. His second, Elizabeth Livesley, bore him at least eight children, four of whom were sons who would carry forward his business and philanthropic ventures. She died on 24 October 1725, recorded by Blundell in a single, spare line: "My dear Wife departed this life with great patience and resignation to God."

His third marriage, to Mary Cunliffe, was brief but deeply felt. They wed on 27 November 1729 in London, at St Benet's Church. Just over three months later, Mary died of consumption, a disease now better known as tuberculosis.[15] It was one of the most feared illnesses of the eighteenth century, responsible for around a quarter of adult deaths in Europe, and especially deadly among women. Its slow, wasting symptoms would later be romanticised in literature, but the reality was one of prolonged suffering and near-certain death.[16]

For Blundell, the loss was immediate and profound. His diary entry, dated Monday, 9 March 1730, reads not like a merchant's record but, as on rare occasion, like a husband's eulogy: "She being a very good woman, one of extraordinary good sense, of obliging deportment and courteous behaviour. But above all, her love of virtue made her not only one of the best of wives and stepmothers, but the best of friends, for which reason her memory will ever be dear to all that had a share in her friendship."[17]

Mary was also the sister of Foster Cunliffe, one of Liverpool's most powerful slave traders. Between 1719 and 1760, Foster and his two sons, Ellis and Robert, oversaw nearly sixty documented slaving voyages to West Africa.[18] He built commercial networks across the American colonies, operated stores in Maryland, and rose to political prominence. He would go on to serve three terms as Mayor of Liverpool.[19]

Loss visited Blundell again the following year. On 13 November 1731, his daughter Hannah Shaw died, aged 35. Widowed young, she had lived with her father for many years, her son Samuel becoming his ward. Blundell's diary records a grief unusually personal and unguarded. He called her "of a good natural disposition, to which it pleased God to give a great deal of His grace… very religious and good." She had devoted herself to acts of charity and quiet piety, "both public and private." Her funeral sermon, he wrote, moved the entire congregation to tears.[20]

"She was always a very good child," he concluded. "My loss is great – but I have received so many mercies from God in the course of my life, that I may say with Job, 'What? Shall we receive good at the hand of God, and shall we not receive evil?'"[21]

These diary passages reveal a man not hardened by grief, but shaped by it: sombre, devout, reflective. They offer a rare window into the emotional life of an eighteenth-century merchant, and into a world where family, faith, and duty were deeply entwined.

The grief was noted, then folded into the margins of daily life.

However, by the late 1730s the world that had enabled his rise was under threat.

Built to Endure

Tensions with Spain had been building for years, fuelled by commercial rivalry and disputes over British smuggling in Spanish America. Then, in November 1739, war was declared.

What began as a dispute over the mutilation of Captain Robert Jenkins, whose severed ear was reportedly presented in Parliament, soon escalated into a wider imperial conflict. The War of Jenkins' Ear, as it came to be known, posed a significant threat to British commerce across the Atlantic, especially the lucrative routes of the slave trade.[22]

As soon as war was declared, Spanish privateers began targeting English shipping, and losses quickly mounted.

Blundell's reputation as a mariner, merchant, and civic figure made him a natural intermediary between Liverpool's commercial elite and the state. That autumn, he joined a delegation of Liverpool merchants who signed the "Traders to Africa" petition, addressed directly to King George II. Their request was plain: deploy Royal Navy warships to patrol the African coast and safeguard British vessels engaged in transporting what the petition called "great Numbers of Negroes" to the colonies. They urged not only protection, but permanence, a standing naval presence to ensure that disruption did not become the default.[23]

This was not a humanitarian appeal. It was a commercial one. The enslaved were cargo. The state was being asked to underwrite their delivery. And Blundell – educator, elder, former mayor – was among those demanding the infrastructure to make it happen.

Liverpool's slaving merchants were no longer simply profiting from the trade; they were organising to defend it and to expand their control.

These efforts continued through the 1740s and bore fruit in 1750, when Parliament passed an act establishing the *Company of Merchants Trading to Africa*.

Two years later, the new company's first register listed Bryan Blundell among its members, with his name recorded alongside those of his sons and grandson. Liverpool now held official parity with London and Bristol in Britain's trade to Africa, and the Blundells were part of its foundation.[24]

Whilst the Company of Merchants did not trade in enslaved people directly, its role was more systemic, and in many ways, more enduring. It oversaw the forts that lined the African coast, negotiated with local rulers, and helped secure Britain's commercial and military dominance in a trade now deemed too vital to leave to chance.[25]

Blundell's membership, alongside that of his sons and grandson, signalled more than a commercial interest. It reflected a deliberate, intergenerational commitment to the infrastructure of enslavement. Every member paid their 40-shilling annual fee not for immediate profit, but for continuity, for access, for control.

Blundell was no reluctant investor. He was a man embedded, connected, and determined to ensure that the system he helped build would endure.

Order at a Price

In the end, order was not only imposed, it was constructed. The ducking stool, the stocks, the proclamations: these were the visible tools, designed to humiliate and deter.

But there were also subtler instruments. Blundell's charity school. His council votes. His name on slaving petitions and probate documents. Together, they helped maintain a broader civic order, that was quiet, enduring, generational.

Blundell was not alone. Liverpool's merchants had worked together for decades to achieve their goals. They wrested control from the aristocracy, invested together and shared risk, sailed in convoy to protect their ships, built docks to expand their trade, and raised defences as the Jacobites approached.

And their system worked. By the 1750s, Liverpool was thriving. Trade flourished. Ships arrived daily from Africa, the Caribbean, and the American colonies.

Their ledgers were full. The merchants' order held.

Chapter 20

The Voice Above

"Sometimes God speaks in a still small Voice, at other Times he speaks in Thunder and Lightning, in Storms and Tempests: and in these latter he speaks so TERRIBLY LOUD, that one wou'd think Men shou'd hear him, and learn Righteousness."

– Christopher Bassnett, 1711

The Caves, Liverpool | Early 1740s

The rocks were slick with seaweed, black and treacherous underfoot. Christopher Bassnett picked his way through the caves at the shore's edge, where the sandstone had been hollowed by centuries of tide.

The water was out. Mud stretched grey and endless toward the Mersey. Above him, somewhere beyond the cliffs, the town continued: ships loading, merchants counting, baptisms waiting to be entered in the register he had kept for more than thirty years.

He could not go back.

For weeks he had been coming there alone, walking the edges of the town. He was 67 years old. His mind was failing him. Or perhaps it was simply refusing any longer to bear what the ministry required.

At the water's edge he stopped.

The river moved cold and restless beneath the darkening sky. No one would question what happened there. An old man losing his footing among the rocks would scarcely raise suspicion. They already knew he had been unwell for years.

He stepped forward.

And then it thundered.

The sound cracked across the estuary, sudden and immense. Bassnett stumbled, catching himself against the rock face, his heart hammering beneath his ribs.

"Can I do this," he cried, "and hear that voice?"[1]

For a moment he stood trembling beside the tide, listening as the thunder rolled westward across the water.

Then slowly he turned back toward the town.

Toward the chapel. Toward the streets above the cliffs. Toward the life he had not yet managed to leave behind.

The Warning Unheard

Born in Chester in 1677, the son of an apothecary, Bassnett arrived in Liverpool as a young minister at the beginning of the century.

Contemporaries described Bassnett as "a homely, useful preacher, with a Puritan unction." He preached extemporaneously, without notes and directly to his congregation, preserving an older Puritan style that was becoming increasingly uncommon among Presbyterian ministers.[2]

For more than three decades, merchants, sailors and tradesmen had gathered to hear his words.

And yet, despite a lifetime of ministry in Liverpool, Bassnett seemed increasingly unable to find peace within it.

His congregation knew he had long suffered periods of profound melancholy. The first had come in 1711, when illness confined him for months. Another followed in 1726, so severe that other ministers were forced to baptise children in his place while he disappeared from public life altogether.[3]

Even in recovery he remained burdened by strain, worn thin by years of ministry in a town whose prosperity sat uneasily against the warnings he had once delivered from the pulpit.

He had preached to sailors before they crossed the Atlantic. To merchants before they sailed for Barbados and Guinea. To men who sat listening beneath the meeting-house galleries before returning to ships increasingly involved in the trafficking of enslaved Africans.

And Bassnett had warned them.

Not with the certainty of later abolitionists, but with the troubled conscience of a minister who sensed the moral current shifting beneath the town long before most others wished to see it.

Few listened for long.

Christopher Bassnett died in July 1744, aged 68.

Liverpool scarcely paused.

Ships still sailed outward on the tide. Merchants still counted profits beneath candlelight. Along the waterfront new fortunes continued to rise from the Atlantic trade, while the warnings Bassnett had once preached were swallowed by the noise of the growing port.

Yet traces of him remained.

In 1717, Bassnett had reflected upon the need for one generation to pass its work and principles to the next:

> "Christ of late has been calling his Ministers very fast to himself. Now we, that are left, should take Care of a Succession: That so the Work may not die with us."
>
> – Christopher Bassnett, Church Officers and Their Mission, 1717[4]

Bassnett would later describe such legacies as a minister's "fruits".[5]

His fruits remained.

In old registers filled with fading ink. In sermons passed quietly between ministers. In the congregations that continued to gather long after his death beneath the same principles he had tried to uphold: that commerce answered to conscience, and that prosperity alone can never justify what a man knows to be wrong.

Liverpool would continue to grow. Its ships would sail farther, its merchants would grow richer, and its involvement in the slave trade would deepen. Yet Bassnett's words endure as a reminder that at least one other voice had existed within the town, one that had questioned where prosperity was leading and what moral cost accompanied it.

More than three centuries later, that voice can still be heard.

Chapter 21

A Town Built for the Trade

"Everybody, my friend, is ready to acknowledge your worth, and to rejoice in your success and prosperity."

Christopher Bassnett, 1711

Liverpool | Saturday, 13 July 1754

This chapter is a historical reconstruction, drawn from contemporary accounts, historical records, the work of later historians, and, where possible, the written reflections recorded in Blundell's own journal. Though his entries grew more occasional in later years, they offer glimpses of a life still deeply entangled with the ships he owned, the causes he backed, and the town he helped shape.

Britain in the 1750s stood on the threshold of empire. That ascent was fuelled by trade, exploration, and the brutal machinery of the transatlantic slave trade.

Liverpool, once little more than a muddy inlet on the Mersey, now pulsed at the heart of that transformation: a port of global reach, driven by tobacco, sugar, and human cargo.[1] Its population had swelled to over 20,000, it was a staggering leap from its modest size in the mid-seventeenth century.[2]

It was now the leading slave-trading port in Britain, responsible for over 40 per cent of all British slaving voyages.

And at its centre stood one man: a 79-year-old merchant whose life had unfolded in tandem with Liverpool's own ascent, a master mariner, shipowner, benefactor, and mayor, now walking more slowly through the thriving port town he had helped shape.

Stillness and Reach

Yet, by that summer, Bryan Blundell no longer moved with the urgency of a man at sea. His pace had eased, his gait grown cautious, but he did not need to hurry. Much of the town already moved to his rhythm.

He left his grand townhouse just after sunrise.[3] The streets were quiet, the town not yet stirring. From the river came the tang of salt and coal smoke, mixed with the faint sweetness of scorched sugar and the acrid scent of charred tobacco. Across the rooftops, a plume rose steadily from the tall chimney in the Custom House Yard, the furnace known as the Tobacco Pipe, where spoiled tobacco was burned, its smoke rising over the waking town.[4]

The bells at St Nicholas had not yet chimed the hour.

He turned along the waterfront, past the place where the Pool had once flowed freely. Now it lay buried beneath docks, timber yards and warehouses.

In the stillness of early morning, the Old Dock worked without spectacle, its stone quays weathered by the traffic of countless voyages. When it first opened in 1715, they had called it the New Dock. But time and trade had overtaken the name.[5]

Others had followed, Canning (1737), Salthouse (1753),[6] and beyond, all dug, paved, and piled within the span of a single generation. Blundell, who had served twice as mayor, and as deputy mayor in the 1730s, as well as town bailiff, helped steer their creation.[7]

He had watched them rise from the mud, swallowing the inlet he had once crossed in a rowboat. The waterfront was no longer a single place. It had become something broader. Deeper. More complex. It was a system, interlinked, relentless, and built to endure.

The Architecture of Empire

He turned up Water Street and along its cobbled rise towards the New Exchange, almost finished but not yet formally opened. Begun five years earlier, the building had risen quickly, a statement of the town's rising confidence.[8]

Blundell paused at the foot of its steps, looking up. The early sun caught the upper windows, gilding the stone in a thin, amber light. But at street level, the building remained cold, its façade still cloaked in shadow. The

Figure 18. *Liverpool Town Hall*, engraving from Bradshaw's *Hand-Book to the Manufacturing Districts of Great Britain* (1854). (*Public domain*)

stone still looked raw: too clean, too perfect, not yet darkened by soot or stained by time.

The columns above him rose in careful symmetry, Doric below, Corinthian above, each line precise, deliberate. He studied the carved African and Indian heads and friezes: elephants, crocodiles, camels, exotic fruits.[9] The source of Liverpool's newfound wealth, etched in stone – a message cast in masonry, to visitor, rival, and heir alike.[10]

That autumn, the merchants would gather for its opening, waistcoats stitched with gold braid, full-bottomed wigs powdered bright, their buckled shoes striking sharply on the new-laid stone.[11] The town would mark the occasion with days of celebration: boat races on the Mersey, public breakfasts, and evening balls.[12]

The building would serve as both the Exchange and Town Hall, a centre of commerce, politics, and civic life.

When Blundell was a boy, Liverpool had been governed by the landed gentry, men of estate and inheritance. Now it was the merchants who held sway.

And he stood not apart from that new order, but at its very heart.

In His Image

Just beyond the pillared arcade, the scent of roasted beans drifted from the Exchange Coffee House. Inside, merchants read shipping lists over cups of coffee sweetened with West Indian sugar. Pipes smoked with Virginian tobacco. Outside, casks of rum were hoisted from the waiting ships. The fruits of empire, cheap, familiar, constant, were everywhere, consumed with scarcely a thought.

Blundell had helped make them so.

He stepped through the door and found a seat near the fire. It was early still; only a few merchants sat with papers, trading talk of insurance rates and customs delays. On the far wall, a boy posted up shipping arrivals in chalk, Kingston, Charleston, St Kitts.

Blundell liked it best this way, quiet, composed, before the day's full weight descended.

He took his drink in silence. He finished slowly, set the cup aside, and stepped back into the street.

By the time he reached School Lane, the town was fully awake. Children in their blue coats lined up in the yard, shuffling into order. Their uniforms stood bright against the grey sky, their voices clipped and cheerful. Soon the boys and girls would settle for morning prayers and lessons, followed by an afternoon of hard labour.

Twelve days earlier, Blundell had attended one of his last quarterly trustee meetings at the school. The room had been full, each man taking his place as the clerk read out the business of the day. Vacancies for boys were noted, apprenticeships approved, and the usual motions passed with the practiced efficiency of a board well used to its work.[13]

Blundell's world was ordered and self-contained. It stretched from schoolroom to workhouse, from ropewalk to quay. He educated the boys, apprenticed the crew, and oversaw the supply of materials – rope, oakum, tar – to keep his ships at sea. It was a system that was as efficient as it was effective. One that allowed Liverpool to undercut its rivals in Bristol and London.[14]

Inside the Blue Coat School, his son Richard, then treasurer, was already at the table, poring over the ledgers.[15] The work suited him, measured, regular, exacting. Blundell offered no advice. There was nothing to add. He had kept the accounts long enough.[16]

He made his way back onto School Lane as the day's rhythm took hold.

On Lord Street, shop shutters banged open. Boys scurried between bakehouses with sacks of flour, and a brewer's dray rattled past, its wheels slick with dew.[17] Ahead, walking alone and upright, a young African boy in a dark frock coat stepped carefully along the kerb. His shoes were polished, his collar starched, and a leather-bound book was tucked beneath one arm. He may have been among the first African youths sent to Liverpool for schooling, a gesture of diplomacy, part of the strange trade in trust between West African kings and the town's merchants. In these boys, they saw both future allies and assurances of continued commerce.[18]

As he walked, a crier called the hour near the old Castle Ditch, once the moat of Liverpool Castle, now little more than a hollow in the ground.[19] The castle itself had been pulled down decades earlier, its stone hauled away, its power long since faded.[20] The sleepy little port of his youth, with its "mouldering Castle," was no more.[21]

Back on Castle Street he walked carefully over the uneven paving. Like much of the town, it was still "narrow, mean, ill-paved, and dirty."[22] On the corner, small knots of gentlemen stood in quiet conversation, cane-handled umbrellas slung over arms, ledgers tucked beneath cloaks. The business of the day was well underway. Behind them, shopfronts displayed Liverpool-made watches and blue hand-thrown pottery, each piece locally crafted for a town growing in confidence. In another window, an ironmonger had arranged his wares: locks, nails, chains and shackles[23] (see Plate 18).

Blundell turned up Dale Street, the town's older artery, once quieter, it was now crowded with carts, clerks, and conversation. He moved slowly, steady in the current, unnoticed by most who passed. These were younger men now, new names, new ideas, but they walked, unknowingly, through a world he had helped shape (see Plate 17).

The Order That Would Not Hold

There were fewer now who remembered what the town looked like before the Old Dock was built. Fewer still who remembered his first voyage.

He did not claim to have built the town. Others had shaped it too, Earles, Cunliffes, Tarletons, Gildarts.[24] But he had helped frame its edges. He had owned ships before there were chandlers enough to supply them. He had funded the school when others still doubted its need.

Now the town was more than masts and merchandise. It was a web of streets, alliances, apprenticeships, leases, and land.

His family ties reached across that web. Marriage, partnership, kinship: by mid-century, almost every significant name in Liverpool's merchant elite could be found in his ledger, or in his family tree.[25]

As he walked, he noticed more noise, more names he didn't know. The shopfronts were smarter, the signs freshly painted, but the talk still echoed old concerns: rent, rumour, reputation. A woman stood quietly in a doorway, not speaking, not moving, but impossible to ignore.

He walked on, unnoticed by many. But he noticed.

He had once believed in discipline, in laws, in tracts, in the shaming power of the ducking stool. But even Bryan Blundell came to recognise the limits of his reach.

In the years after he stepped down as mayor, he watched the order he had laboured to impose begin to fray. His successors, he lamented, were "not so vigilant in suppressing such practices," and soon "they began to grow much in wickedness."[26]

The symbols of civic control he had once helped build were left to decay.

In his journal, he noted it plainly: "The cage was burnt, the ducking-chair broken to pieces, the stocks out of repair." Then, with the cadence of scripture, he added: "We became… like the people of Laish, who dwelt careless."[27]

By now, the town was growing faster than any one man could govern. Streets once walked by clerks and carters now teemed with newcomers. Labourers, seamen, settlers from the countryside arrived in growing numbers, drawn by the promise of work, or wealth, or something in between. And still they came.[28]

Sailors spilled from public houses, drunk, loud, freshly ashore from the Guinea ships and sugar islands.[29] Their pockets briefly heavy with coin. It was not yet noon, but the drink was flowing, the doors wide open, and the street already shifting under the weight of trade, temptation, and noise. These were no ordinary seafarers: the slave trade had forged a breed of men known for their ferocity, restlessness, and readiness to fight. They were hard to manage at sea, and harder still once ashore.[30]

This, too, was Liverpool, the other side of the town he had helped to build. He slowed, watched them a moment, then turned away.

As the bells of St Nicholas rang out, he turned back down towards the river. The church had stood longer than most things in Liverpool. He had been baptised there. Married there. And in time, he would be buried there.[31]

But not yet.

It was here that Robert Styth first spoke to him of founding a charity school, a quiet exchange that would alter the course of his life. His own children had served the church since, as both churchwardens and benefactors. The Blundell pew had grown into a fixture, as solid and enduring as the new spire he helped raise in 1747.[32] It was topped with a 5-foot copper weathervane shaped like a ship, mirroring the one Blundell had erected on the Blue Coat School three decades earlier.

Now, two copper ships, rested above church and charity – still, and glinting in the mid-morning haze.

Names in the Margins

As he walked, he passed the Custom House Yard, low, slate-roofed warehouses lining the quayside. One bore the faded lettering of a Goree merchant, its shutters open to the morning air.[33]

Two Black boys hurried past, each struggling with a crate between them. Breathless and no older than young Bryan had been when he first went to sea, one wore a torn linen shirt knotted at the waist, the other a loose wool coat far too large for him. By this time, their presence on the docks was not uncommon. Some had arrived on ships not as cargo, but as part of the captain's commission. These so-called "privilege slaves," were brought back from the coast as gifts or private trade. In Liverpool, they were sometimes sold, sometimes kept, and often visible in the streets and households of the port.[34]

A clerk stood outside with a ledger, reading out names. The sailors waited in line for their pay, some quiet, some muttering about lost time or short measures. A few leaned against barrels, laughing, swapping stories of Guinea, Martinique, and the Main.[35]

Just beyond the bustle, near the warehouse wall, Captain Charles Pole,[36] Blundell's brother-in-law, stood in quiet conversation with two younger men. He spoke softly, and the boys listened attentively.

At this time Captain Pole would have been seeking crew for his next slaving voyage which was scheduled to leave just two days later. The investors in his ship, the *Nancy*, included Blundell's son, Jonathan, and his grandson Samuel Shaw.[37]

As Blundell passed, Pole looked up. Their eyes met for a fleeting moment, a quiet acknowledgment between men who understood what was being done.[38]

Beyond the bustle, a man lingered with a sketchbook in hand, jotting notes between glances at the ships and warehouses. He watched intently, recording the rhythms of the port in careful strokes. His name was Carl Gottlieb Angerstein, an emissary from Sweden's Board of Mines (an early industrial spy) sent to study Britain's new industries. What he witnessed that morning would later appear in his notes: a town "flourishing" on Atlantic trade, its docks busy with goods, its ledgers full, its course set.[39]

Among the many vessels in the Old Dock that day, four stood out.[40] They all told a story Blundell already knew.

One of his ships, the *Duke of Cumberland,* had arrived four weeks earlier,[41] her timbers thick with salt and barnacles, back from Barbados. She had departed the Gold Coast in Africa with 429 captives. Only 350 had survived the crossing, bound to a lifetime of slavery in Kingston. Now, she was being readied for her next voyage.

As well as himself, the owners included his sons William and Richard, his daughter Elizabeth's husband James Crosbie, and his grandson Samuel Shaw. The captain was John Crosbie, Elizabeth's brother-in-law. It was a family ship.

Alongside her were two more vessels: the *Elizabeth*[42] and the *Nancy*, captained by Mr Pole. Both were fresh from voyages to Bonny and Barbados, and both were part-owned by his family. The *Elizabeth*, launched in Liverpool the year before, had carried 251 captives from Bonny,[43] 36 of whom died before arrival.

All had done as intended. All had delivered. Bonny, and the broader Bight of Biafra, would become the principal source of enslaved people for the Blundell family's future voyages. As the trade passed to the next generation, it was this coast that would supply their ships and fill their ledgers.

Blundell must have been proud. Proud to see vessels being unloaded after successful voyages. Proud to watch his family stepping into the roles he once held. Proud to know that his children's and grandchildren's names were now inked alongside his own, part of a family enterprise built for profit.

At the same time, another vessel waited in the dock: The *Blundell*, almost certainly named in his honour. She sat low in the water, idle but expectant, preparing for her next journey.[44] Within weeks, she would sail for West Central Africa and St Helena. He had never owned her. But his son Jonathan and grandson Samuel Shaw did. She bore his name. And that was enough.

Bryan Blundell did not dwell. He had invested in voyages along the West African coast, to Bonny, the Gambia, and the broader Bight of Benin. He knew what passed through the holds of his ships. He knew what would follow in Barbados, Nevis and Virginia. There was no mystery. He had been there.

A Childhood Shaped by the Sea

By now the dockside was loud with voices – ropemen calling, winches grinding, gulls wheeling above the masts. Barrels rolled. Ledgers were tallied. The ships rocked gently in their berths, their sails furled and timbers drying in the cool summer breeze.[45]

Bryan Blundell paused. He took in the scene: the sweep of the quayside, the bustle of the docks, the pulse of a port that had grown with him, around him, because of him. From somewhere across the quay, a bell chimed the hour.

For a moment, he stood alone in it all.

Then, a gentle tug at his coat.

He looked down. A small boy stood beside him, barely 3 feet tall and flushed from running. His great-grandson, John – curls damp from the morning mist, boots too clean for the quay – had slipped free from his mother's side and crossed the wet stones with determined steps.

John's mother was Ann, the daughter of the preacher, Christopher Bassnett. She had married Blundell's grandson, Samuel Shaw, nine years earlier, just a year after her father's death in 1744.[46]

Blundell turned, smiling. He steadied the child with a hand on his shoulder. Together they stood, great-grandfather and child, facing the ships.

The smells were all familiar: pitch, tobacco, molasses, rope and salt. A capstan groaned nearby. Men shouted across decks, their shirts damp with sweat. A sailor raised a hand in greeting from the rigging. Below, casks thudded against timber, and ropes creaked like breath.

The boy watched, wide-eyed.

Blundell remembered watching like this once, small, silent, the salt wind sharp on his face, the longing in his chest. Then, there had been no dock, only mudflats and anchored hulls shifting with the tide – a far cry from the port he had helped shape. Back then he had only dreamed of such ships. Now they bore his name.

He steadied the boy again, hand firm, his coat drawn warm, his view unbroken. He would never let him fall.

Soon enough, young John would hear stories: of storms and sails, of gold dust and gunpowder, of cannon fire and captured vessels. The old tales of glory. The "gallant" trade.

But for now, Bryan Blundell said nothing. There was no need. One day, the boy's own ships would tell him everything he needed to know. And when he remembered this moment, it would not be the silence he recalled – but the view from his grandfather's arms.[47]

A gust from the river stirred the boy's curls. It was time to go.

Blundell shifted his weight, nodded once to the crew below, and turned, slowly, back the way he had come. The boy walked beside him, small footsteps matching his own, as Blundell's arm settled around his shoulders, gently guiding him. Ahead, the boy's mother waited – the preacher's daughter, standing quietly at the edge – but his path had already been chosen.

Behind them, the dock carried on – ropes creaked, holds filled, men shouted, the ledger of the day still being written in sweat and salt.

Blundell did not look back.

Interlude

A Town Transformed, 1756–1810

From 1756 to 1810, the town of Liverpool underwent the most dramatic transformation in its history. Its involvement in the slave trade deepened, and with the Industrial Revolution underway, wealth poured in.

The docks multiplied. Streets spilled outward. The population quadrupled. Ropewalks, foundries, and taverns rose beside the old counting houses.[1]

New docks were cut into the foreshore, George's (1771), King's (1788), and Queen's (1796). Graving docks and tidal basins followed, pushing the waterfront south to Parliament Street. The water area of the docks increased fivefold in two generations, and each new basin filled almost as soon as it opened.[2]

Still, the slave ships came, over 5,000 in all, carrying more than a million Africans across the Atlantic. Over 40 per cent of Britain's entire slave trade, from one port.[3]

And then, one morning in 1810, the bells stopped.

Chapter 22

The Silence That Followed

"Acting upon wise and calm principles... you are not to be moved with mere hurry and violence... The noise of the seas, the noise of their waves, and after these, you know, comes the tumult of the people."

Christopher Bassnett, 1711

St Nicholas Church, Liverpool | Sunday, 11 February 1810

The Mersey was calm that morning, gleaming silver beneath a dull sky. Above the rooftops, the bells of St Nicholas began to chime, deep and deliberate, its sound rising over the dockyards and echoing between the streets.[1]

At the edge of the churchyard, the iron gate creaked open. The first of the children stepped through.

They came in twos, as they'd been taught, girls from the Moorfields Charity School mostly, buttoned coats, white collars, boots brushing frost from the flagstones. Some glanced upward toward the tower. Others turned their heads toward the water, where the tide had just begun to turn.

A few men stood nearby, hands clasped behind their backs, watching with quiet approval. The sort who arrived early, spoke softly, and noticed small things: the tilt of a bonnet, the chime's odd pitch. One of them pointed toward the spire.

It had stood for generations, medieval stone capped with an octagonal spire added in 1747, part of the council's vision to raise Liverpool skyward. The bells it housed dated back to 1636. Their tone had changed of late, heavier and more distant, as if ringing from somewhere deeper underground.

Cracks had appeared after a lightning strike the year before. Warnings had been issued for years.[2]

Still, the bellringers climbed the tower. Still, the bells rang.

A sound pierced cold, sharp, hollow, unnatural. One of the men turned. The tower was shifting.

It began at the south-western edge. A shudder, a buckle, a tearing from within. For a moment the spire leaned, hesitated, as though undecided. Then it dropped, almost perfectly vertical, a clean plunge into the nave below.

The crash was instant and overwhelming. Stone tore through roof and timber. Lead, slate, brick, and glass collapsed in a single thundering wave. The ringing stopped mid-peal. So did the footsteps in the churchyard. So did the breath in people's throats.

It had taken less than thirty seconds.

Then came the cries.

Faint at first, from beneath the rubble, high-pitched, choked. People rushed toward the churchyard. Dust clouded the air.

Amid the screams of the trapped came the louder wails of parents, sprinting now from side streets, faces wild with disbelief. The crowd swelled, gentlemen, labourers, apprentices, all pushing through, tearing at the debris with bare hands. Sunday clothes were muddied without thought. Beams were lifted. Stones rolled away.

Twenty-eight children were pulled from the ruins. Only three survived.

The dead were laid gently on the grass outside the church, row upon row. Mothers arrived, naming them. Some identified two. One woman claimed three. Their shoes were still buckled. Ribbons still tied.

No one could explain how the bellringers had lived. All but one escaped. The one who returned for a coat, it was said, was found beneath the stones.

The air was thick with grief, raw, stunned, urgent. And then, after the bodies were taken, and the yard cleared, and the dust began to settle, something else crept in.

A silence deeper than any bell could break.

Liverpool mourned and blamed.

The church had long been the town's spiritual anchor, its tower a guide for sailors, its pews filled by merchants. Among them were the Blundells, tied by blood and marriage to the Cunliffes, Tarletons, Shaws, names that had risen with the tide of empire and shaped the town's fortunes from within these very walls.

But the town was changing. And as the spire fell, it seemed to mark the fall of something else: a vision of Liverpool built on scripture and slavery.

The bellringers had ignored the warnings. Just as Blundell ignored the words of the preacher. And the merchants, the cries of the abolitionists.

The bells rang anyway.

Then the stones came down. And in their place: silence.

The Final Accounts

Bryan Blundell died on Tuesday, 27 January 1756, buried in the grounds of the same church whose spire now lay in ruins.

In his time, he had been many things: mariner, merchant, shipowner, benefactor, mayor. He had built ships and sent them westward. He had funded a school and overseen its accounts with fastidious care. He had given thousands to charity and punished women for disorder. He had prayed for his town's soul while profiting from its sins.

No confession. No reckoning. Just ledgers.

He was not alone.

Ships brought profit. Profit built status. Civic duty, often framed as service, but practised as strategy, became the clearest path to respectability. A name revered in Liverpool's Town Hall carried more weight than a prayer.

In a town rising fast and jostling for place, men like Blundell understood that wealth was not an end in itself, it was a way to be seen. To be known. To endure, even if no one remembered the cost.

The slave trade offered returns that few other ventures could match. Profits flowed not just into personal accounts, but into infrastructure, alliances, and power. To own a vessel was to shape the town's rhythm. Funding a school was to anchor one's name in stone.[3] In such a world, morality bent easily under the weight of return.

At the end of every voyage, Blundell meticulously recorded his income in pounds, shillings and pence, often just as plainly as he noted the loss of a crewmember, or the death of his wife. Everything had its place in the ledger.

In 1752, he had sat at his desk and opened his journal. It would be one of his last entries. It began not as reflection or confession, but as a calculation, an inventory of property and possession.

Bryan Blundell's Effects and Estate In 1752[4]

1: Land, Pitch, Tar, and Ships	
– 3½ acres land at the Pitch House, the shed and 2 dwelling houses with carts and horses and other material	£400
– Pitch, tar on hand with …….. due for same	£1,000
– with Mr……………. I suppose may be about	£300
– and with Mr. John Clitherall may be	£200
– the ship *Johnathon* and cargo may be	£800
– Pitch and tar at Dublin and Cork may be	£300
Subtotal 1:	£3,000
2: Houses and Property – Washhouse in Cooper's Row	£330
– The Harrison's house and shop	£300
– Robert Prescott	£300
– Mr. Lor………	£270
– Mr. Baxendale's	£350
– Two houses east end Preeson's Row	£100
– Three houses west side	£300
– The two more houses to be built on	£500
– The others with passage	£400
– My own house and wash house	£650
– Thomas Ward's house	£350
– The Rec……	£60
– My ½ of the Ropery	£560
Subtotal 2:	£4,650
[Subtotal 2 (actual):	£4,470]
3: Debts and Ships – Book debts I suppose may be about	£2,000
– ½ of the ship *Providence* and cargo and affects	£2,000
– 1 sixth part of the ship *Pemberton* and cargo	£900
– ditto *Duke of Cumberland*	£1,000
– ditto *Elizabeth*	£750
Subtotal 3:	£6,650
FINAL LEDGER:	£14,300

The hand that wrote it was not the same as years before. In earlier pages, his script had flowed clean and confident, the letters upright and evenly spaced, the strokes of a practised merchant used to keeping orderly accounts.

By 1752, the change was unmistakable.

The words leaned unevenly, the letters cramped and wavering, the lines crowding into one another. The quill pressed more heavily now, leaving blots where once it had glided. It was the same voice, but slowed, an old man's hand pulling against the grain of the page.

Line by line, he carefully listed his estate in full. It included houses in Preeson's Row, Cooper's Row, and Chapel Street, two warehouses, a half share in a ropery, land holdings, and stores of pitch and tar in Dublin and Cork.[5] He also had part-ownership in two West Indian trading ships, the *Pemberton* and the *Providence.*

And here, in this late reckoning, he noted the two active slaving vessels in his possession: the *Elizabeth* and the *Duke of Cumberland.*

The total value was over £14,000, a considerable fortune by any standard (see overleaf).

Over the course of his lifetime, Blundell also distributed large sums beyond his family. It has been estimated that he gave around £8,000 to Liverpool charities, including the new infirmary (1749) and, above all, the Blue Coat School. His own accounts confirm £2,000 gifted to the school, "a tenth part of which it pleased God to bless [him] with."[6]

The Bitter End[7]

To many in his lifetime, Blundell was the image of a successful merchant and a gentleman of civic virtue: a man who rose from modest beginnings to amass substantial wealth and help build the town's institutions.

But like so many of his contemporaries, he lived a life divided along a sharp line. On one side: Christian duty, charity, discipline. On the other: transatlantic slavery, silence, and suffering hidden in plain sight.

Was Blundell courageous? Undoubtedly. He crossed oceans, risked storms, and faced the dangers of war and privateers head on.

Was he accomplished? Yes. Master mariner, successful merchant, mayor.

Was he charitable? Generously so, by the standards of his time.

Was he a slave trader? Yes. And that too.

Well into the twentieth century, Blundell was still praised as a pious benefactor, his name honoured in histories and civic accounts. As late as the 1950s, historians spoke of him as a model of Christian virtue, with little mention of the ships he owned or the trade they pursued.

Years earlier, a preacher had warned of the storm that follows silence – the tumult that comes not from the sea, but from people and conscience.

Blundell didn't listen.

It would take over 250 years, but eventually the storm would come – gathering slowly, breaking suddenly – and in the end, it carried the man with it.[8]

It is only in recent years that his legacy has been examined more fully, more honestly, and with the discomfort such truths demand. And in doing so, we are reminded that history is not only about the lives we might condemn, but the worlds that made such lives imaginable.

Charity in Stone

The Blue Coat School embodied that very tension. Its motto, *Non sibi sed omnibus*, "Not for oneself, but for all," proclaimed piety and selflessness. Its walls gave shelter to orphans and the children of seafarers. It clothed them in blue coats, taught them their catechism, drilled them in obedience, and prepared them for service. To many, it was the most visible proof of Blundell's benevolence.

But it was also something else.

The timetables of labour and learning were designed not only for salvation but for utility. The boys were apprenticed to merchants and shipowners, many to Blundell himself or his family. Many went on to become clerks, mates, or masters of ships in the very trades that sustained Liverpool's rise. In this way, the school was both sanctuary and supply line for a port town built initially on the trade in goods produced by enslaved labour, and later on the slave trade.

The Blue Coat School was never just a building.[9] It was a statement. An attempt to fuse belief, wealth, and civic purpose into one enduring institution.

In Bryan Blundell, it found its first steward. What remains today is a monument not only to charity, but to the contradictions of its time.[10]

The Man They Might Have Been

Bryan Blundell was not an outlier. His world was full of men who prayed in the morning, counted coin at midday, and signed slaving manifests by afternoon. His faith was real. So was his affection for his family.

He had known loss. Not just in business, but in the private rhythms of family life. He outlived children and wives, and his diary carries traces of real grief. There is affection in his phrasing, devotion in his scripture, and a quiet stoicism in how he accepted each sorrow. The man who traded in men, women and children, almost certainly, also wept in church.

He had grown up in Liverpool, watched the docks rise, apprenticed early, sailed young. He was a cabin boy before he was a captain. He built what he could in the world that formed him.

From his first voyage to Barbados, the goods that shaped his life, sugar, rum, tobacco, were bound to the labour of the enslaved.

He entered a world already entrenched in bondage, long before he had the power to question it.

This was a society sustained by the profits of the slave trade. William Cowper captured that reality sharply in 1788 in his poem *Pity for Poor Africans*:

> I pity them greatly, but I must be mum,
> For how could we do without sugar and rum?[11]

None of this redeems him. None of this absolves. But it complicates the man.

In many ways, Blundell lived the contradictions of his time with a steadier hand than most. He believed in discipline. He believed in God. He believed in family. And he believed, as many around him did, that profit was not only acceptable, it was necessary.

It is easy to condemn him now. But harder, perhaps, to ask what we would have done in his place, faced with the same upbringing, the same culture, the same ledgers.

Dead Reckoning

Blundell's legacy did not end in 1756. His sons, grandsons, and great-grandsons carried it forward. They followed the course he had set, guided not by conscience, but by the same calculation.

From 1721 to 1784, members of the Blundell family were recorded in over 100 slave voyages.[12] Bryan Blundell's sons, Jonathan, Richard, William, and Bryan Jr, became shipowners in their own right. Even his daughter, Elizabeth, invested in two voyages. Their most infamous vessel, the *Blundell*, transported over 2,000 Africans before wrecking off the coast of Africa in 1773. Four hundred and forty-three captives died[13] (see Plate 19).

His grandchildren, like Samuel Shaw, and great-grandsons, Christopher and John Shaw, would also continue the trade.[14] The young boy on the docks in 1754, John Shaw,[15] would become one of Liverpool's last slave traders. In more than 50 voyages, he transported some 15,000 enslaved Africans. He was often in partnership with his brother Christopher and his great-uncle Jonathan Blundell, sailing mainly between Angola, the West Indies and America. John Shaw was later recalled as "a man of immense wealth and intense vulgarity;" he rose to become twice Mayor of Liverpool and was known across the town as "the King of the Council," or simply "King Jack".[16]

By the closing decades of the eighteenth century, however, the tide of opinion had begun to turn. The Industrial Revolution was taking hold; canals and smelting works rose beside cranes and rigging.

Trade winds now carried not only sugar, tobacco and cotton. They also carried questions about justice, suffering and what a moral empire might look like. And with them came a slow reckoning.

Pamphlets circulated. Pulpits thundered. Parliamentary petitions gathered dust, then momentum.

Yet in 1791, when the first abolition bill failed in Parliament, the bells of St Nicholas rang in celebration.[17]

Liverpool's slave merchants, including Blundell's descendants, remained unrepentant and unyielding to the last. Even after Parliament passed the Abolition Act in 1807, one of Shaw's ships continued to sail. His final slaving voyage the *Nicholson* left Liverpool on 1 June that year, only weeks after abolition became law, carrying 279 enslaved people from the Congo to Demerara.[18]

By the time the act was passed, Liverpool ships had carried an estimated 1.4 million Africans into slavery, around 40 per cent of Britain's entire traffic.[19] In that same year, the town's mayor was Henry Blundell Hollinshead, Bryan Blundell's grandson.[20]

The legislation did not end slavery, but it shook the foundations. New laws followed; new industries rose. Voices that had long been raised against the trade, from activists and writers to religious leaders, grew louder. Yet abolition was not achieved by campaigners in Britain alone. Across the Atlantic, enslaved men and women resisted their bondage in countless ways, from everyday acts of defiance to organised rebellions that exposed the violence upon which the system depended. Their actions helped force slavery and the slave trade into the centre of public debate. The victory of 1807 marked a turning point: slavery itself endured in Britain's colonies until 1833.[21]

Nevertheless, the contradictions remained. When emancipation finally came compensation was paid to slave owners rather than to the enslaved. Wealth generated by slavery continued to flow through families and institutions, even as the moral foundations of the system were being dismantled.

Nowhere were those contradictions more apparent than in Liverpool.

A former Blue Coat pupil, the talented painter Richard Ansdell, would later produce one of the era's most iconic abolitionist images.

His 1861 painting *The Hunted Slaves*, first exhibited at the Royal Academy, depicted two fugitives pursued through the American South (see Plate 20). It was accompanied by lines from Longfellow's abolitionist poem *The Slave in the Dismal Swamp*.[22]

That same year, as the American Civil War began, the painting was donated to a Liverpool lottery to raise money during the Lancashire "cotton famine." At auction it raised £700 and was eventually won by a local banker whose family had received compensation as slave owners.[23]

In a single canvas, the Blue Coat School, the slave trade and the movement to abolish it were bound together. They were linked by the hand that painted it, and by the wealth that paid for it.

In the decades that followed, the Blundell name slowly slipped from the forefront of civic life.

But the wealth remained. And so did the buildings. And so did the silence.

The fall of St Nicholas's spire was not caused by Blundell. But its collapse remains a testament to what was once upheld without question: faith and fortune, brought down by time and by denial.

He had been baptised there. Married there. Buried there. His pew had stood for generations.

But when the tower came down, the bells were silenced.

And in that silence, it was not the bells that echoed, but everything that had been left unsaid.

Afterword

What Bryan Blundell left behind was not just a school or a street name, but a set of tensions that still shape the memory of Liverpool: benevolence built on bondage, pride entangled with profit, service shadowed by silence.

He lived in a world that praised charity while enslaving men, women and children; that honoured piety while shipping people in chains. He made Liverpool richer, stronger, more ambitious. Behind the town's rise, however, lay a human cost that history cannot ignore.

We will never know what he thought in his final days. But we know what came after. His family continued the trade. The Blue Coat School prospered (see Plate 21). The docks expanded. A town became a city.[1] And the city grew over its foundations, paved with stone, silence, and selective memory.

For generations, the story remained unchallenged. Blundell was remembered as a founder, a giver, a man of God. And the silence held.

Only now is the ledger, once so carefully kept, being read more fully.

Not just the pages of profit, but the columns of loss: the names missing, the lives erased, the truths long buried. The sea had lifted him, but it had drowned others. His ledgers, though neat, would never balance.

His ships no longer sail. But the city he helped shape must now face its inheritance.

The silence is finally being broken. Across Britain and beyond, the legacies of slavery are being re-examined not as distant history, but as forces still felt in structures, in stories, in who gets heard.

In Liverpool, the redevelopment of the International Slavery Museum stands at the centre of this renewal. The University of Liverpool's Centre for the Study of International Slavery (CSIS) is deepening research into human enslavement and its legacies, supporting work in history, culture, and contemporary society. Recent books, such as Jessica Moody's *The Persistence of Memory* and Malik al Nasir's *Searching for My Slave Roots*, are pushing the conversation forward. Community organisations like the Liverpool Black History Group, and initiatives such as the City Council's contextual panels on contested street names, are widening the public lens.

Together with other academic and community work, these efforts are ensuring that memory is shared more openly, and with greater urgency, than ever before.

Acknowledgment of past wrongs is a beginning, but the true task is to address their consequences today. There is much still to do, work that stretches far beyond the bounds of this book.

Yet for a story built around Bryan Blundell's ledger and its silences, perhaps there is no better place to end than with the warning given to Blundell himself in 1711:

> "*If your Consciences reproach you secretly for the Way that you are in…In the Name of God quit it, and betake yourself to some other Way that you are better satisfied about… For if things must come to Extremities, it were infinitely better to be starv'd than be dammed.*"

Sermon preached to Bryan Blundell
and the crew of the Cleveland.
Christopher Bassnett, 13 December 1711.

Event Timeline

	WORLD	LIVERPOOL	BLUNDELL
1648	Second English Civil War ends	First tobacco cargo lands; the *Friendship* anchors in the Mersey	
1651	Navigation Acts passed — English ships given dominance of trade		
1660	Charles II restored to the throne		
1661	Barbados Slave Codes — enslaved people defined as property in law		William Blundell marries Mary Preeson
1665	Great Plague devastates London		
1666	Great Fire of London	Liverpool merchants seize new trade routes	
1667	Dutch fleet attacks the Medway; English navy humiliated	Southern merchants look north; Liverpool's maritime trade surges	
1668		First sugar refinery established on Dale Street	
1673		Richard Blome notes Liverpool's growing West Indies trade	
1674		New Town Hall built at the High Cross	Bryan Blundell born, 30 December
1675			Baptised at St Nicholas Church, 9 January
1685	James II takes the throne		Inherits house from grandfather, Alderman Thomas Preeson
1687		William Blundell funds gallery in St Nicholas Church	Sails as cabin boy aboard the *Reserve*, aged 12, departing 30 November

	WORLD	LIVERPOOL	BLUNDELL
1688	Glorious Revolution; William of Orange lands in England; James II flees to France	Caryll Molyneux, 3rd Viscount, outlawed for Jacobite sympathies; Robert Styth appointed to St Nicholas Church	*Reserve* arrives in Barbados; Bryan witnesses slavery first-hand; first diary entry, June 1688
1689	William and Mary crowned; Toleration Act passed; Nine Years' War begins; Siege of Derry	Maritime trade moves north as war disrupts southern routes	William Blundell dies; Bryan returns to Liverpool; *Reserve* carries soldiers to Derry; crew lie at anchor off the town for two months
1690	Battle of the Boyne		Sails for Virginia aboard the *Reserve*; promoted to second mate, aged 17
1691			Returns to Liverpool, August, with £50 in wages
1692			Sails for Montserrat; earns respect of Captain Webster
1693			Returns with wages; joins the *Amety* bound for Virginia
1695		New Charter granted by William III; merchants take control of the Corporation; Thomas Johnson Snr becomes mayor	
1696		Thomas Johnson Jnr first mayor elected under new charter; William Preeson (Bryan's uncle) mayor 1696–1697	Marries Samuela Williamson
1697	Treaty of Ryswick ends Nine Years' War		First voyage as master, aboard the *Mulberry*, to Virginia; daughter Hannah born
1698	Royal African Company loses slave trade monopoly; independent traders enter		Virginia voyage aboard the *Mulberry*

	WORLD	LIVERPOOL	BLUNDELL
1699	SPCK founded by Thomas Bray	Liverpool granted its own parish, separate from Walton	
1700		*The Liverpool Merchant* becomes one of the first recorded slaving voyages, under Captain William Webster	Final *Mulberry* voyages
1701		St Peter's Church planned as Liverpool's second parish church	Takes command of the *Lever*; falls ill; carries enslaved people to Virginia
1702	War of the Spanish Succession begins; Queen Anne takes the throne		Further Virginia voyages aboard the *Lever*; evades French privateers and convoy bonds
1703			Joins SPCK as corresponding member
1704	Battle of Blenheim; Marlborough's great victory		First wife Samuela dies while Bryan is at sea
1705	Virginia Slave Codes established	St Peter's Church opens	*Lever* voyage to Virginia
1706			Departs on final *Lever* voyage; commissions the *Cleveland* in Philadelphia
1707	Act of Union; Great Britain created	Key Street Meeting House opens; Christopher Bassnett appointed first minister	*Lever* captured by French privateer; Blundell imprisoned in Dinan; loses £800
1708	Queen Anne knights Sir Thomas Johnson	Styth proposes charity school for Liverpool's poor; town council approves	Sails aboard the *Endeavour* to Philadelphia; witnesses death of Thomas Haddock; the *Cleveland* launches and capsizes; Bryan marries second wife Elizabeth Livesley; donates £25 to new school
1709		Council resolves to build world's first wet dock	*Cleveland* sails to Archangel, Russia; witnesses great fire of Archangel

	WORLD	LIVERPOOL	BLUNDELL
1710			*Cleveland* carries Huguenot refugees with naval escort; engaged by French warship
1711			Bassnett preaches to Blundell and crew of the *Cleveland*, December
1712			*Cleveland* sails for Cork and Barbados
1713	Treaty of Utrecht; new Atlantic trade routes open		*Cleveland* sails to Archangel again
1714	George I crowned; Hanoverian succession secured	Robert Styth dies; Blue Coat School struggles	Final voyage as master; retires from the sea, July; acquires the tar trade from William Clayton
1715	Jacobite Rebellion crushed; Jacobite rebels executed in Liverpool	New Dock opens — world's first commercial wet dock, August	Appointed trustee and treasurer of the Blue Coat School
1717		Blue Coat School opens on School Lane	New school building completed; gallery approved at St Peter's Church; daughter Hannah marries Samuel Shaw
1718			*Cleveland* despatched to Madagascar for enslaved people; grandson Samuel Shaw born
1720	South Sea Bubble bursts; financial crisis across Britain		Involved in eight to ten ships yearly; tar trade expands
1721	Robert Walpole becomes Britain's first prime minister	Slaving voyages resume after South Sea Bubble collapse	Elected Mayor of Liverpool (first term); finances the *Martha* slaving voyage
1723			*Jane and Ellen* sails; 153 enslaved embarked, 131 survive to be sold
1724		Daniel Defoe praises Liverpool's New Dock: "it's like is not to be seen anywhere in England"	

	WORLD	LIVERPOOL	BLUNDELL
1725			Second wife Elizabeth Livesley dies, 24 October
1726			*Good Intention* makes two slaving voyages 1726–1728; over 400 captives carried
1727	George II takes the throne		
1728			Elected Mayor of Liverpool (second term); as mayor oversees fiercely contested election; refuses late voters backed by Brereton; case appealed to Westminster
1729			Marries third wife, Mary Cunliffe, 27 November
1730			Mary dies of consumption, 9 March
1731			Daughter Hannah Shaw dies, aged 35
1732			Blue Coat School builds Liverpool's first workhouse on Corporation land
1733			Son Jonathan carries 40 enslaved Africans from Jamaica to Virginia
1737		Canning Dock opened	
1739	War of Jenkins' Ear declared against Spain		Chancery decree secures Blue Coat School's governance
1744	Second Jacobite Rebellion begins		Preacher Christopher Bassnett dies
1745	Bonnie Prince Charlie reaches Derby		Grandson Samuel Shaw marries Ann Bassnett, Bassnett's daughter
1747			New spire raised at St Peter's; Bryan funds copper ship weathervane
1748			Blue Coat School supports 100 children

	WORLD	LIVERPOOL	BLUNDELL
1749		Liverpool Infirmary founded	Bryan donates to the new infirmary
1750	Company of Merchants Trading to Africa established by Parliament	Liverpool's population reaches approximately 22,000	Bryan listed among 101 founding merchants; grandson Samuel Shaw also listed
1752			Last journal entries; records direct involvement in two slave ships; draws up estate inventory
1753		Salthouse Dock opened	
1754		New Town Hall opens; Carl Gottlieb Angerstein reports Liverpool as "one of the most flourishing ports in England"	Bryan Blundell dies, 27 January; buried at St Nicholas Church
1756	Seven Years' War begins		
1760	George III takes the throne		
1769		William Roscoe, aged 16, praises the Blue Coat School in his poem *Mount Pleasant*	
1771		George's Dock opened; Duke's Dock built for the Duke of Bridgewater's Canal	Family vessel the *Blundell* active in slave trade
1773			The *Blundell* wrecks off Africa; 443 captives die
1775	American War of Independence begins		
1777		Liverpool's population reaches approximately 34,000	
1781		Roscoe publishes *The Wrongs of Africa*; donates proceeds to abolition cause	Grandson Samuel Shaw dies
1783	American War of Independence ends; United States recognised		

	WORLD	LIVERPOOL	BLUNDELL
1787	Society for the Abolition of the Slave Trade founded in London		
1788		King's Dock opened	
1789	French Revolution begins		
1790		Liverpool handles over 40 per cent of Europe's slave trade	
1791		St Nicholas's bells ring in celebration as first abolition bill fails in Parliament	Grandson Henry Blundell Hollinshead elected mayor (first term, 1791-1792)
1793	France declares war on Britain; Revolutionary Wars begin		Grandson Henry Blundell Hollinshead elected mayor (second term, 1793-1794)
1794			Great-grandson John Shaw elected mayor (first term, 1794–1795)
1796		Queen's Dock opened	
1800		Liverpool's population reaches approximately 77,000	Great-grandson John Shaw elected mayor (second term, 1800–1801)
1803	Napoleonic Wars begin		
1805	Battle of Trafalgar; Nelson dies		
1806	Abolition bill passes the House of Commons		
1807	Abolition Act passed by Parliament, 25 March	Roscoe elected MP for Liverpool 1806; votes for abolition; greeted by riot on return; stands down 1807 Last recorded slaving voyage, *Kitty's Amelia*, leaves Liverpool	Great-grandson John Shaw's *Nicholson* sails weeks after abolition — 279 enslaved people from Congo to Demerara Grandson Henry Blundell Hollinshead elected mayor (1807–1808)
1808	West Africa Squadron established to suppress the transatlantic slave trade. Patrolling thousands of miles of the West African coast, it grew to over 25		

	WORLD	LIVERPOOL	BLUNDELL
	ships, intercepting slavers, liberating approximately 150,000 enslaved Africans, and resettling many in Freetown, Sierra Leone.		
1810		St Nicholas Church spire collapses, killing worshippers, 11 February	
1815	Battle of Waterloo; Napoleon defeated	Prince's Dock opened	
1816		Roscoe declared bankrupt; collections sold	
1819			Grandson Jonathan Blundell Hollinshead elected mayor (first term, 1819-1820)
1821		Prince's Dock opened — Liverpool now has seven wet docks	
1824			Grandson Jonathan Blundell Hollinshead elected mayor (second term, 1824-1825)
1829			Great-grandson John Shaw dies; Arrowe Park passes to his nephew (John Ralph Nicholson)
1833	Slavery abolished throughout British colonies		

Appendix A

The Seaman's Character and Calling Consider'd and Improv'd

The Seaman's Character and Calling Conſider'd and Improv'd

IN A

SERMON

Begun to a

Ship's-Company,

Upon *Thurſday, December the* 19th.

The remaining Part Preach'd the ſollowing *Lord's-Day* in the Afternoon, at the New Meeting-Houſe in *Leverpool.* MDCCXI.

By *CHRISTOPHER BASSNETT.*

Is mihi demum vivere et frui Animâ videtur, qui aliquo Negotio intentus, præclari Facinoris aut Artis bonæ Famam quærit. Saluſt.

LONDON.

Printed for *John Clark* at the *Bible* and *Crown* in the *Old-Change*, and ſold by *Dan. Birchall* in *Leverpool.* MDCCXII.

Price, Six Pence.

This letter, reproduced with minor typographical updates for clarity, was written by the Reverend Christopher Bassnett to Bryan Blundell in 1712, as the preface to a printed sermon originally preached to the crew of the *Cleveland* on Thursday, 13 December 1711.

To
Mr Bryan Blundell
Captain of the Cleveland

It was upon your Account, my good Friend, that I preached this Sermon, and the Reason of it appearing in Publick no sooner was the return I have had of Indispositions, which occasion'd some Difficulties as to the Printing of it all. But I have resolv'd at last upon the Publication, not for the Sake of any Curiosity in the Composition, but for the good Example it presents the World with. Could I allege no other Reason, I should reckon it very sufficient that hereby I have an Opportunity of showing to Men of your Profession and Way, the rare and Singular good Pattern that you have set'em who never put out to or return from Sea, but you own God both by Prayer and Praises.

Beside this, I thought it might not be amiss to let some People see, how we spend our Time upon such Occasions, as that which has given Rise to this Sermon. Praying God for Mercies we want, and Praising him for Mercies receiv'd are such clear and Indispensible Duties, even in Natural Religion, that they can hardly ever be unseasonable, and out of Place. To try to Persuade Men to perform the Duties of their Places, and to enforce upon them the great Practical Matters of our Common Christianity, One wou'd think shou'd be no such Criminal Matter as to provoke the Displeasure of any Good Man.

"*Tantane animis caelestibus irae?*"[1]

Were I dispos'd to envy the Establish'd Church any of her Members (which I flatter my self I am not, being a greater, Wellwisher to the Common Christianity, than such a Temper of Mind wou'd express) it should be Gentlemen of your Stamp and Character, who are indeed Her brightest Ornaments and Her truest Honour.

Dat veniam corvis, vexat censura columbas.[2]

It is not the Church, that is shy of owning such for Her True Sons, by only some that would engross that Sacred Name to themselves, who seem more forward to embrace others, that reflect not so true a Lustre upon their Mother.

But as for me, who wou'd not Measure things by their Bulk, but their Quality; Nor by their Weight and Number, but their real Worth and true Value, and had much rather have one Jewel, than a great Deal of Dross; were it put to my choice, I know which I shou'd prefer. It is an Encouragement to Me, and I know it is to many more besides, that some of the best, and most serious of the Establish'd Church, have Favourable Thoughts of Us and our Way.

For your Part to understand Religion, and the Principles you all upon in it; you feel, I doubt not, the Pleasures of Solid Virtue and Unaffacted Devotion; and know that the Spirit and Presence of Christ, is not tied up and confin'd to one Set and Denomination of Christians, and therefore you are not altogether for confirming your Charity and Communion to One; but those that Hold the Head, and call upon the Name of the Lord Jesus Christ in Sincerity, you Love and Reverence. And how Peaceful wou'd the Place of our Solemnities be, if this Temper did not more prevail? Acting thus, upon the Wise and Calm Principles, you are not to be moved with mere Hurry and Violence: These are no proper Instruments to gain upon the Wise, the Sober, the Rational Part of Mankind: However successful they may be in animating the Mobile which naturally runs into Disorder and Tumult; and therefore are joyned in Scripture with a very Unruly Element, which you have had plentiful Experience of; The Noise of the Seas, the Noise of their Waves, and after these you know comes the Tumult of the People.

Every Body, my Friend, is ready to acknowledge your Worth, and to rejoice in your Success and Prosperity. You honour God, and God honours you: And were I to do You Justice in a Character, I might say many great and good Things of you; but I know you will not allow it, and I therefore forbear; but it is impossible so much Virue and such Distinguish'd Merit shou'd be hid. I have done, when I have thank'd, you for the large share that you have allow'd me in your Friendship, and for the tender Sympathy that you express'd towards me, in that very Gloomy Dispensation which of late I have been under, in which I must vindicate God, He is Righteous; and if it but look bright on the other World, it matters not much, how dark it may look on This: Tho' as to the latter, I can Now say that it gives me not one uneasie Thought. I hope you will help me in your Prayers, for a more fancified Use of the Dispensation, and so I take Leave and rest.

Toxteth Park, near Leverpool,
March 1st 1712.

Your Friend
and
Humble Servant

C. Bassnett

The full sermon runs to forty-nine pages in its original printed form. A digitised copy is available via the Internet Archive.

Appendix B

Glossary

This glossary offers a selection of maritime terms and concepts that appear throughout the book. These terms are included here to support the reader's understanding of the nautical vocabulary and operational world of Blundell's time.

Term	*Definition*
About	A sailing term meaning to turn a ship's head through the wind in order to change direction; often used in the command *"come about."*
Aft	Toward the rear (stern) of a ship; the opposite of *fore* or *forward.*
Amidship	The middle part of a ship, halfway between the bow (front) and the stern (back). Often refers to the central area of the vessel, both lengthwise and sometimes across the beam.
Anchor Lights	Lanterns hung from the mast of a ship at anchor to signal its stationary position and avoid collisions, especially at night or in poor weather.
Aweather (helm)	Turning the ship's rudder toward the wind, a manoeuvre to alter course quickly.
Ballast	The heavy materials (often stones, sand, or scrap iron) loaded into a ship's hold to improve stability when not fully laden with cargo.
Bar	A ridge of sand or silt built up at a river mouth or harbour entrance, often hazardous to ships entering or leaving port.
Bare Poles	A state where all sails are removed or furled, often during extreme storms to reduce wind pressure and avoid damage.
Barge	A flat-bottomed vessel used for carrying goods in harbours or along rivers, usually towed or pushed rather than sailed.
Barricado (also Barricade)	A strong wooden partition or fence built across the main deck of a slave ship to separate the crew from the captives and to provide a defensive position in case of revolt. Usually about 8 feet high and constructed of heavy timbers or spars, it was fitted near the mainmast and often reinforced with netting or iron bars.
Beam	The widest part of a ship's hull; also used to describe the structural timbers running across the vessel's width.
Below	Within the body of a ship.

Bilge	The lowest part of a ship's hull, where water collects and must be pumped out.
Bill of Exchange	A written order binding one party to pay a fixed sum to another at a set date, commonly used by merchants to settle debts across ports and colonies.
Binnacle	A waist-high stand or case housing a ship's compass, often containing lamps for night-time use. Magnetic objects nearby could affect its accuracy.
Bitter End	The final portion of a ship's anchor cable, fastened to the bitts, the strong timber posts set into the deck. When a vessel had paid out cable to the bitter end, nothing more remained. In heavy weather, if the strain threatened to tear out the bow or capsize the ship, the cable could be cut at this point, sacrificing the anchor to preserve the vessel.
Bled and Sweated	A period medical practice involving bloodletting and induced sweating (through hot drinks or blankets), believed to restore bodily balance and health. Common among seafarers.
Block	A pulley encased in a wooden shell, used with rope (known as *tackle*) to lift or adjust sails, cargo, or rigging on a ship.
Boom	A horizontal spar fixed to the lower edge of a sail, used to control its angle to the wind.
Boom Grapple	A hooked device or rope used to catch and hold an enemy ship's rigging during an attempted boarding.
Bout	A manoeuvre of a ship, especially in the context of repositioning during naval combat. In seventeenth and eighteenth century seamanship, "to make a bout" often meant to tack or turn a ship, typically to bring it about to face the enemy or to resume a battle course.
Bow	The front end of a ship's hull, designed to cut through the water.
Bowsprit	A spar extending forward from a ship's bow, supporting the foremast and providing anchorage for headsails.
Brig / Brigantine	A two-masted sailing ship with square rigging on both masts. Commonly used by merchants and privateers in the early eighteenth-century. Smaller than a frigate, but faster and more versatile.
Broadside	A full volley of cannon fire from one side of a ship. In naval combat, a broadside could be decisive. Used figuratively to suggest overwhelming force or confrontation.
Bulkhead	An internal wall or partition within a ship's hull, dividing it into compartments for strength and safety.
Bulwark	The solid side or railing along a ship's upper deck, providing protection from the sea and preventing crew or cargo from being swept overboard.

Cable	A thick rope or chain used for anchoring a ship; also a nautical measure of distance, roughly one-tenth of a nautical mile (about 200 yards / 185 metres).
Cable's Length	A traditional seafaring unit of distance, taken from the average length of a ship's anchor cable, approximately 100 fathoms, or about 200 yards / 185 metres.
Capstan	A vertical rotating drum, turned by handspikes or mechanical power, used for hauling heavy ropes or cables such as the anchor or mooring lines.
Careen	The process of tilting a ship onto its side to clean, caulk, or repair the hull. This often involved scraping off barnacles, re-caulking seams with pitch, or applying protective sheathing, essential tasks for keeping a vessel seaworthy.
Cat, Cat-O'-Nine-Tails	A whip made of nine knotted cords, used for flogging sailors as punishment aboard naval and merchant ships.
Caulk	To seal the seams between a ship's planks with fibres and pitch, making the hull watertight.
Chandler	A dealer in supplies and equipment for ships and boats.
Chase Guns	Guns mounted in the bow or stern of a ship, used to fire at an enemy ahead or behind during pursuit.
Clew	The lower corner of a sail where the sheets (ropes) are fastened, used to control the sail's angle and shape.
Clew-Garnet	A tackle used to haul up the corners (clews) of square sails; critical when furling sails in rough weather.
Coamings	Raised borders around hatches on a ship to prevent water from entering.
Commodore	A senior naval officer commanding a small squadron or convoy, ranking below an admiral but above a captain.
Compass	A navigational instrument showing direction relative to magnetic north, essential for steering a ship's course at sea.
Con, Conning	The act of directing the steering of a ship, typically from the helm or a commanding position on deck.
Convoy	A group of merchant ships sailing together under the protection of naval escorts, organised for safety against privateers or enemy vessels.
Cross-Staff (Forestaff)	A hand-held instrument used to measure the altitude of the sun or stars for latitude. Also called a *forestaff*, it required the user to face the sun and align a sliding crosspiece. Gradually replaced by the *Davis quadrant*.
Cutlass	A short, broad-bladed sword used by sailors for close combat and boarding actions.

Cwt (Hundredweight)	A British imperial unit of weight equal to 112 pounds (approximately 50.8 kilograms). Often used for bulk goods and materials.
Dead Reckoning	A method of navigation based on *reckoning* a vessel's current position from its previous position using estimated speed, course, and drift, without reference to celestial observations.
Dissenter	A person who refused to conform to the doctrines of the Church of England, often belonging to Protestant groups such as Methodists, Presbyterians, or Baptists.
Drawing Down	The process of lowering a ship's draft, often by removing cargo or ballast, to expose the hull below the waterline. This allowed the captain or shipwrights to inspect the vessel for leaks, damage, or weaknesses in the planking, and ensure she was watertight.
Driving Out Mast Wedges	A tactic to help shift or adjust the masts' angle to accommodate strain or movement during storms or action.
Ebb	The movement of the tide as the sea level falls and water flows back from the shore toward the open sea.
Ebb Tide	The period during which the tide is receding; the opposite of *flood tide*.
Embargo	An official ban on trade or the movement of ships, usually imposed during war or political dispute.
Embark	To go aboard a ship, or to load passengers and cargo in preparation for a voyage.
Ensign	A national flag flown on a ship to show its nationality, typically from the stern or mainmast.
Entrepôt	A trading port or warehouse where goods are imported, stored, and re-exported.
Factor	An agent who conducted trade on behalf of merchants, usually working on commission. Factors often managed warehouses and extended credit to merchants.
Fathom	A unit of measurement used at sea, equal to 6 feet (about 1.8 metres). Originally derived from the span of a man's outstretched arms.
Fighting Tops	Platforms high on a ship's mast where musketeers or grenadiers could fire or throw explosives onto enemy decks.
Fleet	A group of ships sailing together under one command, whether naval, merchant, or privateer.
Flood Tide	The rising tide; the period during which seawater flows landward, causing the water level to increase until it reaches high tide.
Flyboat	A fast, broad Dutch trading vessel, often used for short voyages or coastal trade. Also employed in convoys.
Forecastle	The forward part of a ship, traditionally where the crew slept; often damp, cramped, and reserved for lower-ranked sailors.

Foremast / Maintopmast	Upper sections of the masts; damage to these could cripple a vessel's ability to manoeuvre.
Foresail	The sail set on the foremast, typically the second mast from the front on square-rigged ships; used to aid forward motion and balance the ship's steering.
Foresheet Blocks	Position the jib sheet to create equal tension on the sail. This position is called the neutral block position.
Forestaff	See *cross-staff*.
Foul, Fouled	Tangled, obstructed, or entangled (especially in rigging or sails).
Freshes	The upper reaches of a river influenced more by freshwater than tidal flow.
Frigate	A fast, medium-sized warship carrying around 30 to 40 guns, used for escort, patrol, and reconnaissance duties.
Furl	To roll up and secure a sail neatly to its yard or boom when it is not in use.
Galley	A long, narrow vessel propelled mainly by oars, used in earlier centuries for war or trade before sailing ships became dominant.
Gunwale	The upper edge of a ship's side (pronounced "gunnel").
Hammock	A canvas or rope bed slung between two points, used by sailors for sleeping aboard ship.
Haul	To pull or drag a rope, sail, or heavy load, especially when adjusting a ship's rigging or course.
Hawser	A thick rope or cable used to moor or tow a ship.
Heave	To haul or pull on a rope, anchor, or other heavy object.
Heave Down	A method of careening a ship by partially submerging and tilting it to expose the hull.
Heave To	A sailing technique used to stop or slow a ship's forward progress without dropping anchor. Often used in storms or while waiting for orders.
Helm	The steering apparatus of a ship, typically the wheel or tiller, by which the helmsman directs its course.
Hogshead	A large wooden cask used primarily for storing and shipping tobacco and other goods; capacity varied by trade but often 100–140 gallons.
Hourglass	A timekeeping instrument used at sea, consisting of two glass bulbs joined by a narrow neck through which sand flows at a steady rate. Known interchangeably as an *hourglass* or *sandglass*, it measured fixed intervals.
Impress	See *press*.
Jib	A small triangular sail set ahead of the foremast, used to help steer and balance a sailing ship.

Keel	The main structural beam running along the bottom of a ship's hull from bow to stern, forming its backbone and providing stability in the water.
Knot	A unit of speed at sea, equal to 1 nautical mile per hour (about 1.15 statute miles). The term derives from the log-and-line method of measuring a ship's progress, in which a rope marked at regular intervals, *knots*, was cast astern and timed with a sandglass. The number of knots that ran out in a set time gave the vessel's speed through the water.
Larboard	The left-hand side of a ship when facing forward; now more commonly referred to as port. The term was phased out to reduce confusion with starboard.
Latitude	A measure of distance north or south of the equator, expressed in degrees, used by navigators to determine a ship's position at sea.
League	A common maritime unit of distance in the early modern period, generally understood as 3 nautical miles (about 5.6 kilometres or 3.45 land miles).
Lee	The side of a ship or an area sheltered from the wind; the opposite of *weather* or *windward.*
Leeward	The direction away from the wind; the sheltered side of a ship or island.
Letter of Marque	A government licence authorising a private ship to attack and capture enemy vessels during wartime, turning merchants into legal privateers.
Lighter	Small flat-bottomed boat used to ferry goods between ship and shore, especially in shallow harbours.
Line of Battle	A naval formation in which warships sail in a single line, allowing each to fire its broadsides without obstructing others, a tactic central to eighteenth-century sea battles.
Log and Line	A method of estimating a ship's speed using a rope knotted at intervals and a floating log. Origin of "knots" as a speed unit.
Longitude	A measure of distance east or west of the Prime Meridian, expressed in degrees; together with *latitude*, it determines a ship's exact position on the globe.
Lowering Yards	Refers to the process of lowering the horizontal spars (yards) that held the sails on a ship's mast. This was typically done to reduce the sail area exposed to the wind, which could be necessary during strong winds or storms to prevent damage to the sails and rigging. Lowering the yards also helped to stabilise the ship and make it easier to control under challenging weather conditions.
Main-Brace	A critical rope or tackle controlling the main yard of a sailing ship.

Mainmast	The tallest and central mast of a sailing ship, carrying the mainsail and often additional topsails above it.
Main Sail	The principal and largest sail on a ship's mainmast, providing the chief source of driving power when under sail.
Main Tack	A heavy rope used to hold down the lower corners of a ship's mainsail, especially on square-rigged vessels.
Main Top	The platform partway up the mainmast where the lower and topmasts join; used as a lookout point and for working the upper sails.
Main Yard	The large horizontal spar attached to the mainmast, from which the mainsail is hung and controlled.
Mainsheet	The rope used to control the angle of the mainsail relative to the wind.
Maintopsail Yard	A horizontal spar holding the topsail on the mainmast, from which sailors often worked.
Man-of-War	A large, purpose-built naval warship of the sixteenth to nineteenth centuries, heavily armed with multiple gun decks and crewed by professional seamen. In the Royal Navy, men-of-war served as the main fighting ships of the fleet, escorting convoys, engaging privateers, and projecting maritime power across the Atlantic.
Master	The commanding officer of a merchant ship, responsible for navigation, crew, and cargo; equivalent to a captain in naval rank.
Master Mariner	A seafarer qualified by experience and certification to command a vessel of any size on any voyage worldwide.
Mate (First, Second, etc.)	A ship's officer ranking below the master, responsible for navigation, watchkeeping, and managing the crew. *First mate* being the senior, followed by *second* and *third mates*.
Mizzen	The aft-most mast on a sailing ship with three or more masts. The mizzen mast supports the mizzen sail, which helps with steering and balance, especially when sailing close to the wind.
Mizzentop	The platform on the mizzenmast (the aft mast of a ship), where the lower and topmasts join; used for lookout and working the upper mizzen sails.
Nonconformist	A Protestant who refused to follow the practices of the Church of England.
Oakum	Loose fibres of old rope, often tarred, used for caulking the seams of wooden ships to keep them watertight.
Overset	Common term used to describe a ship being capsized.
Pink	A small, narrow-sterned ship used mostly for trade; often with a high rear deck.
Pipe	Large cask used for shipping wine, holding around 126 gallons (approximately 477 litres).

Poop	The raised deck at the stern of a ship, above the main deck, often forming part of the captain's quarters or used for observation.
Portage	Goods or cargo carried by a sailor for profit, usually as a personal investment alongside wages.
Powder Monies	A port duty paid by merchants at certain Caribbean ports, such as Barbados, based on the ship's tonnage. The funds were used to maintain powder magazines and fortifications.
Press (Impress)	The forced recruitment of men into naval service, often by *press gangs* acting under royal authority, commonly feared by sailors and dockside workers.
Privateer	A privately owned armed ship authorised by a government (under a *letter of marque*) to attack and capture enemy vessels during wartime.
Prize	A ship or cargo captured during war or privateering, which could be claimed and sold for profit after legal adjudication in a prize court.
Quadrant	A navigational instrument with a quarter-circle arc used to measure the altitude of the sun or stars, helping determine a ship's latitude at sea (also called the Davis quadrant).
Quarterdeck	The aft section of the upper deck, reserved for officers; a site of command and ceremony.
Quarter Galley	The projecting structure near the stern of a ship, often containing toilets or cabins.
Quarter of the Ebb Tide	A stage of the falling tide, useful for navigating out of shallow waters.
Rating	A classification system used by the Royal Navy in the seventeenth to nineteenth centuries to rank warships according to their size and firepower. First-rate ships carried 100 guns or more; fourth-rate ships typically carried 46–60 guns and were large enough to serve in battle formations but often used for convoy escort, colonial service, or as flagships on smaller stations.
Reckoning	The calculation of a ship's position by estimating distance run, speed, and direction since the last known point. See *Dead Reckoning*.
Red Ensign	The flag of the British merchant fleet.
Reef (To Reef) / Reefed Foresail	To reduce the area of a sail exposed to the wind by folding or rolling part of it and tying it securely, often done in rough weather.
Rigging	The system of ropes, cables, and chains that support a ship's masts and control its sails, divided into *standing rigging* (for support) and *running rigging* (for movement).
Ropeyard	A long, narrow workshop where ropes were made by twisting strands of hemp.
Roundhouse	A covered structure at the stern of a ship, often used as a captain's cabin.

Running Fight	A battle between ships fought while both are under sail, each manoeuvring and firing as they move rather than anchoring or engaging broadside at close range.
Sanded Decks	A practice of spreading sand on a ship's deck before combat to soak blood and prevent slipping.
Sandglass	See *hourglass.*
Scoreweight	An archaic unit of measurement; here likely referring to 20 pounds' worth of a given good.
Scow	See *lighter.*
Scraping	Refers to the practice of cleaning a ship's hull to remove barnacles and marine growth, giving the vessel the appearance of a man-of-war and improving speed and handling.
Second Mate	A ship's officer responsible for navigation and assisting in managing the crew.
Shallop	A small, fast boat used for coastal trade and harbour work, often raced by mariners.
Sheathing	Covering a ship's hull (usually with tar and later in the eighteenth-century copper) to protect against shipworm and reduce drag.
Shipworm	See *teredo navalis.*
Shipwright	A skilled craftsman who designs, builds, or repairs wooden ships.
Shoal	A submerged sandbank or reef.
Short Allowance	A reduced ration of food or water issued when supplies ran low; sailors were often granted extra pay or compensation in return for the hardship.
Shrouds	Sturdy ropes or wires that support a ship's mast laterally.
Sloop	A small, single-masted vessel, agile and often used for quick transport of cargo or communications. In Blundell's era, also favoured by privateers and smugglers.
Slops	Ready-made clothing and other basic garments issued or sold to sailors aboard ship or in dockside slop shops.
Soaked the Sails	Refers to the technique of securing the sails by tightening or wetting them to ensure they remain taut and effective in heavy winds or rain. This practice was common among sailors to reduce the risk of sail damage during rough weather.
Sounding	Measuring water depth, typically with a lead line marked in fathoms, to avoid grounding or gauge approach to shore.
Spar	A general term for any strong pole, such as a mast, yard, or boom, and used to support a ship's sails and rigging.
Starboard	The right-hand side of a ship when facing forward toward the bow; opposite of *port.*

Staysail	A small triangular canvas set between the masts.
Stern	The rear part of a ship, opposite the *bow*, often housing the captain's cabin and steering gear.
Stocks	The wooden or metal supports that hold a ship upright during construction.
Stow	To pack or arrange cargo, provisions, or equipment securely in a ship's hold. See *stowage.*
Stowage	The act or method of arranging and securing items aboard ship to ensure safety, balance, and efficient use of space.
Strike	To lower or take down a sail, flag, or mast; also used to mean surrender in battle.
Striking the Union Jack	Lowering the British flag. This was typically followed by raising another, often signalling deception or surrender.
Supercargo	A merchant officer aboard the ship responsible for overseeing cargo and commercial negotiations at port.
Tack	A sailing manoeuvre that involves turning a ship's bow through the wind to change direction. At night, such manoeuvres were dangerous and required signalling to avoid collisions or confusion in convoy formations.
Tackle	A system of ropes and blocks (pulleys) used together to lift or move heavy loads aboard a ship.
Taut	Describes a rope, sail, or rigging drawn tight and free from slack.
Teredo Navalis	Also known as a shipworm, a marine mollusc that burrowed into wooden hulls, weakening them severely.
Toggle	Wooden or metal fasteners used in ship rigging or during hauling operations.
Topgallant	The section of a mast above the topsail mast, supporting the topgallant yard and sail.
Topgallant Sail	The sail set above the topsail, used in light or moderate winds to gain extra speed.
Topsails	The sails above the lowest square sails on a mast; often reefed or furled in strong winds.
Trim	The way weight is distributed on a ship, affecting how it sits and handles in the water.
Trunnels	Short for "tree-nails", wooden pegs used in traditional shipbuilding to fasten planks to frames.
Victual	To supply a ship with food, drink, and other provisions for a voyage.
Wake	The disturbed track of water left behind by a moving ship's hull and propelling motion.

Watch	A duty period during which a portion of the crew is assigned to man the ship; also the system by which the crew's working hours are divided, typically into four-hour shifts.
Ways	The timbered tracks or slip on which a ship is built and launched. A vessel resting on them is said to be *on the ways*, awaiting her launch into the water.
Wear (or Wearing)	To turn a ship away from the wind and bring her around on the opposite tack; the action is known as *wearing ship*. This manoeuvre was the alternative to tacking, used particularly in strong winds or by large vessels that could not tack easily.
Weather Quarter	The side of a ship facing into the wind, particularly toward the stern; often used to describe the wind's direction relative to the vessel during a chase or engagement.
Windward	The direction from which the wind is blowing; the side of a ship or object facing into the wind (opposite of *leeward*).
Yard	A horizontal spar fixed across a mast from which a square sail is hung and controlled.
Yardarm	The outer end of a yard, used for attaching and trimming the corners of sails; also the point from which signals or flags could be displayed.

Appendix C

Family Trees

TREE 1 – THE BLUNDELLS

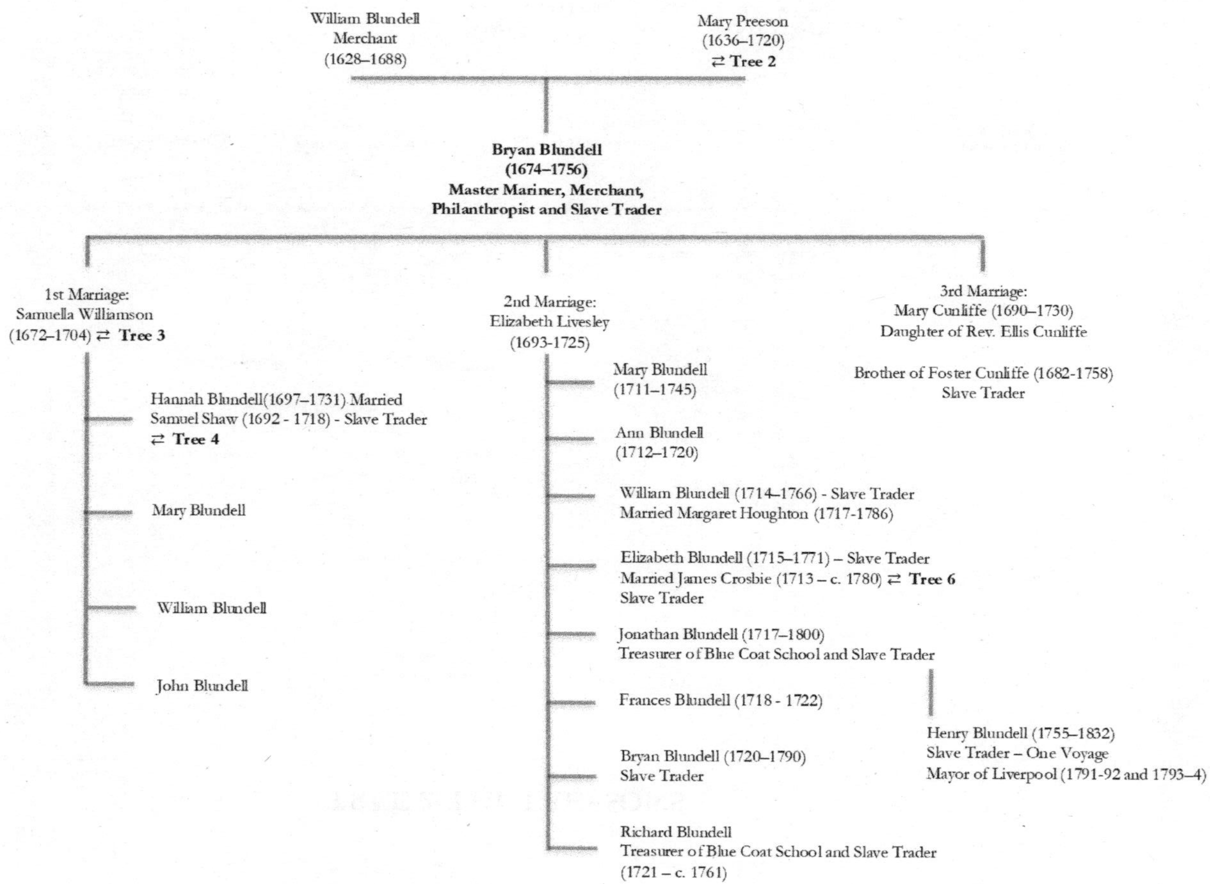

TREE 2: THE PREESONS

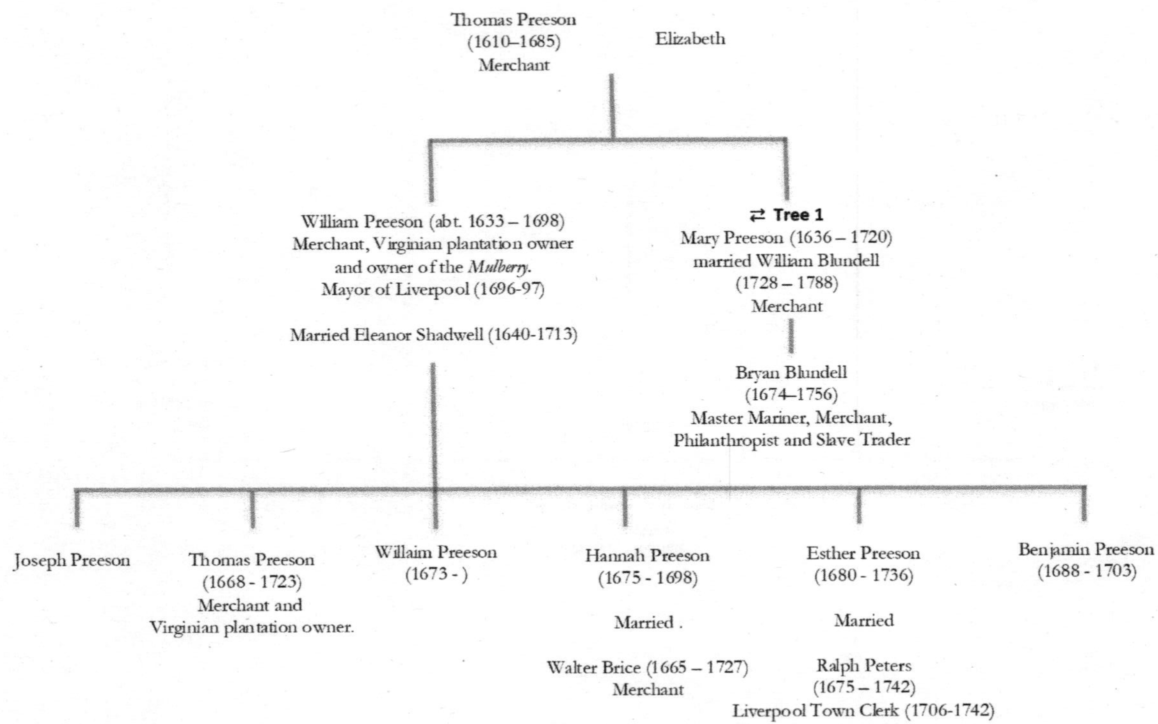

TREE 3: THE WILLIAMSONS

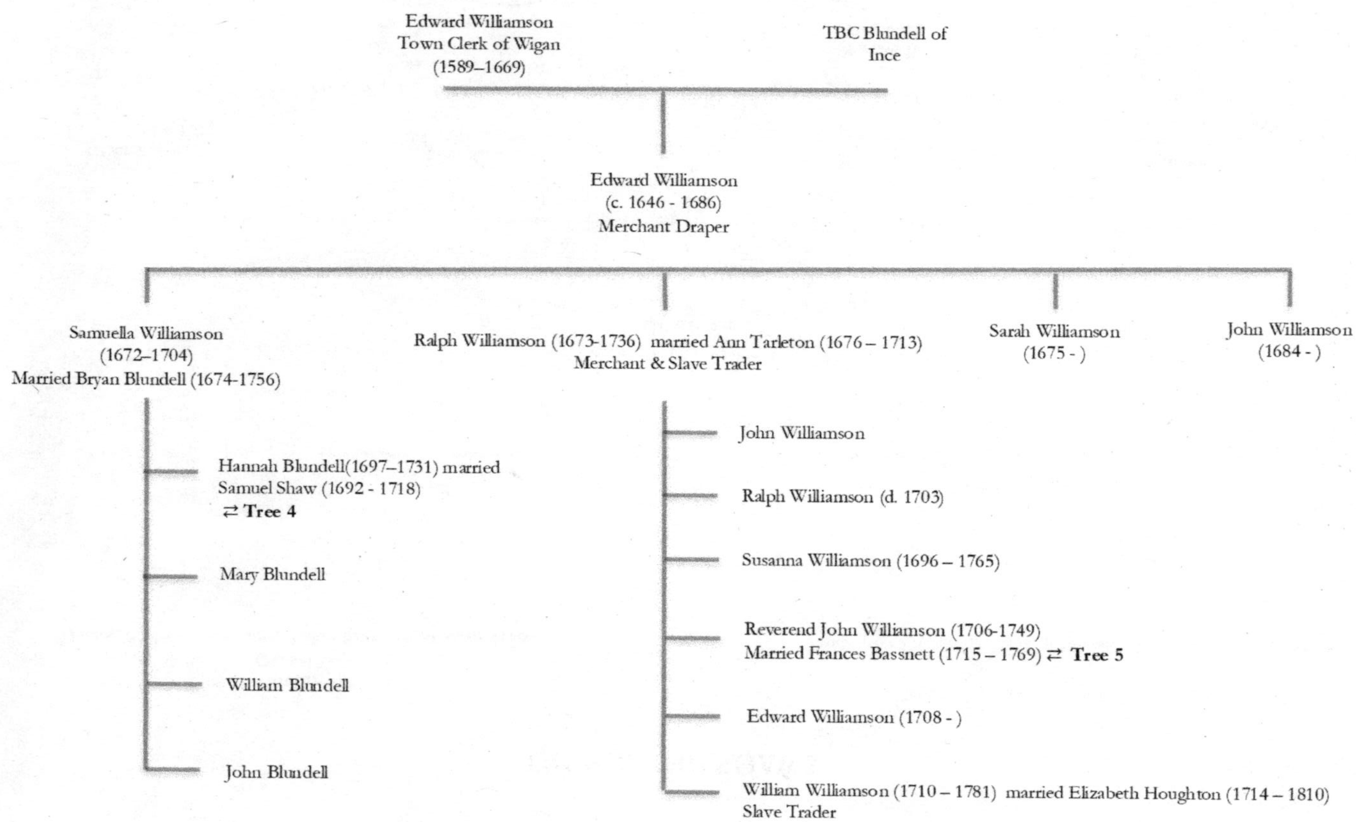

TREE 4: THE SHAWS

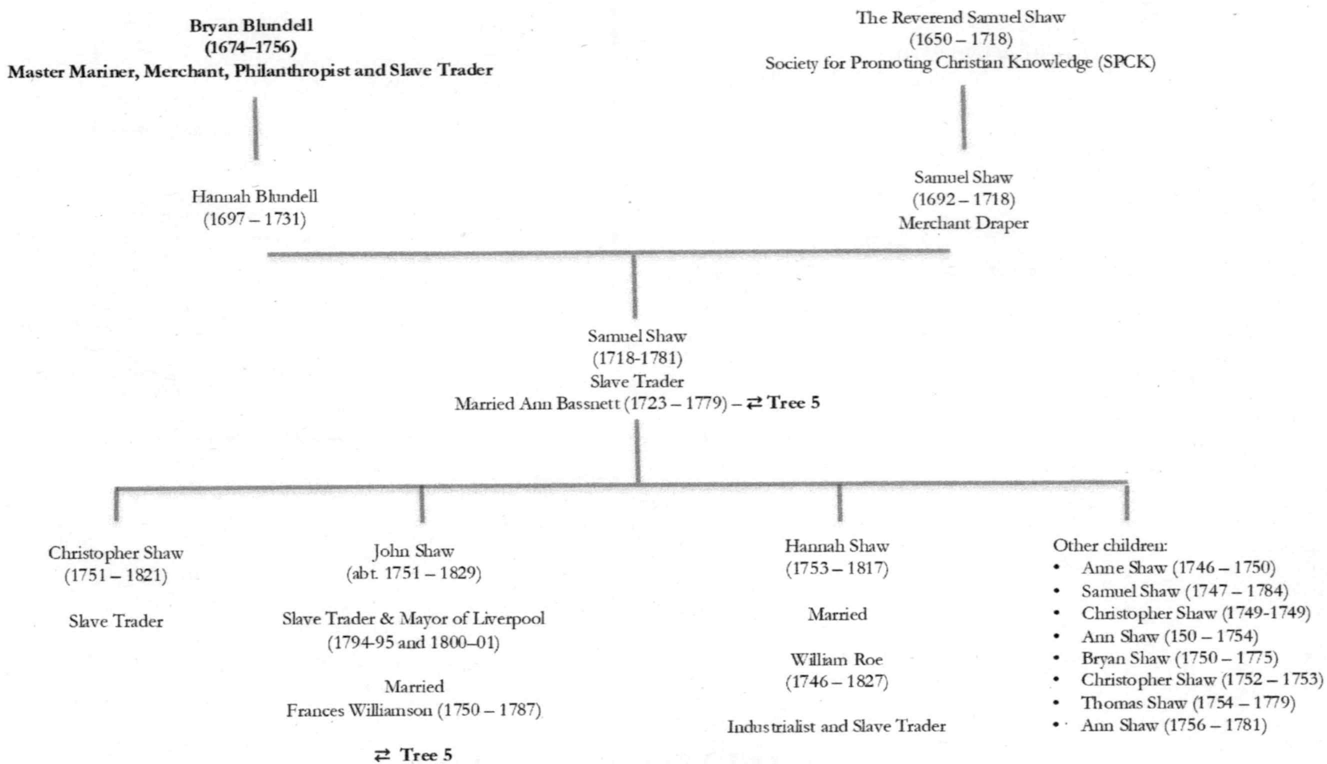

TREE 5: THE BASSNETTS

Nathaniel Bassnett (1626 – 1699)

Frances Richardson (d. 1703)

Other children:
- Benjamin Bassnett
- Joseph Bassnett (d. 1703)
- Susanna Bassnett (1668 -)
- Nathaniel Bassnett (1669 -)
- Catherine Bassett (1675 -)

William Bassnett (1672 – 1731)
Merchant and part owner of the *Laver*

Married Elizabeth Pemberton (d. 1731).
Brother of John Pemberton (1666-1743)
And part owner of the *Laver*

⇄ **Tree 3**
Frances Bassnett
(1700 – 1783)

Married

Edward Cropper (1704 – 1776)
Slave Captain and Slave Trader

Nathaniel Bassnett
(1702 – 1777)
Slave Trader

Married

Ann May

Christopher Bassnett (1677 – 1744)
Minister of Keye Street Chapel
and Society for Promoting Christian Knowledge (SPCK)
Married Anne Eaton

Frances Bassnett (1715 – 1769)

Married

Reverend John Williamson
(1706-1749)

⇄ **Tree 3**

Ann Bassnett
(1718-1718)

Ann Bassnett (1723 – 1779)

Married

Samuel Shaw (1718 – 1781)
Slave Trader

⇄ **Tree 4**

Frances Williamson
(1750 – 1787)

Married

⇄ **Tree 4**

John Shaw
(abt. 1751 – 1829)
Slave Trader
And Mayor of Liverpool
(1794 – 95 and 1800 – 01)

TREE 6: THE CROSBIES

William Crosbie
(c. 1688 – 1732)

Margery Benn
(1688 – 1763)

Other children:

- Jane Crosbie (1711 – 1732)
- Margery Crosbie (1712 – 1732)
- Thomas Crosbie (1715 – 1753)
- Robert Crosbie (1708 – 1732)
- Elizabeth Crosbie (1721 -)

William Crosbie
(1710 – 1785)

Slave Trader

Mayor of Liverpool (1776-67)

James Crosbie (1713 – c. 1780) – Slave Trader
and Mayor of Liverpool (1753-54)

Married Elizabeth Blundell (1715–1771)
Slave Trader
⇄ Tree 1

William Crosbie
(1744 – 1821)

Slave Trader

Mayor of Liverpool (1779 – 80)

John Crosbie
(1746 – 1808)

Slave Trader

John Crosbie
(1716 – 1791)

Slave Captain (*Duke of Cumberland*) and Slave Trader

Mayor of Liverpool (1765-66)

Appendix D

The Recorded Voyages of Bryan Blundell, 1687–1714 – From Cabin Boy to Commander

The Recorded Voyages of Bryan Blundell, 1687–1714

From Cabin Boy to Commander

1687 - 1696

Ship	Role	Journey	Master	Outbound	Inbound	Income	Notes
Reserve	**Cabin Boy**	Liverpool - Dublin - Barbados - London	Master Christopher Moore	30 November 1687	15 August 1688	£0	First voyage at sea and first experience of the slave trade.
		London - Dublin	Master Thomas Riding	16 November 1688 – 21 November 1688	N/A	£0	Short voyage
		Dublin - Liverpool - Derry - Liverpool	Master Thomas Riding	Abt. June 1689	Abt. August 1689	£40	Carried soldiers and spent two months at sea. (Siege of Derry)
		Liverpool - Virginia - Liverpool	Master Christopher Moore	6 November 1690 - 8 February 1691	20 June 1691 - 30 August 1691	£18	Convoy of 130 ships left Virginia.
		Liverpool - Norway - Liverpool	Master William Webster	Departed 15th March 1692	Returned to Liverpool on 29 May 1692	Unknown	
	Second Mate	Liverpool - Monserrat - Liverpool	Master William Webster	14 October 1692 - 16 December 1692	16 August 1693	£50	
Amety	**Second Mate**	London - Liverpool	Master Lewis Jenkins	8 January 1694 - 18 February 1694	10 May 1694 - 27 June 1694	£60	
		Liverpool - London - Virginia - Liverpool	Master Lewis Jenkins	27 November 1694 - 8 February 1695	17 June 1695 – 31 July 1695	£60 (including portage)	
		Liverpool - Belfast - Virginia - Liverpool	Master Lewis Jenkins	5 December 1695 - 4 April 1696	10 July - 13 November 1696	£130	Convoy of 70 – Captain Jackson (*Smyrna Merchant*) and Captain Huckin (*Tiger*)

The Recorded Voyages of Bryan Blundell, 1687–1714

From Cabin Boy to Commander

1697 - 1701

Ship	Role	Journey	Master	Outbound	Inbound	Income	Notes
Mulberry	Master	Liverpool - Virginia - Dublin - Liverpool	Master Bryan Blundell	26 January 1697 - 1 April 1697	7 May - 3 July 1697	£144 + £44 for two servants	Sold two indentured servants on arrival.
		Liverpool - Virginia (Pungiteague) - Liverpool	Master Bryan Blundell	9 November 1697 - 8 January 1698	12 May 1698 - 17 June 1698	£340	
		Liverpool - Dublin - Virginia (Pungiteague) - Liverpool	Master Bryan Blundell	13 October 1698 - 18 January 1699	8 April 1699 - 30 May 1699	£100	18 December: We lost our cook's boy overboard in the latitude of 31° 18' N. Carried three indentured servants on the voyage. Made £100 "but left it in Ireland by selling some tobacco to some men that broke, so that I made but a sorry year's work this year".
		Liverpool - Virginia - Liverpool	Master Bryan Blundell	9 November 1699 - 8 January 1700	12 April 1700 - 3 June 1700	£80-£90	Also had a quarter share in the Lever which cost him £400 but only returned £217.
		Liverpool - Dublin - Virginia (Pungiteague) - Liverpool	Master Bryan Blundell	22 November 1700 - 18 February 1701	11 May 1701 - 16 July 1701	£100	

The Recorded Voyages of Bryan Blundell, 1687–1714

From Cabin Boy to Commander

1701-1707

		Liverpool - Dublin - Barbados - Nevis - Virginia - Liverpool	Master Bryan Blundell	24 September 1701 - Barbados 3 December 1701 Montserrat - 15 December Virginia - 14 January 1702	12 June 1702 - 12 July 1702	£350	Bryan Blundell owned a quarter share of the *Lever*.
		Liverpool - Virginia - Liverpool	Master Bryan Blundell	5 October 1702 - 15 November 1702	26 March 1703 - 26 May 1703	Not recorded	
Lever	**Master and Part Owner**	Liverpool - Virginia (Pungiteague) - Plymouth - Liverpool	Master Bryan Blundell	Autum 1703 - 1704	June 1704 - Abt. September 1704	Not recorded	
		Liverpool - Virginia - Liverpool	Master Bryan Blundell	January 1705	August 1705 - October 1705	Not recorded	
		Liverpool - Virginia - St Malo (France) - Liverpool	Master Bryan Blundell	January 1706 - 20 February 1706	September 1706 – 14 November 1706 Returned 24 January 1706	£860 loss	Ordered the construction of the *Cleveland* in Philadelphia. Captured by French Privateer.
Endeavour	**Part Owner and Passenger**	Liverpool - Virginia	Edward Tarleton	31 March 1707 - 6 June 1707	N/A	£0	Sailed to collect the *Cleveland*.

The Recorded Voyages of Bryan Blundell, 1687–1714

From Cabin Boy to Commander

1707 - 1714

Ship	Role	Journey	Master	Outbound	Inbound	Income	Notes
		Virginia - Liverpool	Master Bryan Blundell	N/A	8 December 1707 - 20 March 1707	£350	First trans-atlantic voyage of the *Cleveland*.
		Liverpool - Belfast - Virginia - Liverpool	Master Bryan Blundell	7 September 1708 - 2 December 1708	13 February 1709 - 17 April 1709	Unknown	Lost Frank Ward overboard on 3 December 1708.
		Liverpool - Archangel - Liverpool	Master Bryan Blundell	17 July 1709 - 17 August 1709	9 September 1709 - 21 October 1709	£950	Witnessed fire in Archangel. Made £1,100 with £150 freight to pay.
		Liverpool - Dublin - Barbados - Liverpool	Master Bryan Blundell	16 December 1709 - 9 February 1710	23 April 1710 - 13 June 1709	£2,400	Battle with privateer.
Cleveland	Owner & Master	Liverpool - Dublin - Barbados - Liverpool	Master Bryan Blundell	23 September 1710 - 25 November 1710	31 January 1711 - 13 July 1711	£1,870	Second battle with privateer.
		Liverpool - Archangel - Liverpool	Master Bryan Blundell	13 July 1711 - 3 September 1711	23 September 1711 - 17 October 1711	£714 (after wages)	
		Liverpool - Belfast - Barbados - Liverpool	Master Bryan Blundell	17 January 1712 - 29 February 1712	29 May 1712 - End July 1712	£1,777 (after wages)	
		Liverpool - Cork - Barbados - London	Master Bryan Blundell	25 November 1712 - 27 January 1713	3 April 1713 - 18 May 1713	£1,259 (after wages and fitting out)	
		London - Archangel - Liverpool	Master Bryan Blundell	27 June 1713 - 30 July 1713	2 September 1713 - 5 October 1713	£497	£650 income (freight) £120 wages £50 damage flax
		Liverpool - Cork - Barbados - London	Master Bryan Blundell	16 January 1714 - 17 March 1714	8 May 1714 - 23 June 1714	Not recorded	"This ends Blundell's seafaring journey".

Appendix E

The Recorded Slaving Voyages of Bryan Blundell and His Direct Descendants,[1] 1722–1808

The Recorded Slaving Voyages of Bryan Blundell and his Direct Descendants
1722 - 1808

Name	Relationship to Bryan Blundell	Via	Tree	Active Slave Trading	Number of Voyages	Total Embarked	Total Disembarked	Mortality during voyage	% Mortality	Notes
Bryan Blundell (1674 - 1756)*	N/A	N/A	Tree 1	1722 - 1756	15	3,419	2,888	531	16%	* Records incomplete between 1729 and 1749
William Blundell (1714 - 1766)	Son	N/A	Tree 1	1745 - 1762	26	8,307	6,681	1,626	20%	
Jonathan Blundell (1717 - 1800)	Son	N/A	Tree 1	1745 - 1780	79	23,343	18,667	4,676	20%	Treasurer of Blue Coat School
Bryan Blundell Jnr. (1720 - 1799)	Son	N/A	Tree 1	1756 - 1776	57	14,500	11,466	3,034	21%	
Richard Blundell (1721 - c. 1761)	Son	N/A	Tree 1	1748 - 1761	21	5,347	4,270	1,077	25%	Treasurer of Blue Coat School
Elizabeth Blundell (Crosbie) (1715 - 1771)	Daughter	N/A	Tree 1	1760 - 1760	2	564	416	148	26%	
Henry Blundell (1755 - 1832)	Grandson	Son of Jonathan Blundell (1717 - 1800)	Tree 1	1784 - 1784	1	597	480	117	20%	Mayor of Liverpool (1791 – 92)
William Crosbie (1744 - 1821)	Grandson	Daughter of Elizabeth Blundell (1715 - 1771)	Tree 6	1767 - 1780	12	3,736	3,037	699	19%	Mayor of Liverpool (1779 – 80)
John Crosbie (1746 - 1808)	Grandson	Daughter of Elizabeth Blundell (1715 - 1771)	Tree 6	1768 - 1768	1	331	270	61	18%	
Samuel Shaw (1718 - 1781)	Grandson	Son of Hannah Blundell (1697 - 1731)	Tree 5	1745 - 1780	76	18,033	14,700	3,333	18%	
Christopher Shaw (1751 - 1821)	Great Grandson	Son of Hannah Blundell (1697 - 1731)	Tree 5	1775 - 1788	8	1,929	1,443	486	25%	
John Shaw (c. 1751 - 1829)	Great Grandson	Son of Samuel Shaw (1718 - 1781)	Tree 5	1774 - 1808	53	15,039	13,364	1,675	11%	Mayor of Liverpool (1794 – 95 and 1800 – 01)
				Unique Total	**185**	**50,153**	**41,736**	**8,417**	**17%**	

Notes

Author's Note

1. Appendix A reproduces Christopher Bassnett's prefatory letter to Bryan Blundell; the full sermon is available online via the Internet Archive. See: Bassnett, Christopher – *The Seaman's Character and Calling Consider'd and Improv'd* (London, 1712), sermon preached 13 December 1711, published 1712.
2. Rates of pay in the late seventeenth century broadly estimated using: Rodger, N.A.M. – *The Command of the Ocean: A Naval History of Britain, 1649–1815* (London: Penguin Books, 2004), pp.618–623.

Chapter 1

1. Before the first dock opened, Liverpool's larger ships anchored in the river and discharged by "lighters"; sailing barges that carried goods through the shallows to the quays at the haven and the mouth of the Pool. Stammers identifies this stretch, from St Nicholas Church to the Pool's entrance, as the town's early anchorage. By 1711, Blundell's vessels were regularly unloading cargo at Hoyle Lake ("Hoylake," as it is called today). See M.K. Stammers, *"Ships and Port Management at Liverpool before the Opening of the First Dock in 1715," Transactions of the Historic Society of Lancashire and Cheshire*, 156 (2007), pp. 32–33, 41–45.
2. "a fairly good consignment in those days": Touzeau, James – *The Rise and Progress of Liverpool From 1551 to 1835* (1910); p.221.
3. See Appendix C – *Tree 1* – William Blundell (1628–1688).
4. The description of Liverpool in the 1640's drawn from: Touzeau, *Rise and Progress*, Section II, pp.220–233.
5. Ibid.
6. Ibid.
7. "lathed and tiered over with lime and hair, and made handsome above, at the town's expense": Touzeau, *Rise and Progress*, Section II, p.243.
8. Detail of early street lighting in Liverpool drawn from: Ibid, p.243.
9. For further detail on Liverpool Castle see: Picton, *Memorials of Liverpool: Historical and Topographical.* Vol. 1 (Longmans, 1873).
10. Peet, Henry – *St Nicholas's Church, Liverpool: Its Architectural History*. (Transactions of the Historic Society of Lancashire and Cheshire, vol. 65, 1913).
11. Liverpool's population figure is estimated from freemen's rolls, parish records, and hearth tax returns. While some reconstructions give lower totals, these often exclude dependents, servants, and women, leading to significant undercounts. See: *The Port of Liverpool in the Seventeenth Century, Transactions of the Historic Society of Lancashire and Cheshire*, Vol. 103 (1951).
12. Touzeau, *Rise and Progress*, p.221.

13. Ibid.
14. For further details on the Navigation Acts, see: Farnell, J.E – The Navigation Act of 1651, the First Dutch War, and the London Merchant Community. *Economic History Review* 16, no. 3 (1964).
15. Owned by William the Blundell "The Cavalier" (1620–1698); likely distantly related to William Blundell (1628–1688).
16. By the mid-1660s, muscovado sugar accounted for nearly 80 per cent of Barbados's sugar-related exports by value. In 1665–1666, muscovado made up 79.3 per cent of such exports, compared with 1.5 per cent for molasses and 6.2 per cent for rum. Eltis, David, The Total Product of Barbados, 1664–1701, *The Journal of Economic History* 55, no. 2 (June 1995): pp.321–338, esp. p.322.
17. Power, Michael – *Creating a Port: Liverpool 1695–1715, Transactions of the Historic Society of Lancashire and Cheshire*, vol. 149 (2000).
18. Ibid.
19. "a house for boiling and drying sugar…": Picton, *Memorials*, p.111; and Muir, Ramsay. *A History of Liverpool*. 2nd ed. London: Williams & Norgate, 1907, pp.138–139.
20. "If this be once done…": Ibid.
21. "divers eminent merchants…": Richard – *Britannia: A Geographical Description of Great Britain and Ireland*. London, 1673, p.134.
22. Wardle, A.R. "Liverpool's Early Customs Collectors." *Transactions of the Historic Society of Lancashire and Cheshire*, p.45.
23. An inventory taken at his death confirms William Blundell was a mariner and shipowner: among his possessions were an anchor, ropes, and rigging. Hignett, Harry – "Liverpool Nautical Research Society Bulletin, Vol. 34, No. 1, Summer 1990," *Liverpool Nautical Research Society Bulletin*, vol. 34 (1990), p.48.
24. Mary Preeson (1636–1720) was the daughter of Thomas Preeson (1610–1685). See: Appendix C – Tree 2: The Preeson Family.
25. Alderman Thomas Preeson built the first house along the edge of Castle Ditch in the seventeenth century. The street that later emerged on the site was named as Preeson's Row in his honour. See Muir, *History of Liverpool*, p.140, and Appendix C – Tree 2.
26. Bryan Blundell (1674–1756) was named after his grandfather, Bryan Blundell the elder (1600–1633), a mariner and merchant active in early seventeenth century Liverpool. See: Hignett, "*Bulletin*", p.48.
27. On Monday, 2 June 1687, William Blundell of Liverpool, mariner, was given a permanent seat in St Nicholas Church, recorded in the indenture between the mayor and aldermen of the borough and Blundell. See Henry Peet, *Abstracts of Deeds Relating to the Sale of Pews in St Nicholas's Church, Liverpool, Transactions of the Historic Society of Lancashire and Cheshire*, vol. 64 (1912), pp.215–216.

Chapter 2

1. Description drawn from: Picton, *Memorials*, p.60.
2. "the great waters": Bassnett, *Seaman's Character*.
3. "bred to the sea": the term was commonly used in British maritime culture from the seventeenth century onward, referring to boys raised for a life at sea.
4. See Manwaring, G.E., "The Dress of the British Seaman," *The Mariner's Mirror* 9, no. 6 (1923): pp.162–173, for a survey of seamen's attire, including slops and caps, and the mixture of official issue and informal supply in the early modern period. See also Kemp,

Peter, *The Oxford Companion to Ships and the Sea* (Oxford: Oxford University Press, 1976), p.742, on coats, breeches, and the protective use of tar in seamen's clothing.

5. The Golden Fleece Inn on Dale Street was mentioned by the diarist Nicholas Blundell in 1706. Blundell, Nicholas – *Crosby Records: Blundell's Diary, Comprising Selections from the Diary of Nicholas Blundell, Esq., from 1702–1728* – edited by T.E. Gibson, Liverpool: G.G. Walmsley, 1895, p.38 and p.127.
6. Bryan Blundell's inheritance from Alderman Thomas Preeson drawn from: Blundell, *Journal* (trans. Hignett), p.ii; Archdeaconry of Chester Probate Records, Will of Thomas Preeson (1610–1685), proved 9 July 1685, LARO WCW/Supra/C245A/19. Also see: Appendix C, Tree 2: The Preeson Family.
7. Bryan Blundell kept an extensive journal, which has been preserved in the Lancashire Record Office – *The Journal of Bryan Blundell* (1674–1756). Unless otherwise specified, all diary quotes are taken from the transcription of Bryan Blundell's journal by Harry Hignett (1991). Cited throughout as: Blundell, *Journal* (trans. Hignett). Specific diary entries are referenced by date only: Blundell, *Journal*, [date].
8. "youthful, deliberate round hand": Bryan Blundell's writing progression is drawn from Harry Hignett's introduction to Blundell's journal. Blundell, *Journal* (trans. Hignett), p.iii.
9. "The wind ruled supreme, without a rival…": from: Aspinall, James – *Liverpool A Few Years Since: By An Old Stager* (1869).
10. For further details on Liverpool's privateers and the techniques used, see: Williams, *Liverpool Privateers*.
11. "wooden world": Rodger, N.A.M. *The Wooden World: An Anatomy of the Georgian Navy*. Annapolis, MD: Naval Institute Press, 1986.
12. Average voyage duration drawn from: Blundell, *Journal* (trans. Hignett), 1991, p.i.
13. Typical voyage detail drawn from: Ibid.
14. Detail on the bilge drawn from: Crow, Hugh – *Memoirs of the Late Captain Hugh Crow* (1830), pp.3–4; and Kemp, *Oxford Companion*, pp.82–83 – "Bilge Water".
15. "…I for one was very sea-sick the greater part of the time": From Crow, *Memoirs*, pp.3–4.
16. "The ship being leaky I was kept almost constantly at the pumps": Ibid.
17. For conditions on board ship and experiences of extreme thirst see: Stanfield, James Field – *Observations on a Guinea Voyage* (1788), p.56; and Crow, *Memoirs* (1830).
18. For more on sea rations and life aboard see: Royal Museums Greenwich – *Life at Sea in the Age of Sail, rmg.co.uk.* For a description of ship's biscuit, see *Kemp, Oxford Companion*, p.85 – "Biscuit".
19. Descriptions of shipboard provisions and their deterioration are drawn from contemporary accounts, including Dampier, William – *A New Voyage Round the World* (London: James Knapton, 1697); and Crow, *Memoirs* (1830). Also see: Royal Museums Greenwich – *Age of Sail.*
20. For further information on disease and illness at sea, see: Royal Museums Greenwich – *Age of Sail.*
21. For further detail see: Bray, R.S. – *Armies of Pestilence: The Impact of Disease on History* (Cambridge: James Clarke & Co., 2004).
22. Captain William Hutchinson (1715–1801) was a respected Liverpool mariner, dockmaster, and early scientific observer of tides and weather. His later publications helped improve navigation and harbour management. In his *Treatise on Practical Seamanship* (1777),

Hutchinson drew on decades of firsthand experience to document both the challenges of sailing and the practices that shaped maritime discipline.

23. "abused and ill-used": Hutchinson, *Practical Seamanship*; footnote p.300.
24. For conditions on board ship and cruelty at sea, see: William, Gomer, *History of the Liverpool Privateers and Letters of Marque with an Account of the Liverpool Slave Trade* (1884); Dampier, *New Voyage*; and Hutchinson, *Practical Seamanship*. Also see: Crow, *Memoirs* (1830) for conditions aboard slave ships; and Grann, David – *The Wager* (Doubleday, 2023), for the sufferings of naval crews.
25. Ibid.
26. Ibid.
27. Some of the imagery in this section is drawn from a sermon preached in Liverpool in 1711 by Christopher Bassnett, addressed to Bryan Blundell and the crew of the *Cleveland*. Bassnett described the Atlantic in vivid, providential terms. Of fair weather he wrote that "sometimes the Sea is bright and smooth, and clear; and affords very delicate and entertaining Prospects," and remarked that on Blundell's most recent voyage "God shone and smil'd upon you in a Manner all the Way." He also marvelled at "the wonders of the deep", its tides, its creatures, and its properties. See: Bassnett, *Seaman's Character*.

Chapter 3

1. Blundell, *Journal*. The month of arrival is not recorded in his journal and has been inferred from his departure from Liverpool on Wednesday, 30 November 1687 (Blundell, *Journal*).
2. Description of arrival in Barbados drawn from: Ligon, Richard – *A True and Exact History of the Island of Barbados* (London: Humphrey Moseley, 1657), pp.20–22.
3. Ibid. At the time, the settlement was officially styled "St Michael's Towne," though "Bridgetown" was already the common name. The name derived from the "Indian Bridge," a crude structure built by the island's Indigenous inhabitants across the Careenage, the tidal inlet that bisects the town. Ligon, *History of Barbados*, p.25.
4. Ibid.
5. "such great drunkards": Larry Gragg, *The Pious and the Profane: The Religious Life of Early Barbados Planters, The Historian* 62, no. 2 (2000): p.270. Contemporary observers frequently criticised Barbadian planters for quarrelsome behaviour, ostentation, and excessive drinking.
6. Richard Ligon, writing in 1657, listed indigo, cotton, tobacco, sugar, ginger, and fustic-wood among Barbados's principal exports. By the late seventeenth century, sugar dominated, though cotton and ginger continued in smaller quantities. Ligon, *History of Barbados*, pp.22–24.
7. Hutchinson, *Practical Seamanship*, pp.24–36.
8. For Barbados population estimates see: Beckles, Hilary – "*The 'Hub of Empire': The Caribbean and Britain in the Seventeenth Century*," in Canny, Nicholas (ed.) – *The Oxford History of the British Empire, Vol. I: The Origins of Empire* (Oxford: Oxford University Press, 2001), p.238. By 1684, Barbados held 46,502 enslaved Africans and 19,568 white settlers. In 1680, over half the arable land was controlled by 175 large planters, each employing at least 60 enslaved workers.
9. Description of slave markets drawn from: Sadler, Nigel – *The Slave Trade* (Shire Publications, 2009), pp.19–21; Radburn, Nick – *HIST241: The Trans-Atlantic Slave Trade, 1500–1865* (2018); Crow, *Memoirs* (1830), p.220; Tibbles, Anthony – *Liverpool*

and the Slave Trade (Liverpool: National Museums Liverpool, 1994); and Equiano, Olaudah, *The Interesting Narrative of the Life of Olaudah Equiano* (1789), p.86–87.

10. Ibid.
11. Sadler, Nigel. *The Slave Trade*. Shire Publications, 2009, p.19.
12. Description of the scramble from: Equiano, *Interesting Narrative*, p.86. Also see: Williams, *Liverpool Privateers*, p.591; and Rediker, Marcus – *The Slave Ship: A Human History* (London: John Murray, 2007). Scrambles might have taken place in a merchant's yard, or even on board the arriving ship.
13. "On a signal given (as the beat of a drum)...": Equiano, *Interesting Narrative*, p.86.
14. "With the ferocity of brutes": Williams, *Liverpool Privateers*, p.591.
15. "The noise and clamour": Equiano, *Interesting Narrative*, p.86.
16. "Seasoned": quote and description drawn from: Sadler, Nigel – *The Slave Trade*. Shire Publications, 2009, p.25.
17. For further information see: Sadler, Nigel – *The Slave Trade*. Shire Publications, 2009; Radburn, Nick, *HIST241: The Trans-Atlantic Slave Trade, 1500–1865*; Rediker, *The Slave Ship*; and Williams, *Liverpool Privateers*.
18. Handler, Jerome S. "Plantation Slave Settlements in Barbados, 1650s to 1834." In *In the Shadow of the Plantation: Caribbean History and Legacy*, edited by Bridget Brereton, Kingston: Ian Randle Publishers, 2002, pp.123–127; and Ligon, *History of Barbados*, p.21.
19. Ligon, *History of Barbados* pp.22–23; and Tibbles, *Liverpool and the Slave Trade*.
20. "appoint them moderate work...": Newton, John. In 1751, Newton, then serving aboard a slave ship, recorded his conversation in Antigua with a plantation owner. He later became an Anglican cleric and abolitionist, best known for writing *Amazing Grace*. Newton, John. *Thoughts Upon the African Slave Trade*. London: Printed for J. Buckland, Pater-Noster Row; and J. Johnson, St Paul's Church-yard, 1788, pp.38–39.
21. "with all possible exactness": Ibid.
22. The Barbados Slave Code of 1661 was the first comprehensive slave law in the English colonies and served as a model for similar legislation across the Caribbean and American South.
23. Blundell, *Journal* (trans. Hignett), p.iv.
24. The Pool of London, the stretch of the Thames between London Bridge and Wapping, was the principal anchorage for sea-going vessels during the seventeenth and eighteenth centuries. For further information see: *Survey of London*, Vol. 15: All Hallows, Barking-by-the-Tower (London County Council, 1934).
25. Ibid.
26. For details of Bryan Blundell's children and family see: Appendix C – *Tree 1: The Blundell Family*.
27. The Reverend Robert Styth served as Rector of St Nicholas Church until his death in 1714. Styth and Blundell would later co-found the Liverpool Blue Coat School in 1708. Their collaboration is explored further in Chapter 15.
28. For further details see: Trevelyan, G.M. *The Glorious Revolution 1688–1689*. Longmans, 1938.
29. The term "Jacobite" derives from "Jacobus," the Latin form of James. It referred to supporters of James II and his descendants, who sought to restore the Stuart line to the throne after James's removal in the Glorious Revolution of 1688.

30. For further details see: The Museum of The Queen's Royal Hussars (qrhmuseum.com) – *The Siege of Londonderry.*
31. Ibid.
32. Henty, G.A., *British Battles on Land and Sea*, Vol. 1 (London: Cassell, Petter & Galpin, 1873), p.399.
33. The *Audit Accounts* for 1691–1692 record widespread public festivities as troops finally returned in May 1691. Touzeau, *Rise and Progress*, pp.336–337.
34. This line appears in Liverpool's audit accounts from May 1694, recording expenditures for festivities marking King William III's return from Holland. These included payments for punch, ale, gunpowder, and bonfires around the Exchange, as well as drink for soldiers and celebratory bell-ringing. The wider context likely included celebrations of William's safe return after campaigns in Ireland, notably following the Siege of Derry (1689) and the later Treaty of Limerick (1691), which secured Protestant control. Ibid.
35. Muir, *History of Liverpool*, pp.145–146.
36. Ibid.
37. Muir, *History of Liverpool*, pp.162–163.
38. Muir, *History of Liverpool*, pp.145–146.
39. For further details see: Pincus, Steven C.A. *1688: The First Modern Revolution.* New Haven: Yale University Press, 2009: Chapter 13. Revolution in the Church.
40. Nine Years' War (1688–1697): Also known as the War of the Grand Alliance, it was fought between France under Louis XIV and a coalition including England, the Dutch Republic, Spain, and the Holy Roman Empire. The conflict marked a major effort to check French expansion in Europe.

Chapter 4

1. Blundell, *Journal*, Monday, 6 November 1690.
2. In his journal Blundell records the stop as "Piel de Foudre," a contemporary spelling of Piel (or Pile) of Fouldrey, the tidal island and castle that guarded the approaches to Morecambe Bay.
3. This passage draws partial inspiration from dialogue in Elizabeth: The Golden Age, screenplay by William Nicholson and Michael Hirst (2007)
4. Blundell, *Journal*, Friday, 6 February 1691: "it bore West 5 degrees southerly from us distant about 6 leagues" (approximately 21 miles).
5. See: *John Smith Explores the Chesapeake*, Captain John Smith National Historic Trail, National Park Service, US Department of the Interior.
6. Whitelaw, Ralph T. – *Virginia's Eastern Shore: A History of Northampton and Accomack Counties* (Richmond: Virginia Historical Society, 1951), p.973.
7. Chesapeake Bay, the largest estuary in the United States, forms a peninsula bounded by the Bay, the Atlantic Ocean, and Delaware Bay. The flat, sandy tract of Virginia's Eastern Shore was known to Indigenous peoples as *Accomac* ("land beyond the water"). Wise, Jennings Cropper – *Ye Kingdome of Accawmache: or, The Eastern Shore of Virginia.* Richmond: Bell Book and Stationery Co., 1911, p.1.
8. Blundell, *Journal*, Wednesday, 14 February 1691.
9. Tobacco was typically harvested between late summer and early autumn, leaving the stalks and stubble in the fields through the winter months.
10. For early descriptions of Chesapeake Bay's approach, depths, and river entrances, see *A Perfect Description of Virginia* (London, 1649); for later accounts of Virginia's mercantile

world around 1700, see Robert Polk Thomsen, *The Merchant in Virginia, 1700–1775* (PhD thesis, University of Wisconsin, 1955); and for descriptions of shipping, river transport, and plantation life in colonial Virginia, see Cerinda W. Evans, *Some Notes on Shipbuilding and Shipping in Colonial Virginia* (Jamestown 350th Anniversary Historical Booklet, no. 22, Williamsburg, 1957).

11. Ibid.
12. Ibid.
13. Ibid.
14. Wise, Jennings Cropper. *Ye Kingdome of Accawmache: or, The Eastern Shore of Virginia.* Richmond: Bell Book and Stationery Co., 1911, pp.2–3.
15. Description of tobacco seasons drawn from Hignett, Harry – Blundell, *Journal* (trans. Hignett), p.v. Also see: Copley, Stephen. "The Bonds of Trade: Commerce and Community in the Liverpool Slave Trade." *Liverpool and Transatlantic Slavery*, eds. David Richardson, Suzanne Schwarz and Anthony Tibbles. Liverpool University Press, 2007.
16. Ibid.
17. Blundell, *Journal* (trans. Hignett), p.v.
18. Ibid.
19. For a description of the merchant's seasons see: Blundell, *Journal* (trans. Hignett), p.iv.
20. Description of shipworms drawn from: Ibid.
21. For details of the Virginian tobacco fleet see: Gray, Stanley – "The British Navy and the Tobacco Trade of Virginia and Maryland," *Proceedings of the U.S. Naval Institute* 62, no. 9 (September 1936). This article draws largely from records at the Public Record Office, the British Museum, and the Bodleian Library. In 1691, during wartime restrictions, the government limited merchant sailings to 300 ships in total, of which 125 were assigned to the Virginia fleet.
22. Ibid.
23. Blundell, *Journal*, Monday, 23 June 1691.
24. Blundell, *Journal*, Thursday, 26 June 1691.
25. Drawn from the journal of Edward Barlow, a mariner whose detailed account of service in King's ships and merchantmen (1659–1703) is one of the richest surviving narratives of life at sea. Barlow, Edward – *Barlow's Journal of his Life at Sea in King's Ships, East & West Indiamen & other Merchantmen from 1659 to 1708*, ed. Basil Lubbock (London: Hurst & Blackett, 1934), pp.60–61.
26. N.A.M. Rodger notes that fewer than one in five sailors could swim. When the *Lichfield* was wrecked, in 1756 only 60 of a ship's company of about 350 survived by swimming: "about the highest proportion that could be hoped for." See N.A.M. Rodger, *The Wooden World: An Anatomy of the Georgian Navy* (Annapolis, MD: Naval Institute Press, 1986), p.53.
27. The Bull, Cow, and Calf Rocks are located off Dursey Island, on the Beara Peninsula, County Cork, Ireland, at the southwestern tip of the island, in the Atlantic Ocean.

Chapter 5

1. Rathlin Sound is the narrow channel between Rathlin Island and the County Antrim coast of Northern Ireland, just north of Ballycastle. Known for its treacherous currents, it marks one of the most exposed parts of the Irish Sea.

2. This section draws on Harry Hignett's own commentary in: Blundell, *Journal* (trans. Hignett), where Hignett describes Blundell's navigational tools and practices, p.iv.
3. Ibid.
4. "The lodestone carries such a mystery…": from Bassnett, *Seaman's Character*.
5. Detail on speed and distance in this section have been drawn from: Hutchinson, *Practical Seamanship*, pp.109–112. Hutchinson measured 50 feet per knot, slightly longer than the 47 feet later used in Admiralty tables.
6. Ibid.; and Kemp, *Oxford Companion*, p.457 – "Knot".
7. Robinson, John, and George Francis Dow. *The Sailing Ships of New England, 1607–1907;* pp.50–55.
8. Ibid.
9. Information on "Dead Reckoning" drawn from: Kemp, *Oxford Companion*, p.234.
10. Blundell, *Journal* (trans. Hignett), p.iv.
11. Detail on the use of the lead line for soundings and sailing by the stars drawn from: Hutchinson, *Practical Seamanship*, pp.77–79 and pp.91–92.
12. Detail on sailors' weather-reading practices drawn from: Hutchinson, *Practical Seamanship*, pp.189–191.
13. Description of the three Ls (Lead, Latitude and Lookout) drawn from: Hutchinson, *Practical Seamanship*, p.77.
14. Blundell, *Journal*, 15 December 1692: "this day at 10 at night we made the island of Désirade and it bore W by N from us distance 4 leagues. It makes at this bearing to have a high point at the southward end and a low dome under that. The northern end is lower with the point sloping a pretty length and from this island we steered away west and W by N."
15. Descriptions of Montserrat's terrain and trade are based on contemporary maps and late seventeenth-century colonial accounts of the Lesser Antilles. By 1700, there were at least 48 sugar estates on the island. Its small size, steep terrain, and limited harbour facilities constrained large-scale development, but planters adapted by establishing compact, diverse estates across the landscape. For further details see: Ryzewski, Krysta, and John F. Cherry – *Struggles of a Sugar Society: Surveying PlantationEra Montserrat, 1650–1850.* International Journal of Historical Archaeology 19 (2015), pp.364–366.
16. Blundell, *Journal*, Friday, 16 December 1692.
17. Ibid.
18. Blundell, *Journal*, Wednesday, 16 August 1693.
19. Blundell, *Journal*, August 1693: "I cleared this with my small venture and upwards £50, the ship was to be sheathed and Mr. Webster would not have me stay till she was done and so put her off, but my friends and the rest of my owners persuaded me to go second master with him, which I did."
20. Blundell, *Journal*, Wednesday, 16 August 1693.
21. Blundell, *Journal*, Wednesday, 5 December 1693.
22. Rappahannock River: a major river of eastern Virginia, rising in the Blue Ridge Mountains and flowing southeast for 195 miles before emptying into the Chesapeake Bay.
23. The town of "Hobb's Hole" was renamed Tappahannock in 1705, from an Algonquian word meaning "the town on the rise and fall of water." See: "*Town History,*" Essex County, Virginia (Essex County Board of Supervisors, 2013, archived version consulted).
24. Blundell, *Journal*, Thursday, 10 May 1694.
25. Blundell, *Journal*, Sunday, 13 May 1694.

26. Blundell, *Journal*, Wednesday, 27 June.
27. "finest shallop racer…": Williams, *Liverpool Privateers*, p.144.
28. Ibid.
29. "Without so much as adjusting the mast, sails, or rigging…": Ibid.
30. Blundell, *Journal*, Monday, 4 February 1695.
31. Blundell, *Journal*. Sighting Cape Henry on Friday, 8 February 1695.
32. Blundell, *Journal*, Monday, 17 June 1695.
33. Blundell, *Journal*. Incident recorded on Tuesday, 16 July 1695.
34. Blundell, *Journal*, Sunday, 28 July 1695.
35. Hartland Point is a prominent headland on the northwest coast of Devon, where the Bristol Channel meets the Atlantic Ocean.
36. Blundell, *Journal*, Wednesday, 31 July 1695.
37. Jonathan Livesley (1653–1719), sometimes spelled *Leivesley*, later became Bryan Blundell's father-in-law following Bryan's marriage to Elizabeth Livesley in 1708. See: Appendix C – *Tree 1: The Blundell Family*.
38. Blundell, *Journal*. Departure from Dublin on Tuesday, 4 February 1696.
39. "Magee Island" (now *Islandmagee*) is a peninsula on the east coast of County Antrim, Northern Ireland, located between Larne Lough and the North Channel. In the seventeenth century, it was often referred to as an island due to its separation from the mainland by water on three sides.
40. Blundell, *Journal*. Arrival in the Potomac River on Saturday, 4 April 1696.
41. Samuela Williamson (1672–1704). See: Appendix C – *Tree 3: The Williamson Family*.
42. In 1651, Edward Williamson (1589–1669) presented an oak chest to St Nicholas Church in Liverpool. The chest was later rediscovered in Ladykirk Church, Berwickshire, in the late nineteenth century. It bears both the arms of the Williamson family and those of the Blundells of Ince, a prominent recusant gentry branch of the wider Blundell family. The presence of both heraldic devices suggests a marital connection between Edward Williamson and the Blundells of Ince. Bryan Blundell himself was likely a distant relative through his grandfather. Bygone Liverpool (wordpress.com) – *Mystery of the Ladykirk Oak Chest*.
43. William Preeson (1633–1698) – Mayor of Liverpool (1696–1697). See: *Liverpool City Halls, "Mayor / Lord Mayors of the City of Liverpool Since 1207," Civic Honours List*. Also see: Appendix C – *Tree 2: The Preeson Family*.
44. William Preeson also owned a plantation in Virginia, though he does not appear to have lived there. He purchased the land in 1682, and it later passed to his son Thomas in 1705, following William's death in 1698. *Peninsula Enterprise* (Accomac, VA), 18 June 1937.

Chapter 6

1. Blundell, *Journal* (trans. Hignett), p.68.
2. Kemp, *Oxford Companion*, p.126 – "Great Cabin".
3. The *Mulberry* was likely of Dutch origin, identifiable by the square loading hatch on the starboard quarter, a design used by Dutch Baltic traders to load long planks of timber. Vessels of this type were frequently captured and sold during or after the Anglo-Dutch Wars. Explanation drawn from: Blundell, *Journal* (trans. Hignett), p.iv.
4. Thomas Preeson was born in Liverpool in June 1668. In later years he would expand the family's tobacco interests in Virginia and died there in 1723. See: Ibid.; and Appendix C – *Tree 2: The Preeson Family*.

5. For further detail on trading in Virginia, see: Thomsen, *The Merchant in Virginia*; and Refford, Brian W. – *The Bonds of Trade: Commerce and Community in the Liverpool Slave Trade, 1695–1775* (San Diego: University Readers, 2008).
6. Blundell, *Journal*. Arrival on Friday, 26 March 1697.
7. Pungoteague and Nassawaddocks were small trading settlements on Virginia's Eastern Shore, located in Accomack County. In the colonial period, both served as minor ports for tobacco shipment and coastal trade.
8. Lundy is a small granite island in the Bristol Channel, approximately 12 miles off the coast of Devon. Though remote, it was strategically significant in the seventeenth and eighteenth centuries, serving at times as a haven for pirates and privateers. For further details see: *The Landmark Trust*, "Lundy – History."
9. Hannah Blundell (1697–1731). See: Appendix C – *Tree 1: The Blundell Family.*
10. For details on child mortality in the seventeenth century, see: Wrigley, E.A., Davies, R.S., Oeppen, J.E., and Schofield, R.S., *English Population History from Family Reconstitution* (Cambridge: Cambridge University Press, 1997).
11. For detail on the role of "credit" in the later eighteenth century slave trade, see: Copley, Stephen. "The Bonds of Trade: Commerce and Community in the Liverpool Slave Trade." *Liverpool and Transatlantic Slavery*, eds. David Richardson, Suzanne Schwarz and Tibbles, *Liverpool and the Slave Trade*, pp.32–33.
12. Ibid.
13. Hockedy, Doreen M. – *Bound for a New World: Emigration of Indentured Servants via Liverpool to America and the West Indies, 1697–1707*, p.116.
14. Blundell, *Journal*, Saturday, 3 July 1697.
15. Hockedy, *Bound for a New World*, pp.122–124.
16. Ibid.
17. The Grand Alliance was a coalition formed in 1689 to oppose the expansionist policies of Louis XIV of France. It included England, the Dutch Republic, the Holy Roman Empire, and later Spain, among others. The Alliance sought to preserve the balance of power in Europe during the Nine Years' War (1688–1697).
18. For detail on The Treaty of Ryswick, see: Lynn, John A., *The Wars of Louis XIV, 1667–1714* (London: Longman, 1999).
19. Blundell, *Journal*. Records their arrival on Saturday, 8 January 1698.
20. Blundell, *Journal*, May 1698.
21. Blundell, *Journal*. Records their return to Liverpool on Friday, 17 June 1698.
22. Blundell, *Journal*. Records their departure on Thursday, 13 October 1698.
23. Walter Brice (1665–1727) married Bryan Blundell's cousin, Hannah Preeson (1675–1698). See: Appendix C – *Tree 2: The Preeson Family.*
24. Blundell, *Journal*, Friday, 4 November 1698.
25. Blundell, *Journal*, Sunday, 18 December 1698.
26. Blundell, *Journal*. Records the "cook's boy" incident on Tuesday, 3 January 1699.
27. Blundell, *Journal*, Tuesday, 18 January 1699: "Had 11 weeks passage and very bad weather. The 19th day we got to our loading place and found tobacco dear at £14 per hogshead."

Interlude: On the Edge of a Century, 1700

1. By the end of the seventeenth century, Liverpool's population had reached over 5,000, with 102 registered vessels totalling 8,619 tons. Picton, *Memorials*, p.147. It was said

that by 1700 Liverpool supplied all the tobacco for Ireland, Scotland, and the north of England. Muir, *History of Liverpool*, p.139.

2. Liverpool's elevation to parish status came in 1699 following a successful petition by the town's Corporation, seeking independence from the parish of Walton-on-the-Hill. As part of its petition for its own parish, the Corporation lamented that "but one chapel… doth not contain one-half of our inhabitants," and that those travelling to Walton "drink in the said village… by which and otherwise many youth and sundry families are ruined." *Picton, Memorials*, pp.145–146.
3. Ibid.
4. Number of vessels in Liverpool in 1700 from: Picton, *Memorials*, p.147.

Chapter 7

1. Blundell, *Journal*, Friday, 19 December 1701: "I, not being well this day or two, have this day bled and sweated." He does not specify the location, though at the time the ship was anchored off Nevis, where disease ashore often led captains and crews to remain aboard their ships.
2. Blundell, *Journal*. Arrival on the evening of Monday, 8 January 1700.
3. Blundell, *Journal*, Monday, 3 June 1700.
4. The *Liverpool Merchant* is widely recorded as the first Liverpool ship to engage in the transatlantic slave trade, departing for Africa in 1700. It was owned by William Clayton (1660–1715) and John Earle. See: "*Liverpool Merchant*" (voyage ID 15122) – Slavevoyages.org – *Trans-Atlantic Slave Trade Database.*
5. Liverpool City Halls. *Mayor / Lord Mayors of the City of Liverpool Since 1207*. Civic Honours List.
6. Blundell, *Journal*, Friday, 22 November 1700.
7. Blundell, *Journal*, Wednesday, 16 July 1701.
8. For further details see: Frey, Linda and Frey, Marsha – *The Treaties of the War of the Spanish Succession: An Historical and Critical Dictionary* (Greenwood Press, 1995).
9. William Bassnett (1672–1731) was John Pemberton's (1666–1743) brother-in-law. See Appendix C – *Tree 5: The Bassnett Family*.
10. Blundell, *Journal* (trans. Hignett), p.68.
11. John Cleveland (1661–1716) was a Liverpool alderman, Mayor of Liverpool (1703–1704), and Tory MP for the borough (1710–1713). A prominent tobacco importer and merchant, he also invested in sugar and rock salt and acquired the manor of Birkenhead in 1700. In this book, he is referred to as *Cleveland*, reflecting the more common modern spelling, though contemporary records show some variation. See: Hayton, D., Cruickshanks, E., and Handley, S. (eds.), *The History of Parliament: The House of Commons 1690–1715* (Woodbridge: Boydell and Brewer, 2002), biography of John Cleiveland (hereafter cited as, *Cleveland*). Also see: *Liverpool City Halls, "Mayor / Lord Mayors of the City of Liverpool Since 1207," Civic Honours List.*
12. Blundell, *Journal*, records that they set sail on Thursday, 24 September 1701.
13. Blundell, *Journal*, Tuesday, 11 November 1701.
14. Blundell, *Journal*, Wednesday, 2 December 1701: "At 6 we put our men ashore at Oistins and lay for our boat till 8. At 8 we set sail and at 10 we came to anchor in the Road." Likely Carlisle Bay, Bridgetown.
15. Blundell, *Journal*, Saturday, 5 December 1691: "Here I must give 6d per ton for it, if I have any," he wrote, "so that I concluded to sell no more here and just what would buy us rum and get it aboard."

16. Detail on rum rations drawn from: Royal Museums Greenwich, *"A Rum Deal: The Origins of Nelson's Blood,"* published 13 October 2015, Royal Museums Greenwich.
17. For further detail on the behaviour and religious life of Barbados planters, see: Gragg, Larry – *The Pious and the Profane: The Religious Life of Early Barbados Planters, The Historian* 62, no. 2 (2000): pp.265–283.
18. Ibid.
19. Blundell, *Journal*, Friday, 11 December 1701.
20. "Nevis" – *Encyclopedia Britannica.*
21. The Leeward Islands operated as a federated colony: a governor-general presided over Antigua, Nevis, St Kitts, and Montserrat, while each island had its own lieutenant-governor, council, assembly, and laws. On Nevis the lieutenant-governor in 1701 was Roger Elrington; he was killed in 1702 after a quarrel with Captain David Chambers of a Queen's man-of-war. See: Qing, Qianwen – *Conflict and Scandal in the British Caribbean, 1680–1720*, p.138.
22. As described by Governor John Hart, who arrived in the West Indies in 1721. Hart explained that the wealthiest and best-educated landowners often lived in England, and those who remained on Nevis were "most obstinate and perverse in their nature and manner". Burns, Sir Alan – *History of the British West Indies* (London: George Allen & Unwin, 1954), p.457, citing *Calendar of State Papers, Colonial, America and West Indies*, 1722–1723, nos. 220 and 417.
23. Soloman Israel Senior (1660–1734). By 1707 Solomon Israel's prominence on Nevis was firmly established. The island census recorded his as the largest Jewish household, comprising family members and thirteen enslaved people. He also played a public role in legal affairs, serving as a jury foreman and as executor for Christian friends. Stern, Malcolm H. – "Some Notes on the Jews of Nevis," *American Jewish Archives* 11, no. 2 (1959): pp.121–134.
24. For further details on Solomon Israel, see: *The Mountravers Plantation Community: Part 2, Chapter 1*. Nevis Heritage Project, pp.60–63 and pp.79–80. Also see: Terrell, Michelle M. – *The Jewish Community of Early Colonial Nevis*. PhD thesis, University of Rochester.
25. Likely Martinique, Guadeloupe, and Marie-Galante.
26. Although European medicine was undergoing rapid change in the seventeenth century, bloodletting did not immediately fall out of use. By the end of the century it had even regained authority, promoted by leading mechanistic physicians and influential teachers such as Herman Boerhaave. For further detail on bleeding and sweating, see: Harrison, Mark – *Medicine in an Age of Commerce and Empire: Britain and Its Tropical Colonies, 1660–1830*. Oxford: Oxford University Press, 2010, pp.121–130 and pp.183–184.
27. Ibid.
28. Blundell, *Journal*, Friday, 19 December 1701.
29. Blundell, *Journal*, Tuesday, 23 December 1701.

Chapter 8

1. Blundell, *Journal*. Records a complex sequence of transactions: at Suggett's Point he bought about 70 hogsheads, followed by 85 more (10 hogsheads on the 12 March, 60 on the 15th, and 15 on the 16th. At Occoquan, in early March, he purchased 33 hogsheads, and later at Rappahannock, in April, he added 91 more, bringing his tally to roughly 150 hogsheads in all. See: Blundell, *Journal*, 1702.

2. An embargo on outward-bound vessels was first proclaimed on 17 September 1701, requiring ships to sail only under the protection of royal convoys: "His Majesties ships, *Lincoln* and *Shoreham,* ordered to act as convoys to ships outward bound; also laying an embargo upon all outward bound vessels, requiring them to sail under convoy" (*Calendar of State Papers, Colonial Series, America and West Indies, 1652–1781*, ed. Cecil Headlam, London: H.M. Stationery Office, 1910, p.75). The measure was reinforced in Virginia the following spring. On 28 May 1702 the council ordered that masters of ships under embargo give bond at the naval office where their vessels lay, binding them to remain until formally cleared to depart (Ibid, p.80).
3. The £2,000 bond acted as a legal surety, payable only if Blundell was caught violating the embargo or sailing without permission. Since he slipped past the Royal Navy unnoticed, no claim was made against the bond and no penalty enforced.
4. Blundell, *Journal,* Thursday, 9 July 1702.
5. Blundell, *Journal,* Thursday, 5 October 1702.
6. Blundell included illustrations of the "Table of Pines" in his journal. This almost certainly referred to the dense stands of tall pine trees that marked the entrance to the Chesapeake Bay. Early explorers such as John Smith described the region as rich in towering forests of pine, oak, and hickory, with little undergrowth and an abundance of wildlife. These wooded headlands provided not only natural shelter but also important visual cues for navigation. See: *John Smith Explores the Chesapeake, NPS, Captain John Smith Trail.*
7. Blundell, *Journal,* Wednesday, 26 May 1703.
8. Clowes, William Laird – *The Royal Navy: A History from the Earliest Times to the Present, Vol. II* (London: Sampson Low, Marston and Company, 1898), p.506.
9. The *Foy (Fowey)* was captured by the French squadron heading towards the Virginia fleet. See: Owen, John Hely – *War at Sea under Queen Anne, 1702–1708*, p.107.
10. Blundell attributed the French squadron to Admiral Jean-Baptiste du Casse (1646–1715), however naval records suggest the force off the English Channel that summer was, in fact, commanded by Captain Marc-Antoine de Saint-Pol Hécourt. See: Owen, *War at Sea*, pp.107–110.
11. "lucky fog…": Owen, *War at Sea*, p.109.
12. William Hutchinson later advised trading vessels to make themselves appear "as big, powerful, and warlike as possible, in order to intimidate," while privateers should do precisely the opposite, concealing their strength until the moment of surprise. Hutchinson, *Practical Seamanship*, p.160.

Chapter 9

1. Blundell's journal does not specify his mode of travel. However, overland journeys between the Chesapeake and Delaware in 1706 were almost invariably made on horseback, given the poor state of colonial roads and the absence of established carriage routes.
2. "History of Philadelphia," *Wikipedia.*
3. For background on early Philadelphia and its shipbuilding industry, see: Dorwart, Jeffery M., *"Shipbuilding and Shipyards," Encyclopedia of Greater Philadelphia* (Rutgers University–Camden, 2013); Evans, *Shipbuilding and Shipping in Colonial Virginia*; and "History of Philadelphia," *Wikipedia.*
4. Ibid.
5. In his journal, Blundell referred to his ship variously as *Clieveland, Cleiveland,* and *Cleveland,* reflecting the inconsistent orthography of the early eighteenth century. The

vessel was named after John Cleveland, a figure whose surname was also spelled in different ways in contemporary documents. In this book, "*Cleveland*" is used throughout for clarity and consistency.

6. By 1720, at least a dozen private yards operated along the Delaware, producing brigs, sloops, and coastal traders of up to three hundred tons. See: Evans, *Shipbuilding and Shipping in Colonial Virginia*; and Dorwart, *Shipbuilding and Shipyards*.
7. For further details, see: Ibid.
8. Ralph Williamson (1673–1736). See Appendix C – *Tree 3: The Williamson Family*.
9. The *Hazardous*, once the French *Hasardeux*, had been captured in 1703 and pressed into British service. On 19 November 1706, as she returned from escorting Blundell's Chesapeake convoy, she was forced ashore in Bracklesham Bay during severe gales and lost. Contemporary salvage recovered 21 guns before the wreck was abandoned in 1707. The site remained unknown for more than 250 years until rediscovered by divers in the 1970s, and it is now a designated protected wreck under Historic England. "The 'Gunnes' of Warship *Hazardous* Prize (1706)," *Historic England Research Magazine*, no. 16 (July 2020); Listing Entry 1000048, *The Hazardous* (formerly *Le Hazardeux*).
10. For details on ships of the line, see: Rif Winfield, *British Warships in the Age of Sail, 1603–1714* (Barnsley: Seaforth Publishing, 2009); and Peter Kemp (ed.), *The Oxford Companion to Ships and the Sea*, p.788, entry: "Ship of the line."
11. Blundell, *Journal*, Thursday, 7 November 1706.
12. Blundell, *Journal*, Thursday, 14 November 1706.
13. Blundell, *Journal*, Monday, 14 January 1707.

Chapter 10

1. Cleveland was Mayor of Liverpool from 1703–1704. See: *Liverpool City Halls, "Mayor / Lord Mayors of the City of Liverpool Since 1207," Civic Honours List.*
2. *Houses of Parliament 1690–1715, John Cleveland.*
3. Blundell, *Journal* (trans. Hignett).
4. Contemporary testimony confirms the advantages of colonial shipbuilding. In 1697 Major Wilson, giving evidence before the Board of Trade, noted that "very good ships were built in Virginia of 300 tons and upwards," with timber of excellent quality and costs far below those in England, though cordage and iron still had to be imported; he added that a cargo of tobacco was often ready for each new launch – See: Evans, *Shipbuilding and Shipping in Colonial Virginia.*
5. Ibid.
6. The *Indian Queen* was owned by Bryan Blundell's brother-in-law, Ralph Williamson. See: Appendix C – *Tree 3: The Williamson Family*.
7. Dorwart, *Shipbuilding and Shipyards*.
8. Blundell, *Journal*, Sunday, 19 June 1707: "Drew 9 feet water abaft and 6 feet forward. She being very thin behind struck very deep so that she stroked the ground pretty heavily with her keel, but went off very well."
9. Whitelaw, *Virginia's Eastern Shore*, pp.1243–1244.
10. Hungars Church, one of the oldest congregations on Virginia's Eastern Shore, stood near the Preeson estate at Nassawadox. The present church, built around 1750, is not the building Bryan likely visited; the earlier structure lay about half a mile away. In 1751 Thomas Preeson Jr. donated land for the current church in return for a pew marked with his initials, *T.P.* 1751. Blundell, *Journal* (trans. Hignett), p.v.

11. See: Appendix C – *Tree 3: The Williamson Family.*
12. Hockedy, *Bound for a New World*, pp.122–124.
13. Two years earlier, in 1705, the Virginia Assembly passed a comprehensive slave code that consolidated and extended earlier laws. It defined slavery as a lifelong, hereditary condition, and explicitly tied bondage to race.
14. Crow, *Memoirs* (1830), p.11.
15. Blundell, *Journal*, Saturday, 20 December 1707.
16. Blundell, *Journal*, March 1708. "Had our passage been longer, it had been very hard with us, for our pump-leather had been very short with us."

Chapter 11

1. Blundell, *Journal*, Saturday, 13 August 1709.
2. Elizabeth Livesley (1693–1725). See: Appendix C – *Tree 1: The Blundell Family.*
3. Ibid.
4. Blundell, *Journal*, Tuesday, 7 September 1708.
5. Blundell, *Journal*. Records Frank Ward's death on Friday, 3 December 1708.
6. Muscovite observers sometimes described Archangel as Russia's "gate to the seas." From its relatively humble start, the White Sea port became the chief outlet for Russian exports during the seventeenth century. Kotilaine, Jarmo T. – *Russia's Foreign Trade and Economic Expansion in the Seventeenth Century: Windows on the World* (Leiden: Brill, 2005), Chapter 5.
7. Blundell, *Journal*, Sunday, 17 July 1709.
8. The Minch is the strait separating the northwest Highlands of Scotland from the Outer Hebrides.
9. Blundell, *Journal*, Saturday, 13 August 1709.
10. Kotilaine, *Russia's Foreign Trade and Economic Expansion*, pp.19–20.
11. De Bruyn, Cornelis. *Travels into Muscovy, Persia, and Part of the East-Indies* (London: A. Bettesworth and C. Hitch, 1737), pp.14–17; and Kotilaine, *Russia's Foreign Trade and Economic Expansion*, pp.19–21. Note: De Bruyn's *gagares* were almost certainly loons or divers (*Gavia* spp.), known in Russian as *gagara* (гагара), whose calls were often compared to the human voice. His *teetars* were likely capercaillie (*tetrao urogallus*), a large woodland grouse native to northern Russia.
12. Blundell, *Journal*, Saturday, 13 August 1709.
13. Ibid.
14. Description drawn from: De Bruyn, *Travels into Muscovy*, pp.14–17.
15. Ibid.
16. Description and quote relating to the townspeople of Archangel drawn from: Blundell, *Journal*, Wednesday, 17 August 1709.
17. Blundell, *Journal*, Thursday, 18 August 1709.
18. Kotilaine, *Russia's Foreign Trade and Economic Expansion*, pp.19–20.
19. "Gost" (гость) was a Russian term for a high-ranking or privileged merchant. In Arkhangelsk, the title often referred to the chief customs officer, typically a member of the state-sanctioned merchant elite. See: Hellie, Richard – *Enserfment and Military Change in Muscovy* (University of Chicago Press, 1971), esp. pp.70–71. Tseloval'niki (целова́льники), by contrast, were local oath-sworn officials, usually drawn from lower-ranking merchant guilds or townsmen, who assisted with customs collection, policing, or tax duties under supervision.

20. Kotilaine, *Russia's Foreign Trade and Economic Expansion*, p.21.
21. Blundell, *Journal*, August 1709.
22. In his journal, Blundell anglicised Solombala as "Solingsburg." Ibid.
23. *Britannica: Arkhangelsk* and *Solombala Shipyard* (Wikipedia). It was the main shipyard servicing Arkhangelsk from 1693.
24. Blundell, *Journal*, Tuesday, 23 August 1709.
25. Blundell, *Journal*, Wednesday, 14 September 1709.
26. The Shiant Isles and Tiree are part of the Inner Hebrides, located off Scotland's northwest coast.

Chapter 12

1. Ecclesiastes 9:11, quoted by Christopher Bassnett in his sermon to Bryan Blundell and the crew of the *Cleveland*, Liverpool, 1711.
2. *Hastings* (1707), "a 44-gun fifthrate of the Royal Navy, was launched in 1707, hulked in 1739 and sold in 1744." *Wikipedia: "HMS* Hastings".
3. Blundell, *Journal*, Monday, 30 January 1710.
4. William Hutchinson described how merchant crews were regularly trained aboard ship. Hutchinson, *Practical Seamanship*, pp.172–178.
5. For contemporary instructions on preparing a ship for action, see: Hutchinson, *Practical Seamanship*, esp. pp.227–228, which details the clearing of decks, the lashing of hammocks for protection against musket fire, the rigging of pumps and shot plugs, tubs of water by the guns, and the sanding of decks before combat.
6. Ibid.
7. In eighteenth-century seamanship, "gun tackles" referred to short sets of rope and pulley (block-and-tackle) used to move heavy gear. In gunnery they were fastened to each cannon carriage, allowing a small crew to haul the gun out to the port for firing and bowse it back in again for loading. Hutchinson, *Practical Seamanship*, p.173.
8. Drawn from: Lavery, Brian – *Nelson's Navy: The Ships, Men and Organisation, 1793–1815* (Conway Maritime Press, 1989); Harland, John – *Seamanship in the Age of Sail* (Conway Maritime Press, 1984); and Falconer, William – *An Universal Dictionary of the Marine* (1769).
9. Blundell, *Journal*, Sunday, 23 April 1710.
10. Blundell, *Journal*, Sunday, 14 May 1710.

Chapter 13

1. "Groots" likely here means "groats": hulled grain, usually oats or barley which could be boiled into a coarse porridge or gruel. It was a common item in naval and merchant victualling lists.
2. Blundell, *Journal*, Wednesday, 31 January 1711.
3. Colonel Thoms Maycock was leaving the island for his new English estate, Redland Court. But the foundation of his wealth remained in Barbados, where he owned extensive "slave-property" in the parish of St Lucy, to the island's northwest. His name endures in Maycock's Bay, a stretch of coastline once part of his holdings. His will, proved in 1732, confirmed that his sons, Thomas and John, inherited not only land but enslaved people and plantations on the island. *Legacies of British Slavery project* – University College London: "Thomas Maycock."
4. Blundell, *Journal* (trans. Hignett), p.56.

5. Blundell, *Journal*, entry for Thursday, 1 February 1711: "We have the winds much northerly, little winds, we stand to the northwest. On 1 February we made St Marie and Martinique. We had the Captain of the man-of-war to dinner."
6. Blundell, *Journal*, entry for Friday, 23 February 1711: "...by the 16th day we were in the Latitude of Bermuda 32° 30' N, then had a good wind to the 23rd day at which time we had a storm. Took us aback at night so that we had some trouble to get down our main and fore-yards. The suddenness of it was surprising to Major Howe who had my roundhouse and was not well that it frightened him, so he was never himself rightly afterwards."
7. This passage draws on imagery from a 1711 sermon by Christopher Bassnett, a Liverpool preacher who described the terrors of a ship in storm as both physical ordeal and spiritual metaphor. Bassnett, *Seaman's Character*. See Appendix A.
8. Ibid.
9. Ibid.
10. Blundell, *Journal*, Friday, 13 July 1711.
11. Based on Blundell's later voyages, the cargo likely consisted of beef, herrings, groots (grouts), and firkins of butter.
12. Vardø (also spelled Vardo) is a small, fortified town on the coast of Finnmark in Arctic Norway. It served as a seasonal fishing station and waypoint for northern trade routes, including those to Archangel.
13. Blundell, *Journal*, Tuesday, 11 September 1711.
14. Blundell, *Journal*, Wednesday, 17 October 1711.

Chapter 14

1. Christopher Bassnett (1677–1744), Presbyterian minister of the New Meeting House on Key Street, was a prominent nonconformist figure in early eighteenth-century Liverpool (appointed 1709). The chapel was a setting made possible by the Toleration Act of 1689, which had allowed nonconformist ministers like Bassnett, whose brother William had sailed with Blundell, to preach openly in towns like Liverpool. The chapel was eventually demolished however it was located near present day Church Street and Basnett Street (named after Christopher Bassnett).
2. Though Blundell remained formally within the Church of England, Blundell and the first minister shared a close personal friendship. In 1716, Bassnett played a pivotal role in establishing a school for the free education of poor children in Liverpool and both men would become related by marriage. Material drawn from: Bassnett, *Seaman's Character*. See: Appendix A and Appendix C – *Tree 5: The Bassnett Family*.
3. All quotes in this section are from: Bassnett, *Seaman's Character*.
4. Cooper, Thompson. "Bassnett, Christopher." In *Dictionary of National Biography, 1885–1900, Vol. 3.* (London: Smith, Elder & Co.). Christopher Bassnett's illness is recorded between: 23 March 1711 and 26 January 1712.
5. Blundell, *Journal*, Monday, 17 January 1712 (incorrectly transcribed as March).
6. Blundell, *Journal*, Friday, 28 March 1712.
7. Needham's Fort, later renamed Charles Fort, was the main coastal defence of Carlisle Bay, Barbados, guarding the approaches to Bridgetown.
8. Blundell, *Journal*, Thursday, 29 May 1712.
9. *Panther* was a 50-gun fourth-rate ship of the line launched in 1703. She had been part of Admiral Sir Cloudesley Shovell's fleet during the Scilly naval disaster of October

1707, when 4 ships were lost and nearly 2,000 men drowned. *Panther* survived and remained in service as a convoy escort in the years that followed. HMS *Panther* (1703), Wikipedia; *Scilly naval disaster of 1707*, Wikipedia.

10. Thomas Lace married Dorothy Blundell, Bryan Blundell's sister, in 1704. She was born in 1664 and died in 1727.
11. Blundell, *Journal*, Friday, 11 July 1712.
12. Blundell, *Journal*, Tuesday, 11 July 1712.
13. Blundell, *Journal*, Tuesday 27, January 1713.
14. Blundell, *Journal*, Thursday, 3 April 1713.
15. Blundell, *Journal*. Records reaching the Bar on Tuesday, 28 July.
16. Blundell, *Journal*, Thursday, 30 July 1713.
17. De Bruyn, *Travels into Muscovy*, pp.14–17; and Kotilaine, *Russia's Foreign Trade and Economic Expansion*.
18. "Very nearly equally yoked as to sailing": Here, *yoked* is used figuratively by Blundell to mean *closely matched in sailing ability*. Blundell, *Journal*.
19. The "Island of Sanina" referred to in Blundell's journal is almost certainly Sanna (also recorded as Sanda), the largest island of the Træna group off the coast of Nordland, northern Norway. Variant spellings were common in English maritime records of the period.
20. Blundell, *Journal*, Sunday, 4 October 1713.
21. "Foyal" (also spelled Fial, Fayal, or Fyal) refers to the island of Faial in the Azores.
22. Blundell, *Journal*, Saturday, 10 July 1714.

Chapter 15

1. Blundell, *Journal*. Described his journey by coach from London in his journal on Wednesday, 14 July 1714.
2. The Clergy Database – *Robertus Styth*.
3. Blundell, *Journal* (trans. Hignett), pp.73–75.
4. Blundell was appointed treasurer of the Blue Coat School in August 1714. Ibid.
5. For further details on the SPCK and Blundell's role in the charity school movement, see: Gómez, Francis Gerald – *The Endowed Schools Of Lancashire From The 17th to the Early 18th Century* (1987), pp.264–285; and Girvan, Michelle – *A Monument to Charity and Piety? Bryan Blundell and the Liverpool Blue Coat School* (2021), pp.10–12.
6. Ibid.
7. Wainwright, Dr Paul. – *Bryan Blundell (bluecoatschoolliverpool.org.uk)*.
8. For further detail on the Lancashire SPCK, see: Gómez, Francis Gerald – *The Endowed Schools Of Lancashire From The 17th to the Early 18th Century*, pp.264–285.
9. Gómez, *The Endowed Schools Of Lancashire*, pp.264–285.
10. St Peter's, erected in 1703 as Liverpool's second parish church after St Nicholas, was regarded as the town's "fashionable" church; Blundell's family held pews in both. The first charity school (1708/1709) seems to have stood on the opposite side of School Lane, on the site now occupied by the Friends Meeting House, before relocating beside St Peter's. Context provided by Bryan Biggs, Cultural Director of the Bluecoat. Also see: Biggs, Bryan, and Belchem, John, eds. *Bluecoat, Liverpool: The UK's First Arts Centre*. Liverpool: Liverpool University Press, 2020.
11. The Blue Coat School in Liverpool was one of around sixty Blue Coat institutions, see: Biggs, Bryan, and Belchem, John, eds. *Bluecoat, Liverpool: The UK's First Arts Centre*. Liverpool: Liverpool University Press, 2020, p16.

12. For further detail on charity school uniform traditions, see: Living London History, "*The Fascinating Story Behind London's Bluecoat Statues.*"
13. Blundell, *Journal* (trans. Hignett), pp.73–75.
14. Ibid.
15. For detail on Blundell's use of his maritime connections to secure subscriptions for the school, see: Girvan, *A Monument to Charity and Piety*, p.3, drawing on his journal and subscription rolls (Liverpool Central Library, 377.BLU/1/1; 377.BLU/5).
16. Blundell, *Journal* (trans. Hignett), pp.73–75.
17. For a detailed account of the construction costs, financing, and Blundell's use of profits from his shipping ventures in building the school and adjoining almshouses, see: Girvan, *A Monument to Charity Piety*, esp. p.1, drawing on Blundell's journal (Lancashire Archives, DDBB/8/4) and his ledger accounts (Liverpool Central Library, 377.BLU/5).
18. Biggs, Bryan, and Belchem, John, eds. *Bluecoat, Liverpool: The UK's First Arts Centre*. Liverpool: Liverpool University Press, 2020, p.16.
19. For detail school meals see: Minute Book of the Board Meetings of the Blue Coat School Trustees and Governors, 1742–1813. Liverpool Blue Coat Hospital and School, LCLA 377.BLU/15/1/1, p.13. Available online at *The Bluecoat* website: "The Blue Coat School" Library section. For detail on a typical school day at the Blue Coat School, see: Blundell, Bryan. *Narrative of the Rise and Progress of the Charity School, or Blue Coat Hospital in Liverpool, written by its co-founder Mr Bryan Blundell, Treasurer, from the year 1709 to near the time of his death*. Liverpool: Liverpool Blue Coat School / Liverpool Record Office (ref. 377 BLU/9); and Gómez, *The Endowed Schools Of Lancashire*, pp.264–285.
20. Ibid.
21. Blundell, *Journal* (trans. Hignett), pp.73–75. Also see: See: Gómez, *Endowed Schools of Lancashire*, p.380.
22. "stand, sit, kneel, and listen to divine service." Hughes, John R. *A Sketch of the Origin and Early History of the Liverpool Blue Coat Hospital*. Transactions of the Historic Society of Lancashire and Cheshire, 1859, p.179.
23. Wainwright, Dr Paul – *Bryan Blundell.* Bluecoatschoolliverpool.org.uk.
24. Girvan, *A Monument to Charity and Piety*, p.10, fn.; citing: Exemplification of the Decree made in the Chancery Court of Lancaster concerning the Government of the Blue Coat School, 27 August 1739, Liverpool Central Library Archives (LCLA), ref. 377.BLU/2/1. The Court of Chancery typically issued rulings on trusts, estates, and charitable foundations.
25. Madam Clayton: Sarah Clayton (1712–1779) was a prominent Liverpool merchant and property investor, and one of the few women in the town to amass substantial wealth in the eighteenth century.
26. Blundell, *Journal* (trans. Hignett), pp.73–75.
27. Girvan, *A Monument to Charity and Piety*, p.11.
28. Quotes from: Blundell, *Journal* (trans. Hignett), pp.73–75.
29. Reverend Samuel Shaw (1650–1718). See: Appendix C – *Tree 4: The Shaw Family*.
30. Samuel Shaw (1692–1718). See: Appendix C – *Tree 4: The Shaw Family*.
31. William Roscoe (1753–1831): A Liverpool lawyer, writer, and later abolitionist. His 1769 poem *Mount Pleasant* was composed while he lived on the street of that name, near the Blue Coat School. He would later campaign vigorously against the slave trade. Yet modern historians caution that his opposition was neither consistent nor wholly separate from the mercantile environment of Liverpool, and that his memory was

reshaped over time in civic narratives that emphasised his anti-slavery credentials. See: Moody, Jessica – *"The Memorial Cult of William Roscoe: Remembering Abolition." In The Persistence of Memory: Remembering Slavery in Liverpool, "Slaving Capital of the World", Liverpool University Press, 2020.*
32. Roscoe, William – *Mount Pleasant* (1769).

Chapter 16

1. It is unclear from the records whether those executed in Liverpool in February 1716 were hanged from fixed gallows or from a cart-based scaffold, as execution practices varied. In the early eighteenth century, the use of a cart was still common: the condemned would stand upon it while the noose was secured, and the cart would then be drawn away, leaving the body to drop. Seal, Lizzie. *"A Brief History of Capital Punishment in Britain." HistoryExtra.* The site of the public executions on London Road was later called Gallows Mills.
2. For further details on the conclusion of the 1715 Jacobite rebellion, see: Muir, *History of Liverpool*, p.163–165; and Robert Patten, *The History of the Late Rebellion* (London: J. Baker and T. Warner, 1717).
3. George Collingwood of Northumberland was hanged, drawn and quartered in Liverpool on 25 February 1716 for his involvement in the 1715 Jacobite uprising. John Hunter was also executed in Liverpool after being wounded at Preston. See: Robert Patten, *The History of the Late Rebellion* (London: J. Baker and T. Warner, 1717), pp.132–139. Historian Charles Hands suggests that the other two men executed in Liverpool were Archibald Burnett of Carlips and Alexander Drummond, gentleman of Logie Drummond's 3rd Regiment of Foot. See: James Hands, "Three Local Windmills," *Transactions of the Historic Society of Lancashire and Cheshire*, vol. 73, p.35.
4. For further details on the conclusion of the 1715 Jacobite rebellion, see: Muir, *History of Liverpool*, pp.163–165; and Patten, *The History of the Late Rebellion*.
5. Ibid.
6. Blundell, *Journal* (trans. Hignett), pp.69–70.
7. Ibid.
8. For detail on port management before Liverpool's New Dock see: Stammers, *Ships and Port Management*, pp.41–45.
9. National Oceanography Centre, *Tidal Range Data for the River Mersey*, Liverpool. See: noc.ac.uk.
10. "the heart of Liverpool": *The Old Dock*, National Museums Liverpool – *The Old Dock Tour*.
11. Thomas Steers (c. 1672–1750) is best known as the engineer of Liverpool's New Dock, but recent evidence suggests he also designed the Blue Coat School building, completed between 1716 and 1725. Girvan, *A Monument to Charity and Piety*, p.11.
12. Nicholas Blundell (1669–1737), the diarist, was grandson of William Blundell, "the Cavalier" (1620–1698), and was likely a distant relation of Bryan Blundell. According to Picton, Bryan Blundell's grandfather was disowned by the Catholic Blundells of Ince for embracing Protestantism. Picton, *Memorials*, p.169.
13. "with great rejoicings…": Blundell, *Crosby Records: Nicholas Blundell's Diary.*
14. Ibid. The *Mulberry* is widely cited as the first vessel to enter the dock in August 1715. Bryan Blundell had previously sailed a ship of that name, though his last known command of her was more than a decade earlier. Some accounts suggest she was still

in his ownership at the time of the dock's opening, though the evidence is inconclusive. Historian Arthur Wardle has argued persuasively that Nicholas Blundell, the diarist, may have misidentified the vessel: what he recorded as the *Mulberry* may in fact have been HMS *Marlborough*, a name often spelt "*Mulberry*" in contemporary sources. *Transactions of the Liverpool Maritime Society*, Vol. IX (1955–1961), p.34.

15. "This is of so great a benefit…": Daniel Defoe writing about the New Dock in 1723 – Defoe, Daniel – *A Tour Thro' the Whole Island of Great Britain*, vol. III (London, 1724–1727), pp.258–259.
16. William Clayton (1660–1715).
17. William Clayton was so influential in the industry that he was nicknamed the "Old Tar Barrel." Hignett, Harry – *Bryan Blundell Shipmaster Merchant Treasurer of the Blue Coat School* (Liverpool Maritime Society Volume 34); and Hockedy, Susan – *Liverpool Shipping and the Tar Trade* – (Transactions of the Historic Society of Lancashire and Cheshire, vol. 144, 1994).
18. Blundell, *Journal* (trans. Hignett), pp.81–82.
19. "I had two or three ships in the tar trade…": Blundell, *Journal* (trans. Hignett), pp.81–82.
20. For further details on the conclusion of the 1715 Jacobite rebellion, see: Muir, *History of Liverpool*, pp.163–165; and Patten, *The History of the Late Rebellion*.
21. "eager mobs everywhere cheered for the Stuarts…": Ibid, p.163.
22. For further details on the conclusion of the 1715 Jacobite rebellion, see: Muir, *History of Liverpool*, pp.163–165; and Patten, *The History of the Late Rebellion*.
23. The Tower of Liverpool, also known as Derby's Tower, stood near Water Street between Tower Gardens and Stringer's Alley. Originally built as a fortified house by the Stanley family (Earls of Derby), it later served as the town gaol. *Tower Building, Liverpool*, Wikipedia.

Chapter 17

1. Blundell does not state where he was when deciding his course after the *Cleveland*'s return on 19 June 1717. However, by this date he had retired from seafaring, was living full-time in Liverpool, and was actively overseeing the construction of the Blue Coat School and engaging in local commerce. The setting of the counting house is therefore inferred from his circumstances and activities at the time, as reflected in his journal and other contemporary records.
2. "a few pipes of wine and some corkwood": Blundell, *Journal* (trans. Hignett), p.70.
3. "A bad voyage": Ibid, p.70.
4. Blundell, *Journal* (trans. Hignett), p.70. Bryan Blundell wrote on 19 June 1717: "Makes a very bad voyage…which is so discouraging that we put the ship in dock for some months…"
5. For further details on postwar commercial pressures and market shifts, see: Williams, *Liverpool Privateers*; and Thomsen, Robert P. – *The Merchant in Virginia*.
6. For more detail on the Golden Age of Piracy, see: Rediker, Marcus – *Villains of All Nations: Atlantic Pirates in the Golden Age* (Boston: Beacon Press, 2004).
7. "We put the ship in dock," he wrote, "and then consulted…": Blundell, *Journal* (trans. Hignett), p.70.
8. For an overview of the end of the Royal African Company's monopoly on the British slave trade, see: Webster, Jane – *Materializing the Middle Passage: A Historical Archaeology*

of British Slave Shipping, 1680–1807 (Oxford, 2023; online edition, Oxford Academic, 23 November 2023), pp.27–53.

9. The "*Liverpool Merchant*" (voyage ID 15122) – Slavevoyages.org – *Trans-Atlantic Slave Trade Database.*
10. For further on Liverpool's slaving voyages, see: Slavevoyages.org – *Trans-Atlantic Slave Trade Database.*
11. For instance, in February 1721, "King" Carter wrote to Blundell to discuss shipping terms, commend his captain, and pass on greetings to fellow Liverpool traders. Berkeley, Edmund Jr., trans., *Robert "King" Carter Papers*, Christ Church Foundation. Letter from Robert Carter to Bryan Blundell, 14 February 1721.
12. Blundell, *Journal*, Friday, 26 December 1701.
13. Blundell, *Journal* (trans. Hignett), p.70; and Wainwright, Dr Paul – *Bryan Blundell – (bluecoatschoolliverpool.org.uk).*
14. For further on Liverpool's slaving voyages, see: Slavevoyages.org – *Trans-Atlantic Slave Trade Database.*
15. "Consulted and determined…": Blundell, *Journal* (trans. Hignett), p.70.
16. Ibid.
17. Drawn from: Eltis, David – *The Trans-Atlantic Slave Trade, 1500–1865* (2009); Crow, *Memoirs* (1830); and Williams, *Liverpool Privateers.*
18. Ibid.
19. Blundell, *Journal* (trans. Hignett), p.70.
20. Ibid.
21. Ibid.
22. Ibid.
23. "humbly represented to 'em the Danger of their Voyage…": Bassnett, *Seaman's Character.*
24. "considerable Difficulties along with it…": Bassnett, *Seaman's Character.*

Chapter 18

1. In his journal Bryan Blundell records that the *Cleveland* sailed from Cork on 14 July 1718 and reached Madagascar by October (Blundell, *Journal* (trans. Hignett), p.70). On a typical South Atlantic passage, vessels took four to six weeks to reach the equator from Europe, depending on winds and calms. This would place the *Cleveland*'s equator crossing in mid- to late August 1718, consistent with her arrival in Madagascar later that year.
2. Blundell, *Journal* (trans. Hignett), p.70.
3. Ibid.
4. Ibid.
5. Ibid.
6. The South Sea Company was granted the *asiento de negros* by Spain in 1713 as part of the Treaty of Utrecht, giving it exclusive rights to supply enslaved Africans to Spanish colonies. Though it never became a major trading force beyond this contract, its collapse in 1720 triggered a wave of financial instability across Britain's emerging capital markets. For further details on the South Sea Bubble, see: Neal, Larry – *The Rise of Financial Capitalism: International Capital Markets in the Age of Reason* (Cambridge University Press, 1993).
7. Slavevoyages.org – *Trans-Atlantic Slave Trade Database.*
8. "the Guinea and West India trades": Ibid.

9. Slavevoyages.org – *Trans-Atlantic Slave Trade Database.*
10. "*Martha*" (voyage ID 62609) – Slavevoyages.org – *Trans-Atlantic Slave Trade Database*; and Blundell, *Journal* (trans. Hignett), p.75.
11. "all condescension, politeness, and civility…": William Butterworth, recalling his recruitment to the slave ship *Hudibras* around 1787, described the hypocrisy of Captain Evans: charming on land, brutal at sea. Butterworth, William – *Three Years' Adventures of a Minor, in England, Africa, the West Indies, South-Carolina and Georgia* (Leeds: Thos. Inchbold, 1831), pp.5–6.
12. For further accounts of slave ship captains and their cruelty, see: Rediker, *The Slave Ship*, pp.202–206; and Crow, *Memoirs* (1830).
13. Ibid.
14. "*Martha*" (voyage ID 62609) – Slavevoyages.org – *Trans-Atlantic Slave Trade Database.*
15. Mackenzie-Grieve, A. (1968) *The Last Years of the English Slave Trade, Liverpool, 1750–1807.* New York: A.M. Kelley, pp.109–111.
16. Ibid.
17. Blundell's journal does not describe the internal modifications of the *Cleveland* or the shipboard preparations for slave transport in detail. The description here is drawn from: Tibbles, *Liverpool and the Slave Trade*, p.33; and Mackenzie-Grieve, *The Last Years of the English Slave Trade, Liverpool*, pp.109–111.
18. See Williams, *Liverpool Privateers*, for additional descriptions of shipboard conversion and crew discipline.
19. "*Martha*" (voyage ID 62609) – Slavevoyages.org – *Trans-Atlantic Slave Trade Database.*
20. Manning, Patrick – *The Slave Trade: The Formal Demographics of a Global System*, pp.258–260.
21. Tibbles, *Liverpool and the Slave Trade*, p.34.
22. Description drawn from: Tibbles, *Liverpool and the Slave Trade*; Radburn, Nick – *HIST241: The Trans-Atlantic Slave Trade, 1500–1865*, Lancaster University (2018); and Crow, *Memoirs* (1830).
23. "When our slaves were come to the seaside…": Phillips, Thomas – *A Journal of a Voyage Made in the Hannibal of London* (1694), p.219.
24. Ibid.
25. "When I looked round the ship…": Olaudah Equiano, formally enslaved and later leading abolitionist, vividly described the terrifying conditions on the Middle Passage in his autobiography. His book offers a firsthand perspective on the sheer brutality of the transatlantic slave trade, amplifying the dehumanising experience endured by millions of African people. Equiano, *Interesting Narrative*, p.43.
26. "I was soon put down under the decks…": Equiano, *Interesting Narrative*, p.57.
27. Butterworth, William – *Three Years' Adventures of a Minor, in England, Africa, the West Indies, South-Carolina and Georgia* (Leeds: Thos. Inchbold, 1831), p.39.
28. "in two rows, one above the other like books upon a shelf": Newton, *Thoughts Upon the African Slave Trade*, p.33.
29. Description drawn from: Crow, *Memoirs* (1830); Newton, *Thoughts Upon the African Slave Trade*; Williams, *Liverpool Privateers*; and Rediker, *The Slave Ship*, pp.244–247.
30. "The article of Women, likewise, contributes largely to the loss of our Seamen…": Newton, *Thoughts Upon the African Slave Trade*, p.11.
31. Ibid.

32. For further detail on slave nutrition aboard ship, see: Walvin, James – *Black Ivory: Slavery in the British Empire* (Blackwell, 2001).
33. "exercise" and "dance": Detail on forced exercise and conditions during the Middle Passage drawn from: *The Middle Passage*, International Slavery Museum, National Museums Liverpool.
34. Ibid.
35. "a dreadful engine…" Newton, *Thoughts Upon the African Slave Trade*, p.17.
36. *Trans-Atlantic Slave Trade Database* (Voyage ID 92609), the *Martha* embarked 142 enslaved people and disembarked 114 in Nevis in 1722.
37. "*Martha*" (voyage ID 62609) – Slavevoyages.org – *Trans-Atlantic Slave Trade Database.*
38. Prices for enslaved Africans varied by age, sex, health, and market conditions. For details on pricing in Nevis in the 1720s, see: *The Mountravers Plantation Community: Part 2, Chapter 2*. Nevis Heritage Project.
39. Brown, Vincent – *The Reaper's Garden: Death and Power in the World of Atlantic Slavery* (Harvard University Press, 2008); also Beckles, Hilary – *Natural Rebels: A Social History of Enslaved Black Women in Barbados* (Rutgers University Press, 1989), for regional comparisons.
40. "*Martha*" (voyage ID 92609): Slavevoyages.org – *Trans-Atlantic Slave Trade Database.*
41. Ibid.
42. "*Jane and Ellen*" (voyage ID 92603): Slavevoyages.org – *Trans-Atlantic Slave Trade Database.* Departed Liverpool, July 1723. The ship embarked 153 enslaved Africans on the West African coast and landed 131 at Nevis in April 1724, a mortality rate of circa 15 per cent.
43. Appendix C – *Tree 3: The Williamson Family.*
44. "*Good Intention*" (voyage ID 95996): Slavevoyages.org – *Trans-Atlantic Slave Trade Database.* Likely incorrectly recorded as "Benjamin Blundell". Two slaving voyages under joint ownership of [Bryan] Blundell and Robert Armitage. First voyage: departed Liverpool late 1726, embarked 226 enslaved Africans at Sierra Leone, landed 204 at Barbados, 1727. Second voyage: departed May 1728, embarked 189, landed 170 at Barbados, December 1728, combined mortality circa 10 per cent.
45. "*Tarleton Gally*" (voyage ID 92385): Slavevoyages.org – *Trans-Atlantic Slave Trade Database.* Likely incorrectly recorded as "Benjamin Blundell". Owned jointly by [Bryan] Blundell, Robert Armitage, and Foster Cunliffe. They were each a past or future Mayor of Liverpool. Departed December 1727, arrived Barbados July 1728. Embarked 273 enslaved Africans; landed 236 (mortality circa 14 per cent). See: *Liverpool City Halls, "Mayor / Lord Mayors of the City of Liverpool Since 1207," Civic Honours List.*
46. "*Jonathan*" (voyage ID 100978): Slavevoyages.org – *Intra-American Slave Trade Database.* Linked to Bryan Blundell through the Intra-American Slave Trade Database. Embarked forty enslaved Africans in Jamaica; thirty-nine were landed in the Lower James River region of Virginia, 1733.
47. In 1752, he wrote that he owned, the slaving vessels, the *Elizabeth* and the *Duke of Cumberland*. Blundell, *Journal* (trans. Hignett), p.83.
48. Slave cargo was routinely insured against loss at sea, including deaths from disease, mutiny, or shipwreck. In notorious cases, such as the 1781 *Zong* massacre, enslaved people were even thrown overboard so their deaths could be claimed as insured cargo loss. For further details, see: Baucom, Ian – *Specters of the Atlantic* (Duke University Press, 2005).

49. For further details, see: Appendix E: The Recorded Slaving Voyages of Bryan Blundell and his Direct Descendants.

Chapter 19

1. This scene is not drawn from a single documented incident but is a plausible reconstruction informed by period sources. Blundell, *Journal* (trans. Hignett), pp.77–78; and Hughes, J.F. *Recollections of Old Liverpool: By a Nonagenarian.* Liverpool, 1863 – which describes the ducking stool at the New Dock.
2. Ibid.
3. "scolds" and "common strumpets": All quotes in this section and the following are drawn from Bryan Blundell's journal, see: Blundell, *Journal* (trans. Hignett), pp.77–78.
4. Description drawn from: Touzeau, *Rise and Progress*, pp.395–396.
5. "The lack of piety and religion": All quotes in this section and the following are drawn from Bryan Blundell's journal, see: Blundell, *Journal* (trans. Hignett), pp.77–78.
6. Blundell, *Journal* (trans. Hignett), pp.77–78; and Hughes, J.F. *Recollections of Old Liverpool: By a Nonagenarian.* Liverpool, 1863 – which describes the ducking stool at the New Dock.
7. "All in a manner do what they please without control": All quotes in this section are drawn from Bryan Blundell's journal. Blundell, *Journal* (trans. Hignett), pp.74–80.
8. Pearce, Edward. *The Great Man, Sir Robert Walpole: Scoundrel, Genius and Britain's First Prime Minister.* p.300.
9. Blundell, *Journal.* Recorded his departure for London on 25 February 1729.
10. Including: Foster Cunliffe (1729–1730 and 1735–1736), Robert Armitage (1738–1739), James Crosbie (1753–1754), John Williamson (1761–1762), John Tarleton (1764–1765), John Crosbie (1765–1766), Henry Blundell Hollinshead (1791–1792 and 1793–1794), John Shaw (1794–1795 and 1800–1801), Henry Blundell Hollinshead (1807–1808), and Jonathan Blundell Hollinshead (1818–1819 and 1824–1825). See: Appendix C – *Family Trees (1–6).*
11. All quotes in this section are drawn from Bryan Blundell's journal, see: Blundell, *Journal* (trans. Hignett), pp.74–80. Also see: Blease, W. Lyon. *The Poor Law in Liverpool 1681–1834* (Liverpool, 1908); Williams, Andrew, and May, Jon – "Racial Capitalism and the Workhouse–Plantation Nexus in the Atlantic World." *Antipode* 57, no. 5 (2025).
12. Blease, W. Lyon. *The Poor Law in Liverpool 1681–1834* (Liverpool, 1908), pp.109–110.
13. Ibid, p.129.
14. For detail on Bryan Blundell's role as executor in twenty wills, see: Ascott, Diana; Lewis, Fiona; and Power, Michael – *Liverpool 1660–1750: People, Prosperity, and Power, pp.110–113.*
15. Blundell, *Journal* (trans. Hignett), p.72.
16. For further details, see: Bryder, Linda – *Below the Magic Mountain: A Social History of Tuberculosis in Twentieth-Century Britain* (1988); and Dormandy, Thomas. *The White Death: A History of Tuberculosis* (2000).
17. "She being a very good woman…": All quotes in this section are drawn from Bryan Blundell's journal, see: Blundell, *Journal* (trans. Hignett), p.72.
18. Transatlantic Slave Trade Database – *Foster Cunliffe.*
19. Liverpool City Halls. *Mayor / Lord Mayors of the City of Liverpool Since 1207.* Civic Honours List.
20. Blundell, *Journal* (trans. Hignett), p.72.

21. Ibid.
22. Wainwright, Dr. Paul – *Bryan Blundell (bluecoatschoolliverpool.org.uk).*
23. Ibid.
24. In 1752, Bryan Blundell, Jonathan Blundell and Samuel Shaw (1718–1781) were listed among the Liverpool subscribers to the Company of Merchants Trading to Africa, which had been established under the African Company Act of 1750 to regulate and support British commercial interests along the West African coast. It is possible that the "Bryan Blundell" recorded here may refer Bryan Blundell's son Bryan Blundell Jr (1720–1790), who was also active in the slave trade by this period. Williams, *Liverpool Privateer,* p.674.
25. Ibid.

Chapter 20

1. "Can I do this and hear that voice": Thomas Raffles later recorded the story: "It is supposed that Mr. Bassnett lost himself towards the close of his life. It is related of him that he used to wander amongst the caves and rocks in the Park on the seashore—and once he had resolved to drown himself, but just as he was about to throw himself into the sea, it thundered. He started at the sound, and cried: 'Can I do this and hear that voice.' He immediately left the shore and went to Mr. Angier's." Raffles, Thomas, manuscript notes, quoted in Roberts, Henry, Hope Street Church and the Allied Non-Conformity of Liverpool (Liverpool, 1905), p.62.
2. "homely, useful preacher, with a Puritan unction": Ibid. p.33 and p.55.
3. Ibid.
4. "Christ of late has been calling his Ministers very fast to himself.": Christopher Bassnett, Church Officers and Their Mission: A Sermon Preach'd at a Publick Ordination (London: Printed for John Clark, at the Bible and Crown in the Poultry, near Cheapside, 1717).
5. "Fruits": Ibid.

Chapter 21

1. Liverpool's growing industrial base by the mid-eighteenth century included five sugar factories, ten potteries, six pipe factories, four glasshouses, ten tobacco works, salt pans, anchor forges, and numerous shoemakers and saddlers. See: Angerstein, Reinhold Rücker – *Reise durch England und Frankreich im Jahre 1754.* Translated and edited by Torsten Berg, 2001, p.336.
2. Fiona Lewis estimates that Liverpool's population had risen to around 22,000 by 1750. Fiona Lewis, *The Demographic and Occupational Structure of Liverpool: A Study of the Parish Regxisters, 1660–1750* (Historical Society of Lancashire and Cheshire, 2001), p.2.
3. There is no surviving record of where Bryan Blundell lived in his later years. This imagined walk begins on the waterfront, just as the narrative did. In the early to mid-eighteenth century, most merchants of his standing kept grand townhouses near the commercial heart of Liverpool: on Castle Street, Water Street, Dale Street, or nearby. See: Mackenzie-Grieve, *The Last Years of the English Slave Trade, Liverpool.* p.6. Contemporary accounts noted the town's architectural ambition. Daniel Defoe wrote admiringly of its elegant streets: "In a Word, there is no Town in England, except Manchester, that can equal Liverpool for the Fineness of the Streets, and Beauty of the Buildings. Many of

the Houses are built of Free-stone, and completely finished; and all the Rest of Brick, as handsomely built as London itself." Defoe, *A Tour Thro' the Whole Island of Great Britain*, p.261.

4. Drawn from: *Bygone Liverpool*, "Goree, Liverpool. Part One," blog post, March 2021. This post draws on Buck's 1728 engraving and the 1750 Lang Plan to reconstruct the Old Custom House Yard, including the furnace known as the "Tobacco Pipe," used to destroy spoiled slave-grown tobacco.
5. As newer docks were developed, the once-celebrated New Dock was relegated to being called the "Old Dock" and was eventually closed in 1826. Its site was repurposed for a grand customs house, and in the twentieth century, the Liverpool One shopping centre. During the construction of Liverpool One, archaeologists uncovered the foundations which can still be visited today. The Old Dock Tour – *Liverpool Museums.*
6. In 1734 work began on a second dock to the south. Unlike the original, this one was not built in a natural inlet and took nineteen years to complete. Primarily intended for the Cheshire salt trade, it stood beside a great saltworks that had long occupied the waste ground south of the Pool, hence its name: Salthouse Dock (1753). See Muir, *History of Liverpool*, pp.177–178.
7. Blundell, *Journal* (trans. Hignett), pp.79–80. In his journal, Blundell records he was deputy mayor in 1732. James Touzeau notes that he also served as deputy mayor in 1735: Touzeau, *Rise and Progress*, p.435.
8. For details on the history and architecture of Liverpool's Town Hall, see: Historic England – *Town Hall, Water Street, Liverpool* – List Entry No. 1360219. Grade I designation amended 2007; and Touzeau, *Rise and Progress*, pp.494–497.
9. Ibid.
10. Council minutes record that the merchants were dissatisfied with the original pediment's bas-reliefs, describing them as "ill-executed." The sculptor, Mr Stephenson, petitioned the Corporation for additional payment in 1756 but was refused. Touzeau, *Rise and Progress*, pp.466–467.
11. Descriptions of the merchants' dress, manner, and presence on Castle Street are based on James Stonehouse, *Recollections of Old Liverpool by a Nonagenarian* (Liverpool: J.F. Hughes, 1863; reprinted by Project Gutenberg, 2007).
12. Touzeau, *Rise and Progress*, pp.466–467; and Mackenzie-Grieve, *The Last Years of the English Slave Trade, Liverpool*, p.6.
13. See: quarterly Trustee Meeting, 1 July 1754. Blue Coat School Minute Book, 1742–1813, p.67.
14. Ramsay Muir notes that Liverpool vessels were typically manned more economically than those of Bristol. Captains and officers were paid lower wages, and a widespread use of apprentices allowed shipowners to staff their crews at minimal cost. These apprentices, often boys, served without pay; in return, the master was expected to "feed and clothe them, teach them their trade, and administer to them such *needful chastisement* as might be required." In some cases, even the junior officers were themselves unpaid apprentices. Muir, *History of Liverpool*, p.183. Daniel Defoe similarly remarked on the town's commercial efficiency, observing that: "The principal internal causes which, as I have been informed, have contributed to the quick growth of commerce here, which in other places rises so slowly, were these: the traders of this place have been remarkable for frugality in management, which enables them to do everything upon the cheapest

terms, and to sell at the lowest prices." Defoe, *A Tour Thro' the Whole Island of Great Britain*, pp.257–258.

15. Richard Blundell served as Treasurer of the Liverpool Blue Coat School from 1752 to 1760, after which his younger brother Jonathan succeeded him. In addition, many of Blundell's relatives would go on to become trustees including: William Williamson (brother-in-law), William Williamson Jr. (nephew), Foster and Ellis Cunliffe (brother-in-law and nephew), Richard Houghton and Ralph Peters (cousins), Samuel Shaw (grandson) and John Shaw (great-grandson). Blue Coat School Minute Book, 1742–1813. See also: Girvan, *A Monument to Charity and Piety*, p.9.
16. Bryan Blundell was treasurer of the Blue Coat School over four decades.
17. By 1766, Lord Street was a bustling thoroughfare lined with brewers, merchants, drapers, and skilled tradespeople. George T. Shaw – *"History of the Liverpool Directories, 1766–1907,"* Transactions of the Historic Society of Lancashire and Cheshire 58 (1906), p.150.
18. From at least the 1730s, the sons of African rulers were occasionally sent to Liverpool to receive schooling. Such visits served a diplomatic and commercial purpose, strengthening ties between African courts and British merchants eager to secure privileged trading relations along the West African coast. Costello, Dr Ray – *"Liverpool Black Community: The Early Years,"* 17 September 2017, Black History Month (UK).
19. Castle Ditch, also called the Potato Market, was a remnant of Liverpool's medieval fortifications, marking the site of the original Norman castle that once overlooked the Mersey. By the early eighteenth century, the ditch had become more symbolic than defensive, partially filled in but still known locally as a reference point near the modern junction of Castle Street and Derby Square. Picton, *Memorials*, p.171.
20. The demolition of Liverpool Castle took place gradually over two decades following the Corporation's acquisition of the site in 1704. The majority of the structure was removed between 1709 and 1717, with the last remaining wall, running across the top of Lord Street, vanishing by 1725. Its removal marked the end of one of Liverpool's most ancient and symbolic landmarks. Muir, *History of Liverpool*, p.175.
21. "mouldering Castle": quote and description from: Muir, Ramsay – *Bygone Liverpool*, with Harold E. Young and Henry S. Young (Liverpool: Young, 1913), Introduction, p.20.
22. "narrow, mean, ill-paved, and dirty": Muir, *History of Liverpool*, p.186. Detail also drawn from: Muir, Ramsay – *Bygone Liverpool*, with Harold E. Young and Henry S. Young (Liverpool: Young, 1913).
23. Mackenzie-Grieve, *The Last Years of the English Slave Trade, Liverpool*. p.15; and Drescher, Seymour – *The Slaving Capital of the World: Liverpool and National Opinion in the Age of Abolition.* Slavery & Abolition 9, no. 2 (1988), p.133.
24. For further details, see: Peter. *The Earles of Liverpool: A Georgian Merchant Dynasty.*
25. Girvan, *A Monument to Charity and Piety*, which draws on the Blue Coat Hospital and School subscription books: First Subscription Roll, 1717, LCLA 377.BLU/1/1; Subscription Ledger, 1756–1780, LCLA 377.BLU/17/1/2; Subscription Ledger, 1781–1813, LCLA 377.BLU/17/1/7. These records show the interlocking merchant families who funded and governed the institution; see also Appendix C (Family Trees 1–6).
26. "not so vigilant in suppressing such practices": Quotes in this section are drawn from: Blundell, *Journal* (trans. Hignett), pp.77–80. In his journal, Blundell wrote: "Most

magistrates all this time being so engaged for one party or the other, that there was not time or thought employed to put the laws in execution against profaneness and immorality. So that whilst the causes of men were fixed as the one thing needful, the cause of God was shamefully neglected, so that the common people was grown to a great height of wickedness…"

27. "Laish": A city mentioned in the Book of Judges (Judges 18:7) whose people are described as "dwelling carelessly," without a ruler, and isolated from others, often interpreted as a symbol of complacency and moral laxity. The Danites later destroyed the city. Quotes in this passage are drawn Blundell, *Journal* (trans. Hignett), p.78.
28. Adapted in part from: Muir, *History of Liverpool*, Introduction p.13.
29. By 1766, Gore's Directory of Liverpool listed six inns on Dale Street: the Golden Fleece, the Woolpack, the Mill Stone and Castle, the Cross Keys, the Golden Lion, and the Angel. Shaw, George T. "History of the Liverpool Directories, 1766–1907." *Transactions of the Historic Society of Lancashire and Cheshire* 58 (1906), pp.141–143.
30. Ramsay Muir described how the rigours of the West India trade produced "a very vigorous, unruly, and warlike type of sailor," often difficult to control while in port. See: Muir, *History of Liverpool*, p.185.
31. Bryan Blundell died two years later, in 1756, and was buried at the Church of Our Lady and St Nicholas in Liverpool, the church of his baptism and marriage.
32. The new steeple of St Nicholas Church prompted the local jibe: "Old church, new steeple, / Poor Liverpool, proud people." Picton, *Memorials*, p.58.
33. "Goree" was a name used by mideighteenth century Liverpool merchants to refer to the waterfront warehouses and stores engaged in African and Caribbean trade. While the grand "Goree Piazzas" were built only later, historians using maps and archival reconstructions have located earlier Goreelabelled warehouse sites near the old Custom House Yard. See: "Goree, Liverpool: Part One," Bygone Liverpool (2021).
34. It was common practice for captains and officers of slave ships to return with a small number of enslaved children. These were sometimes as gifts from African traders, other times as personal acquisitions. These individuals were frequently employed as servants or sold discreetly within the port city. The Blundell family was not exempt. In April 1767, the baptismal register of St Peter's Church recorded the christening of "Thomas Mr Jon' Blundell's Negro About 30 Y' Old." A few years later, in October 1773, *Williamson's Liverpool Advertiser* carried a notice seeking the return of a "runaway Negro Man" named Thomas Gray, approximately 25 years old, for whom Jonathan Blundell was offering a reward of 2 guineas. See: Wainwright, Dr Paul – *Bryan Blundell.* Bluecoatschoolliverpool.org.uk. Liverpool's earliest known Black resident was a man named Abell, who was buried at St Nicholas Church on 1 October 1717. See: *BBC News*, "*Stone Marks Liverpool's First Recorded Black Resident*," 3 October 2020.
35. "The Main" was a common term for the Spanish Main, the mainland coast of the Caribbean Spanish colonies.
36. Charles Pole (1695–1779). Between 1747 and 1757 he undertook between five and ten slaving voyages as captain; and was an investor in at least ten. He became Member of Parliament for Liverpool on 19 March 1756 but lost his seat at the 1761 general election. Pole also served on the Liverpool committee of the Company of Merchants Trading to Africa for the year 1758–1759. Biographical details compiled from *History of Parliament: The House of Commons 1754–1790* (ed. L. Namier and J. Brooke, London, 1964), vol. 3, p.98; and "Charles Pole," *Wikipedia: The Free Encyclopedia.*

37. Transatlantic Slave Trade Database –*Voyage ID 90366 – The Nancy* – part-owned by his son Jonathan Blundell and grandson Samuel Shaw. She would sail for Bonny on Monday, 15 July 1754.
38. William Butterworth, a young sailor drawn into the slave trade around 1787, recalled how he and his friend were baited with advance pay and false promises, "an easy prey to these dealers in human flesh." Butterworth, William – *Three Years' Adventures of a Minor, in England, Africa, the West Indies, South-Carolina and Georgia* (Leeds: Thos. Inchbold, 1831), pp.5–10.
39. Carl Gottlieb Angerstein was an industrial spy working for the Swedish Board of Mines. He visited Liverpool in 1754 as part of a wider reconnaissance mission to observe and report on Britain's technological and commercial advancements. Though his goal was industrial intelligence, his notebooks also captured the atmosphere of the towns he visited. Of Liverpool, he wrote: "It is one of the most flourishing ports in England, and trades particularly with the West Indies and with the African coasts." Angerstein, Reinhold Rücker – *Reise durch England und Frankreich im Jahre 1754*. Translated and edited by Torsten Berg, 2001, p.332.
40. By 1751, Liverpool had 88 ships dedicated to the Africa trade, more than any other British port. This number continued to grow rapidly throughout the 1750s, cementing Liverpool's position as Britain's dominant slaving hub. By the end of the century, the town was responsible for dispatching over three-quarters of all British slave voyages, a total unmatched by London or Bristol. Williams, *Liverpool Privateers*, pp.472–473.
41. Transatlantic Slave Trade Database (Voyage ID 90156). The *Duke of Cumberland*, returned from Barbados on Tuesday, 18 June 1754. She would sail again to Bonny on Friday, 21 February 1755.
42. Transatlantic Slave Trade Database – *Voyage ID 90414 – The Elizabeth* – owned by Bryan Blundell and his two sons William, and Richard. Returned from Barbados on Tuesday, 7 May 1754.
43. Bonny, located in the Niger Delta region of present-day Nigeria, was the most significant embarkation port for enslaved Africans in the Bight of Biafra during the eighteenth-century. By the mid-1700s, it had become a primary hub for Liverpool slave traders, who established enduring commercial ties with local elites. The Blundell family and their associates increasingly relied on Bonny for captives in subsequent decades, with records showing that the vast majority of their slaving voyages originated from this coast.
44. Transatlantic Slave Trade Database – *Voyage ID 90561* – The *Blundell* departed on Friday, 20 September 1754, embarking 352 captives and arriving in Barbados with only 287. In total this ship transported 2,275 enslaved people. However, in 1773, she was finally wrecked off the African coast: 443 captives and 40 crew perished.
45. Description of Liverpool drawn from: James Stonehouse, *Recollections of Old Liverpool by a Nonagenarian* (Liverpool: J.F. Hughes, 1863; reprinted Project Gutenberg, 2007).
46. Ann Shaw (née Bassnett, 1723–1779) was the daughter of the Reverend Christopher Bassnett, a prominent nonconformist minister in Liverpool. She married Samuel Shaw (1718–1781) on 15 April 1745; by 1754, he had become a leading figure in the town's slave trade.
47. John Shaw (c. 1750–1832), great-grandson of Bryan Blundell through the Shaw and Bassnett families, was among the last of Liverpool's slave traders. He completed dozens of voyages between West Africa and the Americas, remaining active in the trade into 1807. His career is discussed further in Chapter 21. Also see: Appendix C – *Tree 4: The Shaw Family* and Appendix E – *The Recorded Slaving Voyages of Bryan Blundell and His Direct Descendants*.

Interlude: A Town Transformed, 1756–1810

1. Muir, *History of Liverpool*, pp.190–195.
2. Ibid.
3. Ibid.

Chapter 22

1. The eyewitness detail in this section is drawn from: Hughes, J.F. – *Recollections of Old Liverpool: By a Nonagenarian.* Liverpool: 1863.
2. By the late eighteenth century, concerns had already been raised about the structural integrity of the spire at St Nicholas. A survey in 1789 prompted repairs costing £20, but the warning signs were not heeded. The tower had not been built to carry the weight of the new spire or the heavy peal of bells installed within. Over time, vibrations from the ringing are believed to have weakened the structure, ultimately leading to its collapse. See: Picton, *Memorials*, p.59.
3. Historian Sophie Jones has calculated that 65 per cent of the Bluecoat School's early eighteenth-century subscriptions were financed either directly from the slave trade or through industries reliant on enslaved labour. See: The Bluecoat. *The Bluecoat and Slavery*. The Bluecoat, Liverpool, 2023 (based on research carried out by Sophie Jones).
4. Blundell, *Journal* (trans. Hignett), p.87.
5. Blundell, *Journal* (trans. Hignett), p.83; and Bryan Blundell's Will: *31 January 1756, Archdeaconry of Chester Probate Records, Testator: Bryan Blundell.*
6. For further details on Blundell's charitable giving, see: Blundell, *Journal* (trans. Hignett), p.76; and Girvan, *A Monument to Charity and Piety*, p.10.
7. In seamanship, the "bitter end" is the last length of cable secured to the bitts, the strong timber posts set into the deck. When a vessel had paid out cable to the bitter end, nothing more remained. In heavy weather, if the strain threatened to tear out the bow or capsize the ship, the cable could be cut at this point, sacrificing the anchor to preserve the vessel. Kemp, *Oxford Companion*, p.86. Here it signals both Blundell's own closing years and the limits of a moral rope stretched too far.
8. On 8 June 2020, protesters in Bristol tore down the statue of Edward Colston, a seventeenth-century slave trader, rolling it into the harbour. This prompted a national reckoning over monuments and legacies linked to slavery. See: "*Edward Colston: Statue of slave trader torn down in Bristol protest*," *BBC News*, 8 June 2020. In Liverpool, scrutiny has also turned toward Bryan Blundell. In 2022, the name "Blundell" was removed from one of the houses at Blue Coat School, where he had long been honoured as its founder. "*Liverpool school renames houses over slave trade links*," *BBC News*, 20 June 2022.
9. The original Blue Coat School building on School Lane still stands today. After its closure as a school in 1906, it became the UK's first dedicated arts centre. It is now a centre for civic and cultural activity as the Bluecoat. The school itself continues to operate in Wavertree, where it moved in 1906, maintaining its charitable foundation and educational mission.
10. For further discussion of Bryan Blundell's role and legacy as founder of the Liverpool Blue Coat School, including tensions between philanthropy, social control, and his wealth from the transatlantic slave trade, see: Girvan, *A Monument to Charity and Piety*.
11. "I pity them greatly, but I must be mum…": Cowper, William – *Pity for Poor Africans* (1788), first published in *The Gentleman's Magazine* (June 1788) and reprinted in *The Poems of William Cowper*, Vol. II (London: J. Johnson, 1798).

12. In 2020–2022, the Bluecoat undertook a detailed investigation into the connections between its founder and the slave trade as part of its *Echoes and Origins* heritage participation project, collaborating with local young people to explore the building's colonial legacies and ties to transatlantic slavery. For a fuller scholarly account, see: Girvan, *A Monument to Charity and Piety*.
13. In 1779, the firm Rainford, Blundell & Rainford (part-owned by Jonathan Blundell) was responsible for importing one in ten of all enslaved people arriving in Jamaica that year.
14. Jonathan (1717–1800), Richard (1721–1760), William (1714–1766), and Bryan Jr. (1720–1790) were the sons of Bryan Blundell and Elizabeth Livesley. All four were actively involved in Liverpool's maritime commerce and slave trading ventures during the middle of the eighteenth century. See: Appendix E – *The Recorded Slaving Voyages Of Bryan Blundell And His Direct Descendants.*
15. See: Chapter 20, John Shaw (c. 1750–1832); Appendix C – *Tree 4: The Shaw Family*; and Appendix E – *The Recorded Slaving Voyages of Bryan Blundell and His Direct Descendants.*
16. "a man of immense wealth and intense vulgarity,": from: Aspinall, James – *Liverpool A Few Years Since: By An Old Stager* (1869).
17. Drescher, Seymour – *The Slaving Capital of the World: Liverpool and National Opinion in the Age of Abolition.* Slavery & Abolition 9, no. 2 (1988), p.133. Liverpool's merchants and its Corporation unfailingly petitioned against every new abolitionist motion in Parliament, whether partial or total, immediate or gradual, regulatory or prohibitive.
18. "*Nicholson*" (voyage ID 82936): Slavevoyages.org – *Trans-Atlantic Slave Trade Database.*
19. Tibbles, Anthony – *Liverpool and the Slave Trade*, p.1.
20. Henry Blundell Hollinshead (1755–1832), grandson of Bryan Blundell, participated in at least one slaving voyage and served as Mayor of Liverpool in 1807–1808, the year Parliament passed the Slave Trade Act. See: *Liverpool City Halls, "Mayor / Lord Mayors of the City of Liverpool Since 1207," Civic Honours List.* Also see: Appendix C – *Tree 1: The Blundell Family.*
21. The Abolition of the Slave Trade Act (1807) outlawed the transatlantic trade in enslaved Africans within the British Empire. However, slavery itself was not abolished until the Slavery Abolition Act of 1833, which freed more than 800,000 enslaved people across the British Caribbean, South Africa, and Canada (though many were required to serve an unpaid "apprenticeship" period until 1838).
22. Slavery in the United States was formally abolished in December 1865 with the ratification of the Thirteenth Amendment. By that time, abolitionist voices had long been part of public discourse. Among them was Henry Wadsworth Longfellow, whose *Poems on Slavery* (1842) offered a restrained yet moral appeal against the institution. *See:* Henry Wadsworth Longfellow, *Poems on Slavery*, 2nd ed. (Cambridge: John Owen, 1842).
23. Richard Ansdell – 11 May 1815 to 20 April 1885. His picture *The Hunted Slaves* (1861) was purchased by Gilbert Winter Moss, a banker whose family had deep ties to slave-ownership and received compensation at emancipation. *National Museums Liverpool, Walker Art Gallery, object record for The Hunted Slaves.*

Afterword: The Silence That Followed

1. Liverpool was granted city status by Queen Victoria on Saturday, 28 August 1880.

Appendix A

1. "*Tantane animis caelestibus irae?*" (from *Aeneid*, Book 1, line 11). Translation: "Can such anger dwell in heavenly minds?" (or more freely: "Is there such wrath in heavenly hearts?"). Context: This line is spoken early in Virgil's *Aeneid* and refers to Juno's divine fury against the Trojans. It expresses amazement that gods, supposedly elevated and divine, can harbour such deep resentment and vengeance.

2. "*Dat veniam corvis, vexat censura columbas.*" (from Juvenal, *Satires*, Book 2, line 63) Translation: "Censure pardons the crows and harasses the doves." Meaning: This satirical line criticises the hypocrisy of moral censors, those in power are lenient to the corrupt (the "crows") while harshly judging the innocent or virtuous (the "doves").

Appendix E

1. All information in Appendix E is based on the Trans-Atlantic Slave Trade Database, *Voyages: The Trans-Atlantic Slave Trade Database*, www.Slavevoyages.Org. Accessed April 2025.

Bibliography

Adkins, Roy and Lesley. *Swimming, Drowning and Amulets: Old Attitudes to Safety at Sea.* Lloyd's Register Foundation (2024).

Agnew, Jean. *Belfast Merchant Families in the Seventeenth Century*. Dublin: Four Courts Press, 1995.

Allen, William Osborne Bird. *Two Hundred Years: The History of the Society for Promoting Christian Knowledge, 1698–1898*. London: SPCK, 1898.

Anderson, Bruce. "The Lancashire Bill System and its Liverpool Practitioners: The Case of a Slave Merchant." In *Trade and Transport: Essays in Economic History in Honour of T.S. Willan*, edited by W.H. Chaloner and Barrie Ratcliffe, 1977.

Anderson, D. "Blundell's Collieries: The Progress of the Business." *Transactions of the Historic Society of Lancashire and Cheshire* 116 (1965).

Angerstein, Reinhold Rücker. *Reise durch England und Frankreich im Jahre 1754*, translated and edited by Torsten Berg, 2001.

Anstey, Roger. "The Volume and Profitability of the British Slave Trade, 1761–1807." In *Race and Slavery in the Western Hemisphere*, edited by Stanley Engerman and Eugene Genovese, 1976.

Arkle, A.H. "The Early Coffee Houses of Liverpool." *Transactions of the Historic Society of Lancashire and Cheshire* 64 (1912).

Ascott, Diana, Fiona Lewis, and Michael Power. *Liverpool 1660–1750: People, Prosperity, and Power*. Liverpool: Liverpool University Press, 2006.

Ashton, William. *The Evolution of a Coast-Line*. 1920. "Liverpool, 1650".

Aspinall, James. *Liverpool a Few Years Since: By An Old Stager*. Liverpool: 1869.

Aughton, Peter. *Liverpool: A People's History*. 1990.

Baines, Thomas. *History of the Commerce and Town of Liverpool, and of the Rise of Manufacturing Industry in the Adjoining Counties*. London: Longman, 1852.

Barlow, *Barlow's Journal of His Life at Sea in King's Ships, East & West Indiamen & Other Merchantmen from 1659 to 1708*, ed. Basil Lubbock (London: Hurst & Blackett, 1934).

Bass, R.D. *The Green Dragon*. Liverpool: 1957.

Bassnett, Christopher. *The Seaman's Character and Calling Consider' d and Improv' d*. London: 1712 (sermon preached 13 December 1711).

Baucom, Ian. *Specters of the Atlantic*. Durham, NC: Duke University Press, 2005.

Beckles, Hilary. *Natural Rebels: A Social History of Enslaved Black Women in Barbados*. Rutgers University Press, 1989.

——. *White Servitude and Black Slavery in Barbados 1627–1715*. 1989.

Behrendt, Stephen D. "Markets, Transaction Cycles, and Merchant Decision-Making in the British Slave Trade." *William and Mary Quarterly* 58 (2001): pp.171–204.

Ben-Porath, Yoram. "The F-Connection: Families, Friends, and Firms and the Organization of Exchange." *Population and Development Review* 6.1 (1980): pp.1–30.

Biggs, Bryan, and Belchem, John, eds. *Bluecoat, Liverpool: The UK's First Arts Centre*. Liverpool: Liverpool University Press, 2020. In this volume, see especially Gavin Davenport, "The Bluecoat Building: Origins and Continuity."

Blome, Richard. *Britannia: A Geographical Description of Great Britain and Ireland*. London: 1673.

Blundell, Bryan. *The Journal of Bryan Blundell, 1688–1756: Master Mariner, Shipowner, Merchant, Mayor of Liverpool 1721 & 1728, Philanthropist, Founder, Principal Benefactor & for 40 Years, Treasurer/Administrator of the Liverpool Blue Coat School.* Transcribed by H.M. Hignett. Crosby: H.M. Hignett, 1991.

Unless otherwise stated, all quotations are taken from this transcription, based on the original manuscript held at the Liverpool Record Office (920 BLU). Cited throughout as: Blundell, *Journal* (trans. Hignett). Entries are referenced by date only: Blundell, *Journal*, [date].

Blue Coat School Records. Minute Book of the Board Meetings of the Blue Coat School Trustees and Governors, 1742–1813. Liverpool Blue Coat Hospital and School, LCLA 377.BLU/15/1/1. Available online at The Bluecoat website: "The Blue Coat School" Library section.

Borucki, Alex, and Greg O'Malley. "Introduction." In *Intra-American Slave Trade Database*. 2018.

Bray, R.S. *Armies of Pestilence: The Impact of Disease on History*. Cambridge: James Clarke & Co., 2004.

Brown, Vincent. *The Reaper's Garden: Death and Power in the World of Atlantic Slavery*. Harvard University Press, 2008.

Bruyn, Cornelis de. *Travels into Muscovy, Persia, and Part of the East-Indies*. Vol. 1. London: A. Bettesworth and C. Hitch, et al., 1737.

Bryder, Linda. *Below the Magic Mountain: A Social History of Tuberculosis in Twentieth-Century Britain*. Oxford: Clarendon, 1988.

Burnard, Trevor. *Mastery, Tyranny, and Desire: Thomas Thistlewood and His Slaves in the Anglo-Jamaican World*. Chapel Hill: University of North Carolina Press, 2004.

Butterworth, William. *Three Years' Adventures of a Minor, in England, Africa, the West Indies, South-Carolina and Georgia* (Leeds: Thos. Inchbold, 1831).

Bygone Liverpool. "Mystery of the Ladykirk Oak Chest." *wordpress.com*.

Clark, Anna. *The Struggle for the Breeches: Gender and the Making of the British Working Class*. London: Rivers Oram Press, 1995.

Clayton, Timothy. *Tars: The Men of the Nelson Navy*. Abacus, 2008.

Clowes, William Laird. *The Royal Navy: A History from the Earliest Times to the Present*, Vol. III. London: Sampson Low, Marston & Co., 1898.

Copley, Stephen. "The Bonds of Trade: Commerce and Community in the Liverpool Slave Trade." In *Liverpool and Transatlantic Slavery*, edited by David Richardson, Suzanne Schwarz, and Anthony Tibbles. Liverpool University Press, 2007.

Crow, Hugh. *Memoirs of the Late Captain Hugh Crow of Liverpool.* London: Longman et al., 1830.

Dampier, William. *A New Voyage Round the World*. London: James Knapton, 1697.

Defoe, Daniel. *A Tour Thro' the Whole Island of Great Britain*, Vol. II. London: 1724–1727.

Dormandy, Thomas. *The White Death: A History of Tuberculosis*. 2000.

Dorwart, Jeffery M. *"Shipbuilding and Shipyards," Encyclopedia of Greater Philadelphia.* (Rutgers University–Camden, 2013).

Earle, Peter. *The Earles of Liverpool: A Georgian Merchant Dynasty*.

Eltis, David, and David Richardson. *Voyages: The Trans-Atlantic Slave Trade Database*. Emory University, 2009–2023. www.slavevoyages.org.

Eltis, David. "The Total Product of Barbados, 1664–1701". *The Journal of Economic History* 55, no. 2 (June 1995).

Evans, Cerinda W. *Some Notes on Shipbuilding and Shipping in Colonial Virginia* (Jamestown 350th Anniversary Historical Booklet, no. 22, Williamsburg, 1957). Reproduced via Project Gutenberg eBook #15648.

Farnell, J.E. "The Navigation Act of 1651, the First Dutch War, and the London Merchant Community." *Economic History Review* 16, no. 3 (1964).

Fox, George. *A New-England Firebrand Quenched*. 1678.

Fox Bourne, Henry. *English Merchants*, Vol. II. London: Richard Bentley and Son, 1886.

Frey, Linda, and Frey, Marsha. *The Treaties of the War of the Spanish Succession: An Historical and Critical Dictionary*. Greenwood Press, 1995.

Girvan, Michelle. *A Monument to Charity and Piety? Bryan Blundell and the Liverpool Blue Coat School,* 2021, the Bluecoat: \https://www.thebluecoat.org.uk/library/artefact/michelle-girvan-a-monument-to-charity-and-piety. Girvan's PhD thesis on the Blue Coat School in the eighteenth century (forthcoming, University of Liverpool) includes detailed research on Blundell.

Gomer, William. *History of the Liverpool Privateers and Letters of Marque With an Account of the Liverpool Slave Trade*. Liverpool: Macdonald & Evans, 1884.

Gómez, Francis Gerald. *The Endowed Schools of Lancashire from the 17th to the Early 18th Century*. 1987.

Gray, Stanley. "The British Navy and the Tobacco Trade of Virginia and Maryland," *Proceedings of the U.S. Naval Institute* 62, no. 9 (September 1936).

Guardian. "Liverpool Must Not 'Shy Away' From Slave Trade Past, Says Museum Chief." *The Guardian*, 2007.

Owen, John Hely. *War at Sea Under Queen Anne, 1702–1708*.

Henty, G.A. *British Battles on Land and Sea*, Vol. 1. London: Cassell, Petter & Galpin, 1873.

Herson, John. *The Mersey and the City: Social and Economic Change in Liverpool 1700–1900.* Liverpool: Liverpool University Press, 1991.

Hignett, Harry. "Liverpool Nautical Research Society Bulletin, Vol. 34, No. 1, Summer 1990," *Liverpool Nautical Research Society Bulletin*, vol. 34 (1990).

HIST241. *The Transatlantic Slave Trade, 1500–1865.* Lancaster University course materials, 2018.

Hockedy, Doreen M. "Bound for a New World: Emigration of Indentured Servants via Liverpool to America and the West Indies, 1697–1707." *Transactions of the Historic Society of Lancashire and Cheshire*, vol. 144 (1994).

Hockedy, Susan. "Liverpool Shipping and the Tar Trade." *Transactions of the Historic Society of Lancashire and Cheshire*, vol. 144 (1994).

Hughes, J.F. *Recollections of Old Liverpool: By a Nonagenarian.* Liverpool: 1863.

Hughes, John E. "Sketch of the Origin and Early History of the Liverpool Blue Coat Hospital." *Transactions of the Historic Society of Lancashire and Cheshire.*

Hutchinson, Captain William. *A Treatise on Practical Seamanship.* London: 1777.

International Slavery Museum. Exhibition leaflets, brochures and guides. Liverpool: National Museums Liverpool, 2007–2020.

John Smith Explores the Chesapeake. Captain John Smith National Historic Trail. National Park Service, US Department of the Interior, n.d.

Jones, M.G. *The Charity School Movement: A Study of Eighteenth Century Puritanism in Action.* Cambridge: Cambridge University Press, 1938.

Kemp, Peter. *The Oxford Companion to Ships and the Sea.* Oxford: Oxford University Press, 1976.

Kotilaine, Jarmo T. *Russia's Foreign Trade and Economic Expansion in the Seventeenth Century: Windows on the World* (Leiden: Brill, 2005).

Laslett, Peter. *The World We Have Lost: Further Explored.* London: Routledge, 2000.

Liverpool Nautical Research Society. *Bulletins and Bluecoat Story Series.* Vol. 30 (1986), September 1717.

Ligon, Richard. *A True and Exact History of the Island of Barbados.* (London: Humphrey Moseley, 1657).

Liverpool City Halls. *Mayor / Lord Mayors of the City of Liverpool Since 1207.* Civic Honours List.

Lynn, John A. *The Wars of Louis XIV, 1667–1714.* London: Longman, 1999.

Mackenzie-Grieve, A. (1968). *The Last Years of the English Slave Trade, Liverpool, 1750-1807.* New York: A.M. Kelley.

Manwaring, G.E. "The Dress of the British Seaman. – II," *The Mariner's Mirror* 9, no. 6 (1923).

Manning, Patrick. "The Slave Trade: The Formal Demographics of a Global System."

Moody, Jessica. *"The Memorial Cult of William Roscoe: Remembering Abolition." In The Persistence of Memory: Remembering Slavery in Liverpool, "Slaving Capital of the World", Liverpool University Press, 2020.*

Moody, Jessica. *The Memory of Slavery in Liverpool in Public Discourse from the Nineteenth Century to the Present Day.* PhD thesis, University of York, 2014.

Morgan, Kenneth. *Liverpool and Transatlantic Slavery.* Liverpool: Liverpool University Press, 2007.

——. *Slavery and the British Empire: From Africa to America.* Oxford: Oxford University Press, 2007.

——. "Liverpool's Dominance in the British Slave Trade, 1740–1807."

Muir, Ramsay. *A History of Liverpool.* 2nd ed. London: Williams & Norgate, 1907.

Muir, Ramsay. *Bygone Liverpool,* with Harold E. Young and Henry S. Young (Liverpool: Young, 1913).

National Oceanography Centre. "Tidal Range Data for the River Mersey, Liverpool." noc.ac.uk.

Neal, Larry. *The Rise of Financial Capitalism: International Capital Markets in the Age of Reason.* Cambridge: Cambridge University Press, 1993.

Newton, John. *Thoughts Upon the African Slave Trade.* London: Printed for J. Buckland, Pater-Noster Row; and J. Johnson, St Paul's Church-Yard, 1788.

Papenfuse, Edward C. *A Biographical Dictionary of the Maryland Legislature 1635–1789,* Vol. 1.

Parkinson, R.B. *Liverpool: A Maritime City in the Making.* London: Historical Society Press, 1985.

Pearce, Edward. *The Great Man, Sir Robert Walpole: Scoundrel, Genius and Britain's First Prime Minister.*

Peet, Henry. "St Nicholas's Church, Liverpool: Its Architectural History." *Transactions of the Historic Society of Lancashire and Cheshire,* vol. 65 (1913).

Phillips, Thomas. *A Journal of a Voyage Made in the Hannibal of London,* 1694.

Picton, James A. *Memorials of Liverpool: Historical and Topographical*, Vol. 1. London: Longmans, 1873.

Pincus, Steven C.A. *1688: The First Modern Revolution.* New Haven: Yale University Press, 2009.

Power, Michael. "Creating a Port: Liverpool 1695–1715." *Transactions of the Historic Society of Lancashire and Cheshire*, vol. 149 (2000).

Prochaska, F.K. *Women and Philanthropy in Nineteenth-Century England.* Oxford: Clarendon Press, 1980.

Radburn, Nicholas. *HIST241: The Trans-Atlantic Slave Trade, 1500–1865.* 2018.

Raleigh, Sir Walter. *A Discourse of the Invention of Ships, Anchors, Compass, etc.* c. 1615.

Rediker, Marcus. *The Slave Ship: A Human History.* London: John Murray, 2007.

Refford, Brian W. "The Bonds of Trade: Commerce and Community in the Liverpool Slave Trade, 1695–1775." *Journal of Economic History*, vol. 64, no. 3 (2004).

Richardson, David. "Merely for Money?" Business Culture in the British Slave Trade.

——. "The Slave Trade, Sugar and British Economic Growth, 1748–1776." *Journal of Interdisciplinary History* 17:4 (1987).

Rivers, Isabel. *Reason, Grace, and Sentiment: A Study of the Language of Religion and Ethics in England, 1660–1780.* Cambridge: Cambridge University Press, 1991.

Roberts, Henry, *Hope Street Church and the Allied Non-Conformity of Liverpool* (Liverpool, 1905)

Rodger, N.A.M. *The Command of the Ocean: A Naval History of Britain, 1649–1815.* London: Penguin Books, 2004.

Rodger, N.A.M. *The Wooden World: An Anatomy of the Georgian Navy.* Annapolis, MD: Naval Institute Press, 1986.

Roscoe, William. *Mount Pleasant.* 1769.

Royal Museums Greenwich. *Life at Sea in the Age of Sail* (rmg.co.uk).

Royal Museums Greenwich. *"A Rum Deal: The Origins of Nelson's Blood"*.

Sadler, Nigel. *The Slave Trade.* Shire Publications, 2009.

Stammers, Mike. *Ships and Port Management at Liverpool Before the Opening of the First Dock in 1715.* Transactions of the Historic Society of Lancashire and Cheshire.

Stanfield, James Field. *Observations on a Guinea Voyage.* 1788.

Survey of London. *Vol. 15: All Hallows, Barking-by-the-Tower.* London: London County Council, 1934.

Sweet, Rosemary. *The English Town, 1680–1840: Government, Society, and Culture.* London: Longman, 1999.

Tadmor, Naomi. "Early Modern English Kinship in the Long Run." *Continuity and Change* 25, no. 1 (2010): pp.15–48.

Thomas, Hugh. *The Slave Trade: The History of the Atlantic Slave Trade, 1440–1870.* New York: Simon & Schuster, 1997.

Thomsen, Robert P. *The Merchant in Virginia, 1700–1775.* PhD thesis, University of Wisconsin, 1955.

Thornber, W. *The History of Lancashire.* (Cited in: "The Bonds of Trade: Liverpool Slave Trade").

Thomsen, Robert Polk. *The Merchant in Virginia, 1700–1775* (PhD thesis, University of Wisconsin, 1955).

Thomson, James. *The Seasons.* Originally published 1730; revised edition 1744.

Tibbles, Anthony. *Liverpool and the Slave Trade.* Liverpool: National Museums Liverpool, 1994 & 2018.

Touzeau, James. *The Rise and Progress of Liverpool from 1551 to 1835.* Liverpool: J. Irvine, 1910.

Trevelyan, G.M. *The Glorious Revolution 1688–1689.* London: Longmans, 1938.

The Bluecoat. *The Bluecoat and Slavery.* The Bluecoat, Liverpool, 2023. https://www.thebluecoat.org.uk/library/the-bluecoat-and-slavery.

The Museum of the Queen's Royal Hussars. "The Siege of Londonderry." qrhmuseum.com.

The Old Dock, National Museums Liverpool. "The Old Dock Tour." liverpoolmuseums.org.uk.

Turman, Nora Miller. *The Eastern Shore of Virginia, 1603–1964* (Onancock, VA: Eastern Shore News, 1964.

Walsh, John. "The Social History of Early Methodism." In *A History of the Methodist Church in Great Britain,* 2003.

Walvin, James. *Black Ivory: A History of British Slavery.* Oxford: Blackwell, 2001.

——. *Britain's Slave Empire.* Stroud: Tempus, 2007.

Wainwright, Dr Paul. *Bryan Blundell.* Bluecoatschoolliverpool.org.uk.

Wardle, A.R. "Liverpool's Early Customs Collectors." *Transactions of the Historic Society of Lancashire and Cheshire.*

——. *The Early Liverpool Privateers.* Liverpool: Historic Society, 1941. Also published as part of *Transactions of the Historic Society of Lancashire and Cheshire*, c. 1920.

Westgaph, Laurence. *Reading the Signs.* London: Historic England, 2014.

Whitelaw, Ralph T. *Virginia's Eastern Shore: A History of Northampton and Accomack Counties.* Richmond: Virginia Historical Society, 1951.

Willis J. Abbot. *American Merchant Ships and Sailors* (New York: Dodd, Mead & Company, 1902; Project Gutenberg eBook #15648).

Wills, Mary and Madge Dresser. "The Transatlantic Slave Economy and England's Built Environment: A Research Audit." *Historic England Research Report Series* 247–2020.

Wise, Jennings Cropper. *Ye Kingdome of Accawmache: or, The Eastern Shore of Virginia.* Richmond: Bell Book and Stationery Co., 1911.

Ryzewski, Krysta, and John F. Cherry – *Struggles of a Sugar Society: Surveying PlantationEra Montserrat, 1650–1850.* International Journal of Historical Archaeology 19 (2015).

Index

Abbreviations for ships:
RN = Royal Navy M = Merchant SL = Slave ship